CULTURAL DIPLOMACY IN U.S.-JAPANESE RELATIONS, 1919–1941

CULTURAL DIPLOMACY IN U.S.-JAPANESE RELATIONS, 1919–1941

JON THARES DAVIDANN

palgrave
macmillan

E
183.8
.J3
D27
2007

CULTURAL DIPLOMACY IN U.S.-JAPANESE RELATIONS, 1919–1941
Copyright © Jon Thares Davidann, 2007.

All rights reserved. No part of this book may be used or reproduced in any manner whatsoever without written permission except in the case of brief quotations embodied in critical articles or reviews.

First published in 2007 by
PALGRAVE MACMILLAN™
175 Fifth Avenue, New York, N.Y. 10010 and
Houndmills, Basingstoke, Hampshire, England RG21 6XS
Companies and representatives throughout the world.

PALGRAVE MACMILLAN is the global academic imprint of the Palgrave Macmillan division of St. Martin's Press, LLC and of Palgrave Macmillan Ltd. Macmillan® is a registered trademark in the United States, United Kingdom and other countries. Palgrave is a registered trademark in the European Union and other countries.

ISBN-13: 978–1–4039–7532–4
ISBN-10: 1–4039–7532–9

Library of Congress Cataloging-in-Publication Data

Davidann, Jon Thares, 1961–
    Cultural diplomacy in U.S.-Japanese relations, 1919–1941 / by Jon Thares Davidann.
        p. cm.
    Includes bibliographical references and index.
    ISBN 1–4039–7532–9 (alk. paper)
        1. United States—Relations—Japan. 2. Japan—Relations—United States. 3. United States—Foreign public opinion, Japanese. 4. Japan—Foreign public opinion, American. 5. United States—Foreign relations—20th century. 6. Japan—Foreign relations—1912–1945. 7. World War, 1939–1945—Causes. I. Title. II. Title: Cultural diplomacy in United States-Japanese relations, 1919–1941.

E183.8.J3D27 2007
303.48′2730520904—dc22   2007010304

A catalogue record for this book is available from the British Library.

Design by Newgen Imaging Systems (P) Ltd., Chennai, India.

First edition: December 2007

10 9 8 7 6 5 4 3 2 1

Printed in the United States of America.

86038280

To Mom and Dad who nurtured my love of learning.

Contents

ACKNOWLEDGMENTS

THIS PROJECT HAS TAKEN LONGER THAN I WOULD HAVE IMAGINED when I started it. Nine years ago I began research. Given the length of time that has elapsed, inevitably I have incurred many debts to institutions, colleagues, friends, and my family. My wife Beth and son Eli have borne the greatest burden. The project took time away from them and at times turned me into a crabby, tired professor when I was with them. I appreciate their loving patience. Hawai'i Pacific University made this book possible by supporting my work with many Trustees Scholarly Endeavors awards. I would like to thank in particular President Chatt C. Wright and Senior Vice President for Academic Administration John Fleckles for their support and understanding. It is not often when the leadership of an institution so readily embraces and supports the study of history. Writing a historical account can be lonely work. It is mostly individual work. Thus, the listening ear and timely words of encouragement can mean the difference between continuing and abandoning a project. This project was strengthened immensely by the insight and support of many colleagues. I would like to thank professors David Noble, Jerry Bentley, Pat Manning, Emily Rosenberg, Prasenjit Duara, and James Matray for their continuing support of my scholarship and of this particular project. Other scholars read all or parts of the manuscript and improved it through suggestions and comments. Professors Akira Iriye, Dan Headrick, George Oshiro and Associate Professor Paul Barclay took time out of their busy schedules to read the manuscript and suggest improvements. I had excellent support from archivists at the Kautz Family YMCA archives in Minneapolis, the Yale Divinity School Library Archives, the Japanese YMCA Archives, the National Diet Library in Tokyo, the Columbia University Rare Book and Manuscript Library, and Houghton Library at Harvard University. Student assistants contributed in innumerable ways to the completion of this book. Very simply, I would not have finished without their support. Thanks to Marc Gallows, Trevor Tresselle, Stephanie Orr, James Uregen, and Arian Whitley for their hard work and persistence.

NOTE ON CHINESE AND JAPANESE NAMES

CHINESE NAMES ARE GIVEN IN WADE-GILES FORM AS THEY APPEAR MOST OFTEN in the sources for the interwar period. Pinyin versions appear in parentheses following the first appearance. Japanese names are given in Japanese name order last name first, except in the notes where they are given as they appear in the sources.

THE SEEDS OF WAR

WHEN FAMOUS AMERICAN PHILOSOPHER JOHN DEWEY VISITED CHINA IN 1919, more than twenty years before the Pacific War, he saw the seeds of war in the Pacific being sown.

> But in the interests of truth it must be recorded that every resident of China, Chinese or American, with whom I have talked in the last four weeks has volunteered the belief that all the seeds of a future great war are now deeply implanted in China.[1]

China and Japan were increasingly antagonistic toward each other. The Chinese protested against Japanese intrusion in North China, while the Japanese believed their presence was justified by the roiling instability there.

These Sino-Japanese tensions damaged U.S.-Japanese relations, according to Dewey. He thought the China issue more central to the threat of a U.S.-Japan conflict than tensions over Japanese immigration into the United States. "It cannot be too often repeated that the real point of friction between the United States and Japan is not in California but in China . . ."[2]

Dewey avowed that an unofficial "diplomacy of peoples" and properly educated public opinion could provide a better solution to the conflict than could official diplomacy. But he also acknowledged that public opinion informed by cultural bias or manipulated by "apologetics" or propaganda could be turned into a powerful and dangerous tool if not informed by "goodwill and wisdom."[3]

Dewey's "great war" came to pass when Japan invaded China in the summer of 1937. Dewey's assertion that conflict between China and Japan imperiled U.S.-Japanese relations also foreshadowed an even greater war, the Pacific War in 1941. Finally, his hope mixed with caution about unofficial diplomacy and public opinion mirrors the initial success, struggles, and ultimate failure of cultural diplomacy in U.S.-Japanese relations in the interwar period.

* * *

What caused the Pacific War? This deceptively simple question has tantalized historians ever since the war ended. Many historians emphasize the diplomatic and military developments of 1939–1941 such as the Japanese Axis Pact with Germany and Italy, the course of war in Europe, the role of the Soviet Union in Japanese strategic thinking, and the American oil embargo.

The American oil embargo against Japan was crucial in the march to war, because without oil, the Japanese war machine would grind to a halt. The Japanese bought over 80 percent of their oil from the United States. So the embargo became a provocative act in 1941. Closer study of the embargo reveals that it was a response not only to Japanese aggression in Asia, but also to American public opinion heavily in favor of an embargo. Calls for a strategic embargo by influential private citizens began much earlier in the decade. The decision lay in not just in the hands of official diplomats and President Franklin Delano Roosevelt but also with the U.S. populace.

However, historians have traditionally undervalued the role of public opinion and unofficial diplomacy in explaining the Pacific War. Without denying the importance of formal diplomacy and geopolitics, this book studies these neglected areas to see how they contributed to the cause of war.

First, the interwar period witnessed disturbing trends in the American public's views of Japan, views that contributed to alienation between the United States and Japan. In addition to shifting from generally positive to quite negative by the 1930s, the popular debate also shifted in its content. Some Americans thought the Japanese were moving ever closer to the American model of a modern democratic nation, while other Americans saw the Japanese as having only a façade of modernity underneath which they were prisoners of a past dictated by feudal militarism. Although neither argument accurately represented the Japanese situation, the latter came to dominate American public opinion by the time of the Pearl Harbor attack. Both arguments mistakenly viewed the Japanese through the lens of culture and filtered the political and economic crises Japan faced in the interwar period through that lens instead of confronting these problems on their own terms. The Japanese for their part initially saw Americans as different from the untrustworthy European powers, but by the 1930s grouped Americans with the European powers as enemies of Japan.[4]

Second, U.S.-Japan private citizen diplomacy broke down in the interwar period. In the 1920s, internationalist organizations such as the Institute of Pacific Relations (IPR, 1925) were founded to solve the problems of

U.S.-Japanese relations. However, these unofficial efforts were undermined by official tensions between the United States and Japan, national loyalties, and links to official diplomacy. In addition, a web of connections between American and Japanese private citizens developed by the early 1920s. For instance, American historian Charles Beard, and Japanese politician and intellectual Tsurumi Yusuke became friends in the 1920s, referring to one another in letters as "Mutt" and "Jeff" after the well-known cartoon of that period. However, these connections, badly frayed by events such as immigration exclusion and the Manchurian Incident, were broken by the time of Pearl Harbor. Beard and Tsurumi ceased communicating in 1932, after the Manchurian Incident. As unofficial relations between Japan and the United States weakened, the failure of informal diplomacy in the 1930s meant that communication between the two countries flowed less often through unofficial channels, shaping a more limited and negative understanding of the other.

Third, China appears at the center of many U.S.-Japanese tensions. Although the role of China has at times been downplayed, China was actually of vital concern to the relationship. Because the focus is on nonofficial relations and public opinion, China emerges as a third partner, albeit many times silent, in U.S.-Japanese tensions.

Fourth, examination of public opinion and private diplomacy forces us to broaden our perspective to include the entire interwar period (1919–1941), not just the years right before the war (1939–1941).

By 1939, with private diplomacy having failed to bring the two nations closer and public distrust of one another at an all-time high, the seeds of war were planted. The Sino-Japanese War, the Axis Pact with Germany, the Japanese occupation of Indochina, the American oil embargo against Japan, and the Japanese attack on Pearl Harbor caused those seeds to germinate into a vicious war in the Pacific. By 1941, alienation and distrust between the two powers made war all but inevitable and put the relationship beyond resolution not only by private citizens but also by formal diplomacy.

DEMOCRACIES AND PUBLIC OPINION

Nations go to war in the modern age, not just armies or governments. We are once again learning this in the wake of the September 11, 2001 terrorist attacks. The "war on terror" has initiated changes in many parts of American life including new limits on our civil liberties and generous funding for any project that includes national security.

In the premodern period, war was the domain of professional soldiers. Subjects of the realm had no voice in the decision to make war, although they often suffered the brunt of war. With the rise of modern nations, wars became projects of the whole nation, involving more often than not the whole population of the nation in a patriotic effort. In the time of the American Revolution (1775) and later, the population was expected to make sacrifices for the war effort. France became the first nation to conscript troops from the general population in the French Revolution (1789).

By World War I, governments had to mobilize entire populations to fight the war. The massive scale of World War I made it impossible to win without the public will to fight. Politicians of all stripes had to be much more sensitive to whether the population was ready to make the sacrifices war demanded. This change in the nature of war emphasized the influence of public opinion in the discussions of war and peace. This was even more true in the period between World War I and World War II. Thus, the public, as it bore the brunt of war, had to give its consent to war.

The public approval of war was starkly demonstrated in the United States in 1937 when a constitutional amendment was proposed that would have required a popular referendum before an American president could declare and prosecute a war. The Ludlow Amendment, as it was called, only applied to offensive wars. However, the amendment would have greatly tied the hands of the American president. A poll showed that the Ludlow Amendment had the support of 70 percent of the American population. In addition to demonstrating the public's desire to be influential in the decision of war, the support indicates the strong isolationist tendency prevailing in the American population. According to this view, the European and East Asian troubles were not the United States' problem and Americans should not get involved. The Ludlow Amendment died in Congress because President Roosevelt campaigned against it. Its failure does nothing, however, to diminish the power of its message that the average American had to be consulted in case of war. And this conclusion in turn confirms the importance of studying public opinion in the developments leading to the Pacific War.

In the same year as the airing of the Ludlow Amendment came an urgent telegram to the State Department from Joseph Grew who was the American ambassador to Japan at the time. Grew's cable was in response to a Japanese initiative inviting him to mediate peace negotiations between Japan and China in the early stages of the Sino-Japanese War. He sought State Department approval to act as intermediary. State cabled back in the negative, stating that the American people were so strongly anti-Japanese that they would not support a U.S. negotiated settlement that might favor the Japanese.

The public therefore played an important role in the shaping of foreign relations in the United States before World War II and cannot be easily dismissed. However, the difficulty is in finding out what the populace thought. Up until 1935, public opinion polling was almost nonexistent and polls thereafter have to be examined carefully for accuracy. For instance, two different polls taken in the 1936 presidential election predicted totally different outcomes. A *Literary Digest* poll predicted Franklin Roosevelt would be soundly beaten, while Professor George Gallup's poll was more accurate predicting Roosevelt's victory. Another approach is to study the writings of public opinion leaders and make inferences about the direction and weight of public opinion from them.[5]

Like those in the United States the public of Japan was a significant player in the making (or unmaking) of official diplomacy. Japan had developed a democratic political system with a parliament (Diet) and prime minister and the Japanese public often made its opinion felt in the political arena. In 1905, the American-brokered settlement of the Russo-Japanese War, thought to be too lenient on Russia, provoked large protests and riots in Tokyo and caused the Katsura government to fall. Again in 1918 at the end of World War I, almost 700,000 people participated in protests, this time against high rice prices.

Japanese public opinion was divided between westernized elites within cities and impoverished peasants in the countryside who supported the military. Japanese rural areas suffered from grinding poverty in the interwar period. Absentee landlords living in cities raised rents to the point that tenant farmers struggled to pay the rents and feed themselves from the same crop. The Japanese army set up the Imperial Military Reserve Association to sustain impoverished villagers and build its own political support.[6] Thus, rural areas became captive to the concerns of the militarists. In 1931–1932, rural youths from a right-wing organization called the Blood League carried out assassinations of political and business leaders thought to be too pro-Western or corrupt.

Within large cities many Japanese supported and/or benefited from Westernization. They saw no contradiction between Westernization, loyalty to the emperor, and support for the Japanese Empire. These liberals and moderates were likely to be from the growing Japanese middle class. They lived in an urban Japan that was becoming modernized. Large factories and office buildings dominated the skyline and automobiles and electric trolleys ran on the streets of the large cities of Japan. Western style dress was common and American jazz music could be heard from bars and clubs along Japanese sidewalks.

The political parties gained support from the urban population in the 1920s, maintaining open diplomacy with the West and working to improve relations between the United States and Japan. They desired peaceful economic penetration of northeast Asia and feared that the work of the military would undermine their efforts. Under Shidehara Kijuro, who was foreign minister between 1924 and 1927 and again between 1929 and 1931, foreign policy was moderate and conciliatory toward Western nations. Cooperation with the West was pursued throughout the 1920s but lost popular backing in the late 1920s as anti-Western sentiment rose and the Japanese public began to see cooperation with the West as appeasement detrimental to Japan.

PRIVATE CITIZEN DIPLOMACY

In what ways did private citizens affect U.S.-Japanese relations? They met with like-minded people on the other side, exchanged letters, participated in international organizations such as the Young Men's Christian Association (YMCA) and the Institute of Pacific Relations (IPR), and created resolutions and agreements. Through speeches and diverse writings, which included books, magazines articles, book reviews, pamphlets, and circular letters, private citizens also communicated with particular segments of the public.

In comparing Japanese and American private citizen diplomacy, one major difference comes to mind. In Japan, influential private citizens often either worked with or at least consulted Japanese government officials (most often the Japanese Foreign Ministry) in promoting U.S.-Japanese relations. In the United States, private citizen diplomacy rarely took the form of lobbying or consultation with State Department officials, and never took the form of actually working for the State Department until immediately before the Pacific War. Japanese informal diplomats, like Americans, communicated downward toward massed public opinion, but unlike Americans, they also communicated upward with government officials.

How significant was the activity of private citizens in U.S.-Japanese relations? This is a difficult question to answer precisely. Certainly on both sides there were influential private citizens involved in what John Mott called "person-to-person diplomacy." Mott, who was the head of the YMCA and a missionary leader in the United States, traveled dozens of times to East Asia to organize mission work there. He became so prominent in American political life that he was offered the ambassadorship to China in 1913 by the then newly elected president Woodrow Wilson. He turned the job down saying that he could do more good in China as head of the YMCA than as ambassador.

In addition to John Mott, Sherwood Eddy and Sidney Gulick were very influential informal diplomats who helped shape American policy and public opinion through their writings. Gulick, a former missionary to Japan, led the fight against Japanese immigrant exclusion and other anti-Japanese measures in the United States in the 1920s. Although he was unable to stop the American Congress from passing a law that essentially banned Japanese immigration in 1924, his influence helped Americans understand the Japanese view that a grave injustice had been done to them. Sherwood Eddy, a former YMCA missionary leader and prolific writer on East Asia, was in Manchuria when the Manchurian Incident took place in 1931. He sent urgent cables back to the United States describing Japanese trickery in its invasion of Manchuria. His strong denunciation of Japanese actions strengthened the opposition of Americans to the Japanese takeover in Manchuria.

In Japan, Shibusawa Eiichi and Nitobe Inazô were powerful informal diplomats in the early interwar period. Shibusawa, a wealthy textiles manufacturer who in retirement took up the cause of improving U.S.-Japanese relations, became head of the Japan branch of the U.S.-Japan Friendship Committee formed in 1916 (the name is indicative of how important friendly contacts with the United States was in the Japanese view). He was also present at the Washington Conference as an adviser to the Japanese delegation. He was friendly to American-centered organizations in Japan such as the YMCA and the IPR. Shibusawa met regularly with officials in the Foreign Ministry to give updates on the informal contacts he had with Americans. He was asked to chair various ad hoc committees formed by the Foreign Ministry. He was never paid by the Foreign Ministry but this is irrelevant because Shibusawa was a very wealthy man and supported himself easily from his own income. The connections between the Foreign Ministry and Shibusawa remained very strong until his death in 1931.

Nitobe Inazô, like Shibusawa, was an influential unofficial diplomat. Nitobe was one of the best-known internationalists in prewar Japan. He spent his career attempting to teach the rest of the world about Japan. For his efforts, he was sometimes referred to as Japan's "bridge" to the outside world.[7] Nitobe was a renaissance man. An intellectual, Nitobe wrote many books. Written in English, *Bushido*, his most famous book, became a bestseller in the West as well as in Japan. He also worked as an administrator in the Japanese colonial government in Taiwan, studied in the United States, married an American Quaker and became one himself, became head of the prestigious First Higher School, joined Tokyo Imperial University as professor, and served as under-secretary-general of the League of Nations for seven years in the 1920s. Nitobe also met with foreign ministry officials periodically to consult about Japanese policy.

We can see from these examples that informal diplomats on both sides exercised substantial influence on public attitudes and sometimes on official diplomacy, probably more so in the Japanese than in the American case because of the connection between unofficial and official diplomats.

CONTENTS AND CONCLUSIONS

The two main subjects of this book, public opinion and private diplomacy, are explored in detail in the chapters that follow. Chapter 1 studies the two main arguments made by Americans about Japan in the interwar period.

Chapter 2 explores Japanese views of the United States and responses to American Orientalist views and accusations of militarism. John Dewey's trip to China and talk of war, between the United States and Japan over China issues comprises chapter 3 and chapter 4 reassesses the impact of the Washington Conference on public opinion. Chapter 5 focuses on the rise of an anti-Japanese movement in the United States and the effects of the American immigration exclusion clause and the Kanto earthquake on Japanese opinion. The aftermath of immigration exclusion is examined in chapter 6. Chapter 7 looks at the way Americans responded to the enthronement of Hirohito in Japan as well as the struggles to contain increasing tensions over Northeast China. The cataclysm of the Manchurian Incident and its impact on U.S. and Japanese opinion and private diplomacy takes up chapter 8. Chapter 9 studies new tensions wrought by the rise of Japanese militarism, the hope for a liberal turnaround after the failure of the February 26, 1936 coup d'état in Japan, and new suspicions of spying in the mid 1930s. Chapter 10 examines the outbreak of the Sino-Japanese War, public responses on both sides, and the rupture of U.S.-Japanese informal diplomacy. The immediate causes of the outbreak of the Pacific War are examined in chapter 11 and last-ditch efforts to avoid war are revealed. Finally the epilogue makes connections to the Pacific War and the American occupation of Japan after World War II.

*   *   *

One can draw several conclusions from this study of U.S.-Japanese relations. Using the Japanese media to shape public opinion, Japanese conservatives and militarists used several events to shape a negative opinion of Americans. The Washington Conference Treaties that most American observers believed to be a win for the Japanese and especially for Japanese liberals was interpreted by the right wing as a questionable appeasement. The so-called exclusion clause of the U.S. Immigration Act of 1924 mobilized conservatives and created strong antagonism toward the United States. Resentments that had built up after continually being slighted by the West exploded with immigration exclusion. Japanese burned the American flag, staged protests in all major Japanese cities, and July 1, the date of the law's implementation, was renamed National Humiliation Day. This was the beginning of strong anti-American sentiment and it grew stronger throughout the rest of the interwar period.

Japanese liberals believed that they held sway in the 1920s. They followed the lead of the West and encouraged cooperation with the West to ensure Japan's trade networks there. However, liberals never believed that Japan was becoming just like the United States. Nor did they endorse the Orientalist exoticism of the West. Nitobe and others openly tried to dissuade Westerners from thinking about Japan in these highly stereotyped ways. The Japanese had passed a Universal Manhood Suffrage Law in 1924 that seemed to under-line the power of liberals in Japan. However, they underestimated the strength of militarists. Their approach of cooperation with the West was undermined not only by the actions of the militarists but also by the American approach in the Washington Conference and immigration exclusion. A force for stability in U.S.-Japanese relations, liberals eventually lost power to the militarists and became marginalized.

The shifting views of the American public also played an important role in the decline of the relationship. The more favorable view put forward by missionaries and others that the Japanese were becoming more like the United States was overtaken by a more negative view that the Japanese maintained a façade of modernity under which they were really not modern at all but bound by a feudal past of militarism and blind obedience. The belief that Japan was becoming a modern Westernized nation was undermined by the actions of the Japanese Kwantung Army in Manchuria such as the assassination of Chang Tsolin (Zhang Zuolin) and the Manchurian Incident. By the 1930s, Americans began to be persuaded that the Japanese were not like them after all.

The consequence of this shift was an increasingly anti-Japanese American public. The impact of this antagonism was felt concretely by official diplo-mats in the State Department. In 1931 during the Manchurian Incident, again in 1937 at the outset of Sino-Japanese War, and finally in 1941 with the American oil embargo against Japan, the response of the American government to events in East Asia was shaped by public outcry against the Japanese.

Finally unofficial diplomacy failed to bridge the gap that developed between the United States and Japan. The same events that shaped public opinion also shaped and limited the ability of private citizens to change the direction of U.S.-Japanese relations. The period began with the high aspira-tions of John Dewey and many others that private citizens would fulfill their democratic potential by solving the problems that beset the world through a "diplomacy of peoples."

With hopes raised by President Woodrow Wilson's vision of a new world order of peace and collective security after World War I, internationalism, like unofficial diplomacy, gained new strength. Many individuals pursued both. Although many Americans embraced Wilson's ideas and the League of Nations, Japanese liberals expressed skepticism about the new international-ism. They wondered if the words were simply new labels placed on the same old European system of secret alliances and war that had previously mistreated Japan.

The immigration debacle in 1924 galvanized unofficial diplomats on both sides. The IPR was founded in the aftermath of it and devoted a great deal of energy to immigration issues in its first two conferences. Tsurumi Yusuke spent over a year in the United States giving lectures designed to convince Americans to reconsider their punitive law. Sidney Gulick too campaigned to roll back the law.

However, private citizens could not escape the interests and loyalties of their nations. Many Americans considered immigration to be an internal matter and immigration exclusion remained. The IPR research program became an expression of the American and Japanese rivalry instead of an opportunity to collaborate on an internationalist research agenda. Although the IPR's Kyoto meeting in 1929 calmed tensions between Japan, the United States, and China over Manchuria, and seemed to justify faith in unofficial diplomacy, ultimately, Japanese liberals sided with their emperor as Japan began to expand into Manchuria by force of arms in September 1931. In 1932, Nitobe traveled to the United States to explain the Manchurian Incident to an outraged American public. Instead of calming antagonism, Nitobe further angered his American audience with a defense of the Japanese Empire and accusations that the Americans suffered from unjustified self-righteousness. Americans accused him of abandoning his commitment to internationalism.

Japanese private diplomats moved closer to official diplomats in the 1930s by amalgamating the IPR and the Japan International Association, an arm of the Foreign Ministry. Japanese IPR leadership saw this move as an opportunity to become more influential. However, American IPR members intimated that the close links between the IPR and the national government eroded the IPR's effectiveness as an "impartial" instrument of private citizen diplomacy, without any "political character." During the Sino-Japanese War, the Japanese IPR became a tool for Japanese propaganda. In general, unofficial diplomacy became discredited as a means of resolving U.S.-Japanese tensions in the 1930s.[8]

At the moment of war in 1941, a last-ditch effort to save U.S.-Japan relations was initiated by Japanese Christians. Kagawa Toyohiko and other Japanese Christians traveled to the United States in 1941 on a whirlwind tour, but the conferences and meetings that had no discernable impact on U.S.-Japanese relations.

CHAPTER 1

AMERICAN PERCEPTIONS OF JAPAN: LIBERAL MODERNITY OR FEUDAL MILITARISM

BY THE END OF WORLD WAR I IN 1918, THE JAPANESE AND AMERICANS HAD contemplated each other for close to seventy years, from the time of Commodore Perry's opening of Japan in 1853. In this time both developed strong images of the other. Though these images did not accurately or completely reflect the reality of the other, they were nonetheless powerful because they represented the building blocks of the unofficial U.S.-Japanese relationship. Although it would be inaccurate to say the United States and Japan went to war over mutually antagonistic images, perceptions of the other help us begin to piece together an explanation of tensions that made war seem inevitable by 1941.

Americans' views of Japan were shaped mostly through the media available to the American reading public. To be certain, there were a few Americans who traveled once or twice or even frequently to Japan. An even smaller minority went to live in Japan either permanently or for long periods of time. Most prominent in this group were Christian missionaries. Those who lived in Japan and learned the Japanese language could call on more information to reach conclusions about the Japanese as a people. Only when Americans decided to stay long-term in Japan as missionaries, businessmen, or diplomats were their impressions of Japan shaped more by the Japanese flow of information and Japanese relationships. These cases were more infrequent but still influenced American perceptions of Japan.

Americans could choose from a wide variety of sources of information to find out more about Japan. Almost 80,000 newspaper articles with the word "Japan" in them were published in *The New York Times* alone from 1919 to 1941. In the same period, there were 2,897 magazines articles on Japanese domestic politics, society, and on U.S.-Japanese diplomacy. This number was slightly less than the number of articles published on China and slightly more than the number published on France. More articles were published on Germany and Great Britain, but the large number of articles on Japan tells us that there was a substantial amount of information available on Japan in the interwar period. One article per week for the entire interwar period could have been read. This fact runs against the traditional assumption that Americans suffered from a lack of information about Japan.[1]

In addition, several dozen books were published with Japan as one part of the subject or the whole topic. Book lists with Japan as the subject were available in *The Literary Digest, The New York Times Current History, The Missionary Review of the World,* and *The Japanese Student* (a publication of Japanese YMCA students in English printed in the United States by the American YMCA). Beyond that, missionaries wrote circular letters that were sent back to home congregations in the United States. These letters had small circulation but a large impact on the people who read them. Parishioners were expected to give donations to missionaries and so paid close attention to the work they supported. Missionaries also returned home for extended periods of time to rest and recuperate, and they often went on lecture tours explaining their work in Japan. This information reached an interested listening public.

Recent Japanese history held the interest of the American public. The Meiji Restoration of 1868 and the Japanese campaign of modernization that followed it provided a dramatic introduction. The Japanese political leadership had guided Japan from a position of vulnerability threatened with takeover by the European powers to great power status for themselves by the end of World War I. They had achieved this great height through thorough political, economic, and military modernization. Americans were greatly impressed. However, the rapidity of Japan's modernization left them with lingering questions about how modern the Japanese really were.

Certainly Americans interested in Japan knew of the stunning victory of the Japanese in the Russo-Japanese War of 1904–1905. This victory gave the Japanese legitimacy in the eyes of the Western powers. It also marked the beginning of rivalry between the United States and Japan, a rivalry that was very much alive in 1919. After American president Theodore Roosevelt negotiated the Portsmouth Peace Treaty between the Russians and the Japanese and won a Nobel Peace Prize for his efforts in 1905, he reinforced the American fleet in the Philippines, saying, "Japan is an Oriental nation and the individual standard of truthfulness in Japan is low." In 1906, Roosevelt initiated WAR PLAN ORANGE which was the army's strategic plan to fight the United States' most threatening enemy. The plan focused on Japan.[2]

The fears of Americans about Japanese immigrants on the West Coast of the United States also plagued U.S.-Japanese relations. Japanese immigrants in California, who had become successful farmers, faced economic resentment, racial prejudice, and open discrimination there. In the aftermath of the Great San Francisco earthquake in 1906, the San Francisco School Board forced all Asian students to attend a separate school. In 1907, Theodore Roosevelt negotiated the Gentlemen's Agreement with the Japanese government to outlaw further immigration to the United States from Japan in almost all cases. Later in 1913 the California legislature passed the Alien Land Act that barred Japanese immigrants from buying or leasing land there. The Japanese, well aware of these actions, were offended by them.[3]

ORIENTALISM

Most of the information Americans gathered about Japan was tainted by stereotypes. Sheila Johnson has called much of American image-making about Japan "dangerously antiquarian and exceptionalist."[4] The stereotypes began with first contact between Japan and the West in the sixteenth century, but were greatly strengthened by reports from Westerners in the nineteenth century after the Meiji Restoration (1868). Missionaries brought back stories of Japanese sexual promiscuity that made American Christians blanch. A.B. Simpson, in a book ironically entitled *Larger Outlooks on Missionary Lands* (1893), found the Japanese in general to be a "frightfully immoral people" whose women wore kimonos "quite too open at the bosom" and whose "habits and customs in public baths are said to be grossly improper."[5]

The Japanese were often grouped together with other races, ethnic groups, and nations into the category of "the Orient," spanning the Middle East and East Asia. This grouping allowed Westerners to speak and think of those who lived in the Orient as people with a common way of life and a common spirit. It drove Western interpretations of the region.[6] However, this approach badly misrepresented the diversity and variety of those so labeled. In addition, the characteristics of this supposedly common Oriental culture were often portrayed in negative terms. For instance, Orientals had too few morals and too much sensuality. Orientals lacked honesty and therefore the Orient was full of corruption. However, these stereotypes took a variety of forms. Not all Americans saw Japanese culture so negatively.[7]

Historian Joe Hennings, who has studied nineteenth-century American views of Japan, examined those "orientalists" who saw traditional Japanese culture in a more positive light. He notes that antimodernists in the West abhorred rising industrialism and the disintegration of traditional ways of life admired Japanese traditions.[8]

At its most extreme, this rejection of Western industrial modernity created a phenomenon of "going native." For example, Lafcadio Hearn, who came to Japan as a journalist, ended up staying permanently, marrying a Japanese woman, and taking a Japanese name. Hearn tended to idealize old Japan and emphasize the exoticism of it. He was important because he published several books on Japan that sold many copies in the United States in the late nineteenth century, at a time when much less information was available on Japan.[9]

Americans were fascinated with Japanese art. In the early years of Japan's opening to the West, art curator Ernest Fenollosa from Harvard University became entranced by Japanese art and took a teaching job at Tokyo Imperial University. Fenollosa worked for the preservation of Japan's traditional art and became curator of Imperial Art Museum of Japan. Like many Western art aficionados of the time, Fenollosa also took a large number of Japanese art objects out of Japan back to Boston's Museum of Fine Arts where he became curator of Oriental art. In addition, American women became very interested in art trinkets from Japan and they sold well in the United States in the interwar years.[10]

In the magazine *Current Opinion*, Dr. Frank Crane, a Presbyterian minister and columnist who had become well known for pithy maxims about life, cast traditional Japan in a positive light. Crane was a fan of Okakura Kakuzô, a famous Japanese writer who extolled Japan's traditional virtues and bemoaned the onslaught of crass moneymaking of modern capitalism. Writing of traditional Japan, Crane stated "Their civilization automatically produces quietness, peace, contentment, and the riches of the thought-life, while ours has a constant product of turmoil and dissatisfaction, for we are so preoccupied in acquiring the means to live that we forget life itself . . ." J.O.P. Bland, an old China hand, wrote of the Imperial Palace in Tokyo. "It is as if the spirit of the ancient East were here invulnerably entrenched, a treasure-house and strong hold of Asian mystery, protected by invisible hands against a world of impious change."[11] These nostalgic views constructed a dreamworld around Japan that hindered a clear view of Japan during the interwar period.[12]

William Elliot Griffis, one the most prominent of the commentators on Japan, lived in Japan in the 1870s and wrote *The Mikado* (1876), perhaps the most influential book written on Japan before World War II. *The Mikado* made it on most readings lists of Americans seeking knowledge about Japan. Rejecting the antimodernist perspective, Griffis took a positive view of Japanese modernization. Although he died in 1928, Griffis' writings continued to appear into the 1930s. His writing on Japan—numbering fourteen books, many of which were reissued more than once in his lifetime—and his long experience of Japan gave him a broad view of Japan's changes. Even though Griffis clearly endorsed Japanese modernity, as he was close to his own death, he seemed to invite nostalgia for the old Japan that he had known when he arrived in Japan in 1872. One of his essays, "Japan, Child of the World's Old Age," appeared in the *National Geographic Magazine* in 1933 and came out a year later as a book. The essay had many pictures of old Japan and a nostalgic tone.[13]

Even the well-known missionary Sidney Gulick, who welcomed modernity in Japan, commented, "For it is safe to say that no Japanese lady ever appears quite so attractive in a foreign gown as in her own picturesque costume."[14]

Another book read by many Americans was Nitobe Inazô's *Bushido*. Nitobe wrote the book in English and intended it for a Western audience, and it was also tinged with nostalgia for old Japan. It was translated from English into five other languages and went through several editions. Immensely popular, the book focused on the decline of Japanese samurai traditional ethics Nitobe termed "bushido" or the way of warrior. In the view of Nitobe and other Japanese, the demise of bushido was the result of the rise of modern values such as individualism and the selfish greed of capitalism. *Bushido's* imagery of hara-kiri or ritual suicide was fascinating to Western audiences, and its descriptions of the samurai's unerring sacrifice, honor, and self-denial were an ode to the Japanese warrior way of life.

Increasingly, however, as U.S.-Japanese relations failed and Japanese militarism arose in the 1930s, bushido became a symbol of antiquarian and dangerous attitudes in Japan, at odds with modern life. William Chamberlin, an American journalist covering Japan in 1937, thought he saw bushido's influence on the Japanese military-officer class in their ascetic personal habits.[15]

Thomas Millard, a native of Missouri, worried that nostalgic Westerners got the wrong impression of Japan. Having served as a journalist in Shanghai between 1895 and 1915, Millard founded his own journal there in 1917 and found time to write seven books on East Asia between 1905 and 1931. According to Millard, this nostalgia obscured the truth that Japan was a military oligarchy intent on the domination of East Asia.

> How much I wonder, of geisha girls, of cherry blossoms, of politeness of servants and rickshaw coolies anxious for a tip or desirous of smoothly cover-ing a pecuniary exaction, of lotus blooms, of old palaces and temples, of crude surprise and astonishment at commonplace facts and circumstances of Oriental life, of the beauty of a scenically delightful land, is included in the pre-sent Western conception of Japan and her policy? Too much; entirely too much I think.[16]

George William Knox critiqued Asian culture in his book, *The Spirit of the Orient* (1906). Knox, who had attained his doctorate and taught theology at Presbyterian College in Tokyo from 1877 to 1900, stated

> The East has lacked the power of organization, of attention to detail, of thoroughgoing discipline, of patient working to great and distant ends. It has been absorbed in the contemplation of "the Ultimate and the Absolute" and it has submitted in the present world to more militant races.[17]

At a deeper level, Orientals did not learn much from other cultures and maintained their own culture in a kind of immutability which made them prisoners of the past. "The weight of the past is too heavy, and the bondage of custom too strong for emancipation to win, and the 'native' remains unconvinced and unimpressed."[18]

Finally Knox summarized his work with a sweeping statement.

> During long centuries Asia remained unchanged, or slowly and steadily deteriorated. There seemed no inherent power capable of producing new life. Thought revolved perpetually around the same subjects; literature repeated the same stories, centered its poetry in the same themes, and found delight in increasing minuteness of style and ornament.
>
> Government discovered no new system, and wars or revolutions simply replaced one set of rulers by another. In neither rulers nor ruled were great ideals of human liberty or progress produced. So was it in India and in China and in Japan . . . The spirit of Asia had exhausted itself; it had no new inspirations and no new visions. Its thought of the universe was of a vast living organism circling round and round forever; over all was Fate, ruling spirit and body alike.[19]

As "Oriental" as Japan seemed, Knox believed the Japanese had escaped. Japan had modernized itself on the Western model and looked not at all like the Orient but more like the modern West. "But Japan has proved itself possessed in high degree of the very qualities which we have regarded as peculiarly belonging to the Occident."[20]

Historian Akira Iriye has commented that the question of how non-Westerners could participate in modern life vexed Westerners.[21] Knox found an answer to the question in the Westernization of Japan. By framing Japan's modernization within an Oriental-Occidental divide, Knox made modernity the exclusive domain of the Occidental. In so doing he linked cultural assumptions about "the spirit" of Japan to whether or not Japan was capable of modernity, assumptions that we have seen were distorted by the lens of Orientalism. As long as Japan abandoned its Oriental culture and became Occidental, its place in modern life was assured. The question became whether Japan had truly become Occidental. This culturalist interpretation became a litmus test for the authenticity of Japan's modernization.

What weight can we place on Knox's conclusions? Certainly it would be untrue to suggest that all Americans thought as Knox did. Given the high quality of the binding and higher price, Knox's work was a small to medium circulation book. It reached a serious reading audience curious about Asia. Given the large number of newspaper and magazine articles published on Asia, we can assume the reading public was a substantial market. Knox had an advanced degree and an attentive audience as a scholar of Christianity in East Asia. So we must take Knox's ideas seriously.

Knox's damning critique of the Orient and his positive assessment of Japan reflect two different arguments Americans made about the Japanese. The first, made by missionaries to Japan and others, recognized the great Japanese achievement of modernization and saw it as transforming not just Japan's political and economic systems but also its social system and basic outlook. In short, Japan had been liberated from the Orient by embracing Western modernity.

The second argument, put forward by journalists and others, saw Japanese modernization as limited to the mechanics of the political and economic systems and questioned its genuineness. This view questioned the depth of Japanese modernization because it seemed so unlike the situation in the rest of the Orient that "steadily deteriorated" as Knox indelicately put the matter. Could the Japanese really be so unlike their ancestors and near relatives in the Orient? According to this argument, Japan's geographical location in East Asia was a historical anchor that prevented true modernization. The possibility that the Japan had not escaped the Orient gave rise to the suspicion that they were not really modern in spite of the trappings of modernity. This became the basis for the argument that Japan was in the grip of feudal militarism. It produced a sense of betrayal and distrust of Japan among a sizeable segment of the American public in the 1930s.

LIBERAL MODERNITY

Several of the most important missionary voices of this time period, Sidney Gulick, Sherwood Eddy, and Galen Fisher, all articulated the positive view of Japanese modernity. Gulick, who was perhaps the best known of these, at least concerning Japan, grew up in a missionary family, serving the American Board of Foreign Missions as missionary from 1887 to 1913. In 1906 he began teaching at Doshisha University, a Christian University in Kyoto, and also taught at the Imperial University of Kyoto, returning to the United States in 1913. Gulick was among the most prolific and well-known writers on Japan. He wrote nine books concerning Japan and several more on other topics. His books were generally large-market books published with prominent presses. They made their way onto recommended readings lists for those interested in Japan and had a devoted following in the United States.[22]

In 1905, Gulick wrote a book in response to the rise of the anti-Japanese movement in California, sometimes called the Yellow Peril. Cleverly entitled *White Peril in the Far East* (1905), the book argued in an anti-imperialist vein that Europeans and Americans endangered East Asia more than Orientals endangered the United States Gulick went to some length to point out that not only had Japan modernized but the whole cultural system had been converted to a Western outlook. Japan had become individualistic and more democratic and this was sound evidence for its successful modernization.

Gulick's evidence for this transformation was the Russo-Japanese War of 1904–1905 when the Japanese treated their Russian prisoners of war with care and respect, giving medical attention to their wounds, while the Russians allowed 2,000 wounded Japanese soldiers to die on the battlefield in August 1904. Asking the question "Is Japan Oriental or Occidental?" Gulick stated,

> Oriental signifies that type of civilization which does not recognize the value or rights of the individual person as such. It represents autocratic absolutism in government; it emphasizes the rights of the superior and the duties of the inferior; it ranks men as inherently superior to woman; it has no place for popular education or for representative government, and it esteems military virtue as the highest type known.

On the other hand there was Occidental

> civilization which recognizes and builds on the inherent value and inalienable rights of the individual person. . . . In its logically developed forms, Anglo-Saxon civilization emphasizes constitutional and representative government. Obedience to law, inherent equality and liberty of all men . . .[23]

Then Gulick asserted that Japan could no longer be Oriental because of the way it valued individualism. "So far then as we judge Japan's treatment of Russian prisoners to be the genuine expression of her inner life must we count her as belonging to the occidental rather than to the oriental system of civilization."[24] In Gulick's view, Japanese modernization was a success story, but it is also clear that he shared a caricatured view of Oriental culture with commentators like George Knox.

Sherwood Eddy was second only to Sidney Gulick in popularizing East Asia to the American public, although Eddy was much more of a generalist than Gulick. Gulick focused on Japan and Eddy covered virtually all of Asia, including Russia, in his writings. Eddy had spent a great deal of time in Asia, working in India for several years as a YMCA secretary there and making missionary tours to both China and Japan. By the early 1930s Eddy had written several books about the region. He showed a talent for turning notes from his tours into books very rapidly, and excelled at public speaking, so he soon rose to the leadership ranks of the missionary movement. In addition to his books, Eddy spent many hours in church basements throughout America relating his travels and ideas, and he became very influential in framing Japan and East Asia to the American public.

In the early post–World War I period Eddy expressed a hopeful view of Japan and U.S.-Japanese relations. He visited Japan in 1922 and found that while industrialism had created profound strains, Japan was making great strides. Later, in *The Challenge of the East* (1931), he remarked on the breathtaking rapidity of the Japanese march to modernity. "In nearly all departments of life, Japan's advance during the last sixty years has been phenomenal." The empirical reality of Japanese modernization was stunning to Westerners.[25] In another characterization that was often repeated, Eddy painted a picture of Japan throwing off feudalism for modernity. "Like a chick breaking from its shell, the liberal Japan is today breaking through the hard and crusted repression of feudal militarism and a new nation is coming to birth."[26]

Galen Fisher, who had served as a missionary to Japan from 1901 to 1919 as head of the Japanese YMCA there and was later head of the Institute of Social and Religious Research, made the same argument in his 1923 book, *Creative Forces in Japan.* Fisher's book was a small-market book published by the YMCA Association Press. However, his ideas confirm Eddy's. In a chapter entitled "Militarism, Reaction and Liberalism," Fisher began with the unsubtle statement that "Japan came into the family of nations fifty years ago with a big handicap. For ages she had been brought up by the rod and the straitjacket of feudalism and she has had a hard time learning how to behave in a family where self-government is the rule." According to Fisher's version, the break came with the Meiji Restoration. When Fisher looked upon Japan in 1923 with his accumulated experience he saw much the same trend as Gulick and Eddy had identified. In fact Fisher was fairly open about what the Americans wanted to see in Japan.

> But for us, as we seek evidence that liberalism will ultimately prevail in Japan, the most significant facts are not the edicts of the government, but the voluntary activities of the people—the development of the press, the gradual creation of an intelligent public opinion and the tireless fight for freedom of speech and for party government.[27]

These missionaries saw Japan through the prism of American democracy and liberalism. So Japan was a mirror for American liberals. In his approach,

Fisher indicates some of the intense struggles of American liberals in this period. Not only did the world need to begin to look like the United States In turn, Americans had to protect and enlarge liberal and democratic ideas at home. In reality, Fisher's somewhat fevered analysis indicates that liberals were not completely comfortable with political and social conditions within the United States in what was to be a fairly conservative time in American life in the 1920s. Linking change in Japan to the American situation became troublesome because vulnerability and reaction at home and abroad became indivisible. Unable to see the limits of American and Western influence upon Japan, Fisher succumbed to the fiction that American and Japanese destinies were inextricably linked.

Though missionaries who stayed for long periods in Japan might have had a clearer view of Japan, their general commitment to a liberal view and the fact that Japanese friends of the missionaries were liberal and Westernizing skewed their perceptions about the potential for a liberal and democratic future in Japan. They were quite likely to underestimate the power and influence of the militarists in Japan.

JAPANESE FEUDAL MILITARISM

Journalists and others who had less direct experience in Japan were less likely to perceive Japan becoming modern. What emerges from their writings is an extended critique of Japanese modernization. The problem is that the critique was not based upon deep knowledge of Japan in most cases but upon commonly held assumptions about the nature of Japanese culture. Writing on the basis of one or two short visits to the Japanese islands, those who took the negative view made the opposite mistake of the missionaries. They overestimated the power of the military instead of underestimating it. This view played directly into the assumption that nothing much changed in Japan. The militarists of the present were direct descendants of the feudal samurai of the past. Whereas the missionary view emphasized change, the negative view of journalists and others saw the Japanese as an unchanging people stuck in the past.

Putnam Weale's *An Indiscreet Chronicle of the Pacific* (1923) discussed the military men of Japan to frame Japan's unchanging past. "The men [Japanese] of five centuries ago had therefore almost precisely the same characteristics as today . . ." Putnam Weale is the pen name of Bertram Lennox Simpson, an Englishman who worked in the political section of the office of the president of China. He worked in China under Sir Robert Hart who was the head of the trade and currency exchange section of the Chinese government. Released by a very successful British publisher, this book probably circulated widely in England where it was published but was less popular in the United States

It is likely that those in either country who knew East Asia were attracted to the book by the relative prominence of the author.[28]

In addition to Weale, J.O.P. Bland discussed Japanese political and social modernization in a negative light as well in a book *China, Japan and Korea* published by the large New York press Scribner. The book made the *New York Times Current History* magazine recommended reading list.[29] Generally, political protest and labor unrest—widespread in Japan in the years immediately after World War I—were interpreted as signs of the growth of a democratic mentality. Bland disagreed, stating,

> Observers on the spot seem to be so impressed by the growth of political ferment and labor unrest that they are liable to lose sight of the inherent vitality and cohesive value of the family system, on which the whole structure of Japan's society is based.

Bland saw the family system in Japan as too strong to be overcome by Western values.

> It [the family system] constitutes beyond all doubt the strongest moral and political force in Japan; so deep in the past lie its roots, so strong are its inherited impulses of obedience and loyalty, that I cannot bring myself to believe that Western civilization will ever dominate or destroy it.

According to Bland, modernization would never penetrate the Japanese political or social values as long as the Japanese family and clan system maintained its grip upon Japan.[30]

Another writer, Stephen King-Hall rejected the view that Japan was becoming more liberal and democratic in its politics. King-Hall, an Englishman with a scholarly interest in East Asia, focused upon Japanese politics and on Shintoism in *Western Civilization and the Far East* (1925). In discussing Japanese politics, he asserted that nothing fundamental had changed in Japan.

> As we shall see, even the so-called Restoration of the Emperor at the close of the shogunate period did not affect the existence of this peculiar system, but merely altered the personalities of the actors, substituting for the men who had controlled the shogun and therefore the Emperor a body of bureaucrats who by means such as Shinto and a constitution modeled on Bismarck's ideas, were destined to govern Japan autocratically from 1870 until now.

King-Hall asserted the Japanese people would follow their leaders obediently.

> It was easy, necessary, natural, for the values of Japan to be autocratic. They could and did change their policies with impunity, secure in the knowledge

that the people, politically negligible, bewildered and blinking at their emergence from the twilight of feudalism into the glare of Western civilization would do as they were told with sheep-like fidelity.[31]

In another blow to the modernization argument, King-Hall believed Japanese Shintoism held back the nation.

It is a fact from which great consequence may arise that the [Shinto] cult which is considered by the Japanese rulers as the principal cement of national morale, is antithetic to the whole spirit of modern western thought. It is unscientific; it is intensely official and centralized; it is imperialistic; it is militaristic and undemocratic; it is intolerant.

If Japan is to develop along those democratic lines, which so far as one can judge are, with occasional set-backs, the lines of future political development throughout the world, it is difficult to suppose that this national cult of Shinto can remain as the foundation of Japanese morality.[32]

King-Hall did concede that the spiritual aspect of any nation-state is important for national unity, comparing the Japanese to other situations such as American Republicanism, the French commitment to their own artistic and intellectual genius, and the German interest in scientific industriousness.

One can see in King-Hall's arguments two different paths. He saw the power of Shinto to captivate the Japanese and predicted the rise of Japanese militarism and war. However, the distinction that King-Hall drew between Japanese Shintoism-militarism and Japanese democracy oversimplified the situation. In 1925, the year that King-Hall published his book pointing to Japanese autocracy, the Japanese moved to universal manhood franchise, enabling all adult Japanese males to vote for the first time in Japanese history. In fact the move to militarism in Japan later in the 1930s was not characterized by the destruction of democracy. Elections continued and governments rose and fell even during World War II. The 1930s in Japan were characterized not by the end of democracy and the assertion of autocracy as King-Hall argued but by a greater alignment between democracy, support for the Japanese Emperor, and expansion abroad. After all, successful modernization and the existence of a democratic political system were no guarantee against militarism. The fact that Adolf Hitler was elected democratically in 1932 and maintained tremendous popular support throughout the 1930s illustrates the point.[33]

Marguerite Harrison commented widely on Japanese society and politics in her book *Yellow Dragon and Red Bear* (1924). Harrison was a journalist and adventurer of a kind not often found in the 1920s. Her father was a shipping tycoon who made a fortune in the transatlantic trade. Harrison raised a family but after her husband died, she became determined to break the mold of an upper-class life. She worked for a short time for the *Baltimore Sun* but when World War I broke out she volunteered to work as an agent in the Military Intelligence Division of the U.S. Army while posing as a newspaper correspondent. She had little experience of Japan but in 1921 she traveled there on the way to Soviet Russia where she was arrested and imprisoned by the Bolshevik government.

Harrison, in spite of her slight experience of Japan attained a remarkable range of description. Her book is one of the better sources we have of American descriptions of Japanese society and culture in the 1920s. Women, geishas, theater, storytelling, the writing of poetry, sports, and dancing in Japan all occupied Harrison's pen. Harrison pointed out that most women were considered lower than men and common prostitutes in Japan were little more than slaves, although she also remarked on the considerable freedom and prestige of the geisha.

When Harrison discussed Japanese storytelling or Kodan entertainment, she noted that tradition held sway amidst modernity.

> Except for the fact that beer was served instead of sake, that the lanterns were lit by electric bulbs instead of rush lights, and that some of the men wore European undergarments or American B.V.D.'s instead of the haori and the hakama, they might have been their own ancestors . . . The men who listened were modern Japanese of the middle and lower classes. They read the daily papers and the latest books; they also probably enjoyed the American movies a few doors away; but the past had lost none of its charm for them and still held them as firmly as ever under its spell.[34]

Marguerite Harrison added the point that the Japanese military was influential and Japanese of all stripes saw expansionism as indispensable to the survival of the state.

> The Japanese have always been a military people. The average Japanese will tell you that militarist imperialism was largely stimulated in their own country by the example of other countries and by the instinct of self-preservation. I talked with many Japanese on the subject, from extreme conservatives down to Socialist leaders like Kagawa and Suzuki Bundji [*sic*], and I never found a man or woman who did not firmly believe that the Sino-Japanese War, the Russo-Japanese War and the acquisition by Japan of Formosa and Korea were absolutely essential to the preservation of the Empire.[35]

Stanley Hornbeck straddled the divide between those who believed in and those who were skeptical of Japanese modernization. Hornbeck, who received a Ph.D. from the University of Wisconsin went onto a distinguished career in government service as a diplomat, but in the early 1910s–1920s he remained a scholar of East Asia, writing a book on Japan and China, *Contemporary Politics in the Far East* (1918). Hornbeck divided the book into two major sections, historical and contemporary politics, siding with the missionary view in constructing his argument about the history of Japanese modernization and joining the skeptics when discussing the contemporary situation.[36]

Hornbeck suggested that the change in Japan came during the Russo-Japanese War of 1904–1905. Here Japanese modernization went from benign to dangerous because Japan became an imperial power. It is perhaps not a coincidence that at this point in time Japan also became a much greater threat to the United States, which began to see Japan as a rival for power in the Pacific thereafter.

What conclusions can we draw from these expressions of skepticism about Japan's modernity? Asserting that Japan was the same as centuries before in essential ways, most of these writers underestimated the great changes that had taken place in Japan since the Meiji Restoration. In many ways the changes that had taken place in Japan made discussion of whether Japan was modern a silly exercise. Japan had centralized its political system and educational system, built a modern industrial economy, and created a modern army based upon the Prussian model.

Some scholars have claimed that proof of Japan's lack of modernity can be seen in the brutal atavism of Japan's warfare. The soldiers were barbaric because they had not mastered modernity. However, the twentieth century demonstrates that nothing is so brutal as modern warfare. The brutality of the Japanese Army likely had more to do with the inhumane hazing Japanese officers inflicted upon new recruits. They were beaten regularly, sometimes daily, as a way to toughen them. As a consequence, soldiers treated the victims of war in the same way that they were themselves treated.

Other scholars argue that Japanese soldiers were imitators of samurai in their self-sacrifice and devotion to nation. This argument carries more weight but must be understood within the context of the rise of Japanese nationalism in the late nineteenth century. The samurai were loyal to their lord and region and did not have a modern concept of a Japanese nation. Only in the era of modernity when loyalty was inculcated nationwide through public schools, nationwide media, and military training was deep loyalty to the Japanese Emperor created. Some Japanese did not even know of the existence of the Japanese Emperor before the national indoctrination campaign of the late nineteenth century.[37] Imperial loyalty was not an ancient tradition, but a very modern practice of molding the entire population, creating a nation of loyal subjects. The loyalty that one glimpses in any modern nation especially in time of war is the direct result of this practice. It is true that modern nationalists often use references to ancient traditions to bind populations.

But this is not an actual return to the past but an invention of a past that never existed in the quite the same form. A perfect example of this is Nitobe Inazô's samurai ethics in his book *Bushido*. The word Bushido did not even exist in the premodern period in Japan. Under Nitobe's hand it became a modern way to remember the values of the samurai. Thus, those who saw Japan as a feudal nation possessing only a thin veneer of modernity distorted Japan's recent past to fit this view rather than confronting squarely Japan's recent history.

Comparing Japan to other nations also helps to dispel the accusation of feudal militarism. The 1930s were characterized by the rise of militarism not only within East Asia but also within Europe. Germany and Italy became fascist, devoting great amounts of money to building their armies. And yet no one claimed at the time that either Germany or Italy was stuck in or returning to their past. These Europeans used the past to create loyalty and a mystique of the nation. They invented a past to serve the needs of their nation.[38]

In the United States, no militarism arose. However, the forces for the rise of a militant fascism similar to Germany existed in the political careers of Huey Long and Father Charles Coughlin, both of whom were right-wing populists with large constituencies. Franklin Delano Roosevelt outmaneuvered them in the 1936 election. Coughlin's movement, the National Union for Social Justice, faltered at the polls. Huey Long disappeared from the political scene after he was assassinated in 1935.

Therefore, the rise of militarism in Japan can be accounted for by the same conditions under which it arose within Europe and had the potential to arise within the United States. The instability of industrial capitalism and the devastation the Great Depression wrecked on all of these nations gave rise to right-wing forces in Japan as it did in Europe and the United States.

Russell Weigley, a noted military historian, has remarked that

> too often American observers of the Japanese army saw only the stereotypes they had carried in their heads from the United States, not the real Japanese army. Japanese bayonet training for example, was reported to be merely an adaptation of traditional Japanese techniques of the sword and therefore surely unsuited for combat against Western armies.[39]

The assumption that Japan hid its true feudal nature under a cloak of modernity was the foundation of this stereotype.

The Japanese, well aware of the stereotypes emanating from the United States about Japanese militarism, sought to counter those perceptions.

CHAPTER 2

JAPANESE RESPONSE TO ORIENTALISM

BY THE INTERWAR PERIOD, THE JAPANESE HAD ACCESS TO A WIDE VARIETY OF information about the United States and Europe. Japanese youth were known to be voracious readers, devouring great volumes of books. Reading Western literature, philosophy, and history, Japanese were well educated about Western ideas. However, American critics suggested that the number of books did not equal quality and fell back on Orientalist assumptions to describe Japanese reading habits. Robert Nichols, who had recently taken over Lafcadio Hearns' old post as the chair of English Literature at Tokyo Imperial University, stated his opinion unabashedly.

> It is a curious and in some ways pathetic sight to observe these young men and women swimming before the great glass cases [of Western books]. They appear to select at random—so much of what the Japanese do seems done at random . . . It is in many ways a primitive and naïve race.[1]

Some claimed that the old emphasis on Confucian readings was being displaced by focus on Western ideas.

> The old bookstores, containing the Chinese classics and other writings in the Chinese, are no longer, as they once were, the cornerstone of culture in Japan . . . The younger generation not only takes little interests in books in Chinese, but they find difficulty in reading them.[2]

Tsurumi Yusuke, an important prewar liberal intellectual and politician, explained the power of Japanese newspapers and other media. He estimated literacy in Japan at over 95 percent of the population. Total newspaper circulation was around 6–7 million; the *Osaka Mainichi* with daily circulation of 1.25 million and combined with *Tokyo NichiNichi* at 2 million; the *Tokyo*

Asahi and *Osaka Asahi* with a combined circulation of 1.25 million. These newspapers were all national in scope. And many newspapers carried book advertisements for popular Western books. Magazines were not nearly as popular as newspapers. The most popular Japanese magazines obtained a circulation of 200,000. One of the popular magazines *Reconstruction* had a circulation of between 60,000–70,000 and often ran articles that were critical of Japanese society, politics, or even more radical critiques of capitalism in Japan. Even occasional scholarly articles appeared in magazines and newspapers. Taken together this indicates a well-read and well-informed Japanese reading public. As a result we can safely assume that newspapers in Japan were very influential in shaping public opinion. Though scholars have questioned whether Japanese civil society was viable, this is evidence of a strengthening civil society and democracy in the 1920s.[3]

Japanese views of the United States and the West, though neither completely unified nor static before World War II, were influenced greatly by its experience of foreign relations in the Meiji period (1868–1912). Japan arrived at modernization in part by avoiding the fate of other East Asian nations. China had come under the hegemony of Great Britain at the end of the Opium Wars in 1842. Then Westerners came seeking trade privileges and resources, exploiting China's weakness by imposing new unequal treaties at every opportunity. Japan seemed destined for the same fate when American commodore Mathew C. Perry sailed into Yokohama harbor in 1853 forcibly opening Japan to the West. Later in 1858, the Americans and Japanese signed an unequal treaty similar to the Chinese unequal treaties.

The initial opening of Japan by the Commodore Perry and his black ships in 1853 was a shock. This shock could be interpreted in many ways. Maruyama Masao the famous postwar interpreter of Japanese modernization construed it as a positive shock that pushed Japan to modernize itself on the Western model. The Perry expedition was interpreted more negatively by other Japanese as an early blow in a war of Western imperialists against East Asians that put Japan at risk. Both the positive and negative interpretations saw Commodore Perry's arrival as a turning point that produced change.

The Triple Intervention of 1895 produced a second shock. The Germans, Russians, and French forced Japan to give the Liaotung peninsula back to China after it had been received as a result of Japan's great victory over China in the Sino-Japanese War of 1894–1895. The intervention embedded itself in the Japanese national memory as a sign that the West could not be trusted. Once again after the Russo-Japanese War, resentment against the West appeared when the terms of the peace negotiated by President Theodore Roosevelt seemed too lenient on the Russians. Huge protests in Japan marked the signing of the Portsmouth Treaty. These memories never disappeared and were later used to argue against cooperation with the West.

The victory of Sino-Japanese War (1895) encouraged patriotic feelings within Japan helping to fuel a nationalist revival in the 1890s. Issued in 1889, the Imperial Rescript on Education laid down the basic relationship of the Japanese Emperor and his subjects and established the divinity of the emperor. The new nationalism resulted in patriotic unity between those who favored more contact with the West and those who favored less contact. Called Westernizers and conservatives, these groups disagreed about much, including how Japan should expand its empire—through force or peaceful economic exploitation—but remained unified in their loyalty to the emperor and in their support for the growth of the Japanese Empire. Only Marxists in Japan rejected this dual commitment, condemning the emperor system and Japanese expansionism. But in the late 1920s as the Communist movement in Japan grew more vocal, Japanese authorities began to round up the leaders. The Marxist leadership spent the rest of the prewar period in jail and lost much of their influence.

In economic terms, Japan's experience after World War I was pivotal. Japan's economy boomed during the war but slid into recession afterward as Europeans began to produce for their own markets the items they had previously imported from Japan. Along with record labor unrest in 1919, the recession demonstrated the fragility of the Japanese economy and its dependence upon foreign markets and resources. In turn, it reemphasized the argument that its empire, especially Manchuria, provided Japan with significant resources, and therefore was a "lifeline."

This was a volatile time in politics as well. Japan suffered from great political protests after World War I both from those who wanted to open up the political system and make it more democratic, the so-called Taisho Democracy Movement—named for the Taisho Emperor's rule (1912–1926)—and from those who simply had difficulty in making ends meet. Large riots in Tokyo over the rising cost of rice and a trolley ride indicated tough economic times. Though liberals wanted a more open political system, fair governance of Japan's Empire, and peaceful expansion in East Asia through investment and trade, militarists wanted to control politics through bureaucratic management and expand the empire through force. The difference was sometimes compared to the difference between the Western European Enlightenment and German Romanticism. Ito Hirobumi, a Meiji oligarch who wrote the Japanese Constitution, took as his model the German Constitution, not the English or American Constitution. Referring to his approach, he once stated, "The situation in our country is characterized by the erroneous belief that the words of English, American, and French liberals and radicals are eternal verities . . . I have acquired arguments and principals to rectify the situation." The contest between liberals and conservatives was nothing less than a battle to define the character of Japanese modernity, although significantly, it was not about whether to return to the past.[4]

Japanese liberals often criticized not only the lack of democracy in government but also the domination of the government by clan politics. Clan politics had its origins in premodern Japan. Warlords who were the heads of the ruling clans of the various regions controlled the political system. Many Japanese believed that the Japanese government was still controlled by the two clans who had overthrown the Tokugawa in the Meiji Restoration, the Satsuma and Choshu. Ruling through bureaucrats who were not accountable to the Japanese people, clan politicians were considered a major danger. This was not an issue of more democracy but whether Japan's government ruled as the constitution specified or through some extra-constitutional and unelected clique hidden behind the scenes. As a consequence, the 1920s were a period of political contest and economic decline for Japan. This is not the traditional picture of Japan in the 1920s as a prosperous and increasingly democratic country, a view held by many foreigners, especially American missionaries.

CRITIQUE OF WESTERN PERCEPTIONS

The Japanese saw the United States differently than the rest of the West. The Americans were seen as more democratic and more willing than Europeans to treat Japan fairly and with respect, although the American role in the Portsmouth Treaty made some Japanese think otherwise. This positive view of American treatment of Japan changed gradually to one of suspicion over the interwar period.

Gauging their place in the world, the Japanese were sensitive to foreign interpretations of Japan. As we have seen, many Americans defined the Japanese as exotic Orientals. This was of concern to Japanese interested in creating better relations with the United States because they believed the stereotypes created false and damaging impressions. They responded by communicating directly with the American public to correct or downplay stereotypes, defending their culture and nation, and justifying their actions in East Asia by arguing that Japan produced progress and modernity there. Japanese elites who were fluent in English wrote articles in American journals and magazines countering the prevailing perceptions of Japan. From more popular magazines such as *Asia* or *The Living Age* to smaller journals such as *The Japanese Student*, which was a publication of Japanese foreign students studying in the United States, the Japanese communicated their views to the American public. It is difficult to measure the impact of these publications on the American attitude toward Japan. To read the views of Japanese themselves in English had been until recently somewhat unusual for an American audience. One can surmise that among Americans interested in Japan, these articles were read carefully.

The liberal Nitobe Inazô spent much of his time in this period as an internationalist working to improve U.S.-Japanese relations. But he also supported the imperial system of emperor and empire. Nitobe was critical of Japan's brutal handling of its colony Korea during the 1919 uprising and encouraged a more benign policy, but never suggested a Japanese withdrawal. Even more telling, Nitobe defended Japan's Manchurian invasion in 1932.[5]

As Nitobe had so much contact with the United States, he was very sensitive to the ways in which Americans exoticized Japan. Nitobe noted in an article on Japanese Westernization, "A good lady missionary once remarked to a friend of mine. 'Everything is different in Japan,' she said, 'cats have no tails, dandelions are cream-colored and chickens' feathers grow the wrong way.'" Nitobe went on to explain that in each case, the apparent difference was either an import from elsewhere or simply not a difference at all.[6]

Nitobe analyzed the nature of Japan's Westernization in an essay entitled "Character of the Occidentalization of Japan." Westerners believed that Japan was wholly dependent upon the West for innovation and change. Nitobe pointed out that while Westerners might believe that Japan "absorbed foreign ideas much like a sponge sucks up water," he asserted that "the last fifty years of Japan's progress will show that Occidentalization has been a systematically planned work." He pointed out what was going on in Japan could be described as "the Europeanization of Japan or, not unfitly [sic], the Japanization of European influences." Nitobe also made quick work of the overall assumptions about Occident and Orient by suggesting that both were too broad. Europe was different from America, Catholicism different from Protestantism.

> Just as, upon first approach, all Japanese look alike to a European and vice versa, simply because racial characteristics strike us first and individual peculiarities grow clearer only after close acquaintance, so was Aryan culture undivided in Japanese eyes and the whole white race one.[7]

When Nitobe refuted the notion that the West alone was responsible for Japan's progress, his assumptions were rooted in rudimentary anthropology. Nitobe introduced the reader to two terms, "convergence" and "affinity," to explain Japan's rapid assimilation of Western thought and institutions. Although Nitobe did not explain convergence satisfactorily, convergence buttressed his argument that Japan was not an inert receptor but actively engaged the West as it converged upon the West, and the West was also converging with Japan. "Affinity" meant that any humans who responded positively to the progressive West could acquire modernity, even primitive tribal peoples. Nitobe then argued that Japan had a preexisting natural "affinity" toward Western ideas. In fact, he asserted that "response means affinity," and thus,

Japan's rapid response to the West was evidence of its affinity for Western progress. However, a nation or race of people had to first possess this quality of affinity. Nitobe took pains to point out that in Russia, where various Tsars had been trying to Westernize the Russian people for centuries, the response there had been pitiful, and therefore no natural affinity existed.[8]

Nitobe also argued that feudalism and the modern concept of liberty were not as opposite as they seemed. "But strange to say, in the isolated feudal state, and in graded feudal society there was no small amount of liberty." In Japan, according to Nitobe, feudalism had offered some substantial forms of freedom, and here was the underlying affinity to the West: feudal freedom foreshadowed the Western concept of liberty. Nitobe turned Western assumptions about Japan upside down with this argument. While Westerners believed that the impulse for modernization came entirely from the West, Nitobe, using the example of the Japanese concept of liberty, argued that the roots of Japanese modernization lay in Japan and that the Japanese could direct modernization.[9]

Tsurumi Yusuke, one of the most talented of the younger generation of Japanese liberals and internationalists, was a student of Nitobe. As Nitobe had, Tsurumi became fluent in English and it seemed his destiny to become a cultural diplomat like Nitobe. Tsurumi became a writer and politician. After marrying the daughter of powerful moderate politician Goto Shimpei, Tsurumi also became well connected. He traveled many times to the United States to cultivate the U.S.-Japanese relationship. Tsurumi assumed that educating Americans to the truth about the Japanese would transform American attitudes toward them. Like Nitobe, Tsurumi recognized the danger of Western stereotypes about Japan. He began an inspection of the most common assumptions in a chapter facetiously called "The Mysterious Oriental Mind," published in a book called *Contemporary Japan* (1927). The book was written in English and intended for an American audience.

As Tsurumi noted, even though the term Oriental covered the geographical space from the Middle East to East Asia, the peoples included were in fact quite different from one another and should not be lumped together. To the notion that the Japanese were inscrutable because they were quiet and did not like debate, Tsurumi patiently explained that the basis for Japanese culture was harmony. He also suggested that the Japanese loved abstraction and were highly emotional but strove to control their emotions. Tsurumi might have been accused of substituting one stereotype for another at this point.[10]

Tsurumi also included a chapter on Japanese humor. Noting that Westerners assumed that the Japanese lacked any sense of humor, Tsurumi pointed out the myth of Japan's origins, which was tinged with humor. After recounting the story of the Sun Goddess retreating to a dark cave to escape her mischievous brother, Tsurumi explained she was lured from the cave by peals of laughter as the whole nation burst out at a funny dance given by one of its countrymen. Tsurumi told another story, this one contemporary, of a candidate for parliament who announced that the country must take a "bold forward step," and as he stepped forward he slipped and fell into the audience to great shouts of laughter. He was later voted into office. Tsurumi told many such funny stories. His point was that the Japanese did indeed have a good sense of humor. Westerners simply made assumptions without much knowledge of the Japanese.[11]

In an editorial in the March 1919 issue of *The Japanese Student*, Kato Katsuji, a Japanese student studying in America stated the very real peril that resulted from Western assumptions about Japan.

> Time was when it used to be the fashion among Americans to talk about that little island empire of Japan, characterizing it as a "land of cherry blossoms" and its people as "polite" and what not. We appreciate our American friends in praising what little we have in the way of Oriental Civilization, and thank those who have kindly taken trouble to write volumes of books on Japan. Most of these productions, however, are putting undue emphasis upon nonessentials, the mere outward expressions of a few Oriental traits. Up until the time of the Russo-Japanese War in which Japan emerged as a victor, Japan had been an object of curiosity to many a casual observer of things Oriental and the little Japan, unable to place herself in the position of foreign observers to see how she would appear from a distance, took not a little pride in being thus flattered. But that time is now gone. Japan is no longer an object of curiosity and of petty love; Japan is now often considered as a dangerous nation, and certain Americans are bent on attacking Japan on the presumption that the Japanese traits are at best detrimental to the progress of the world.[12]

Kato accurately gauged a shift in Western opinion after the Russo-Japanese War and understood clearly that Japanese success in empire-building had eroded Japan's innocence in Western eyes.

In a later issue of *The Japanese Student*, by then renamed *The Japan Review*, Kawashima Saijiro, editor of *Dai Nihon*, an influential and conservative monthly journal published in Tokyo also wrote of Western perceptions of Japan. Although he admitted that there was a "tendency abroad to credit Japan with crafty villainy," Kawashima believed that Japanese actions in expanding to East Asia could be explained within the context of the threats to Japan from an unstable East Asian continent. Kawashima argued that it was not Japanese duplicity but rather just the opposite, Japanese innocence and lack of guile in international relations that caused tension with the West. He saw two sides to the Japanese people, one side filled with courage, activity, and fortitude, the other characterized by weakness and shallow-brained thoughtlessness. Kawashima unwittingly contributed his own Orientalist perceptions of the Japanese here. Kawashima believed that many political and military leaders in Japan had too much of the bad side of the Japanese character. He criticized the Japanese "habit of silence" that he believed led to many misconceptions about the Japanese.[13]

These misunderstandings were of concern to Shibusawa Eiichi as well. Shibusawa was a great promoter of the U.S.-Japanese relationship. Shibusawa made a fortune in the early Meiji period, founding a bank and buying at a discount several government-built textiles factories that became very profitable. Building the nation through business prosperity, Shibusawa exemplified the patriotic Japanese businessman. He retired in 1909, after which he developed a strong interest in U.S.-Japanese relations. Shibusawa understood that Japan with few natural resources and a small domestic market needed more of both and should seek them in the West. He had many American friends in Japan and the United States such as John Mott the head of the American YMCA. In 1916, Shibusawa founded the U.S.-Japan Friends committee. This committee was associated with the Japanese Foreign Ministry. In the 1920s Shibusawa traveled to the United States several times, including the Washington Conference in 1921–1922. Until his death in 1931, he advocated closer relations between the two countries.

In a January article for the Japanese journal *Taiyo* that was reprinted in *The Japanese Student*, Shibusawa discussed the issue.

One of the most regrettable things which has been pressing upon my mind even before the late war was the fact that Japan, in spite of her rapidly ascending position in the comity of the nations, is still treated on bases decidedly inferior to other powers . . . The differences in race and religion has also contributed to this situation.

Such a situation as this however, cannot be silently overlooked by Japan. From the standpoint of physical equipment and appearance, we may be inferior, but these outward traits are never the criteria of ability of characters.[14]

Although he had no ready answers for the problem, Shibusawa understood that the perceived inferiority of Japan could do great damage to Japan's diplomacy with the West.

Ozaki Yukio, an old opponent of clan politics, also shared a concern about how the Japanese were perceived in the West. Ozaki was associated with the popular rights movement of the 1880s that had pushed Japan toward a parliamentary system and later became famous as the longest serving parliamentarian in the history of the Japanese Diet. He continued to serve through World War II and the American occupation, dying in 1954. Ozaki was convinced the Satsuma and Choshu clans still ruled behind the scenes and championed truly constitutional government to overcome clan rule.

Traveling in the United States in 1919, Ozaki noted that Japanese toys there were cheaply made and fell apart easily. Ozaki was embarrassed by this. He also saw that many American shops were unwilling to sell Japanese made goods anymore. Perceiving that the Japanese were no longer popular in America, Ozaki believed that the Chinese seemed to be more popular. But he did not blame this on American racism. Instead he stated,

> But this time I found it was the Japanese who were conceited. By now, in contrast, the Chinese had lost their arrogance. They had shown much more adaptability. So while the Japanese were not popular, the Chinese now were liked. Japan and China had reversed the positions in the thirty years since I had made my first visit abroad.[15]

Ozaki saw much to admire in the United States, unlike Europe. He admitted to being envious of the American approach to World War I. He saw the United States as decisive in entering the war and unselfish in not demanding reparations from the war.

> Americans are a remarkably resolute people. They do not appear to mind risking their lives. In the Great War, they spent an enormous amount of money and lost many lives, but they seem to regard war as being rather adventurous and exciting. Men and women routinely carry guns and use them against each other, often fatally. It is a great mistake to think that the women are weak.[16]

He even thought the decision for prohibition showed resoluteness.

Asakawa Kan'ichi, a distinguished scholar and the first Japanese to take an academic position at an American university (Yale), reflected on attempts to reeducate Americans about the Japanese. Asakawa came to the conclusion that in spite of these efforts, Americans clung to their preconceived ideas about Japan. He was skeptical that these notions could be overcome. Instead, he believed that only the interchange of serious scholars could over a longer time period be effective.[17]

REJECTION OF MILITARISM

Yoshino Sakuzo, liberal democratic leader and Christian, also weighed in about Western perceptions. Yoshino honed in on the perception that Japanese modernization and liberalization was superficial and underneath Japan was a militarized and bureaucratic state in a November 1919 *The Living Age* article. The origin of the text is unclear although it could have been part of a series of public lectures Yoshino gave to Tokyo Imperial University students on democracy in Japan.

> Nothing is a greater source of regret to the Japanese at large than to see their country represented abroad, especially in America, as wedded to militarism and bureaucratism. Some of them [Japanese] deprecate such a characterization

of Japan because they believe in liberalism and wish her to shape her course in accord with the principles of democracy, while others do so because they fear that the knowledge that Japan is intent on conquest may obstruct their militaristic ambitions. But whatever the reasons, it is undeniable that the majority of the Japanese are agreed in regretting that Japan is regarded as for [sic] a militaristic country in foreign lands . . . It is not without reason that a superficial observer, whose vision does not penetrate the surface of things, might come to the conclusion that Japan is an out and out follower of militarism. This is, needless to say, an unfair statement of the case; for if an observer is sufficiently keen-visioned he will have no difficulty in discerning on every side the fermentation of a new idea, a new mode of thinking, which is a flat denial of Japan's traditional way of thinking.[18]

Rejection of militarism and bureaucracy and an embrace of democracy had penetrated into significant portions of the Japanese population, especially Japanese young people, according to Yoshino.

Yoshino rejected the Western assumption that militarism in Japan was based on the inherent nature of the people. Instead he argued that the Japanese were essentially a peace-loving nation, and support for militarism arose out of the recent history of Western imperialism in East Asia and its threat against Japan. Yoshino might have had a more powerful impact on U.S.-Japanese relations but he died in 1933.[19]

Baron Fujimura Yoshiaki made the same point as Yoshino about Japanese militarism in a slightly different way.

Japan and Japanese militarism are not the same thing. No people are more convinced and sincere in their condemnation of the militaristic principles of administration than the Japanese. A few days ago a gathering of politicians, businessmen, journalists and professors was held. In our discussions we disagreed on many subjects, but we were absolutely at one in condemning the military diplomacy and were of the opinion that the militarists ought to confine their activities strictly within the sphere of their proper function.

Much like Yoshino's critiques, Fujimura saw Japan's political system as a work in progress with the potential for much positive growth but with a violent strain of militarism. He and Yoshino were responding to Japan's mishandled and brutal military occupation in Siberia in 1918—great tensions almost erupted into skirmishes between Japanese and American troops, there to support the anti-Bolshevik white Russian government in Siberia—and the military's vicious suppression of the March 1919 uprising in Korea. Finally Fujimura pointed out that militaristic elements existed in every nation including Europe and the United States.[20]

Others argued that the history of Japan was mainly peaceful, not warlike, pointing out that Hideyoshi's expedition into Korea in 1592 was the only instance of imperialistic war in Japan's history and it ended in failure. Of the Sino-Japanese War of 1894–1895 and the Russo-Japanese War of 1904–1905, a Japanese author asserted, "It must however be remembered that these wars were forced on Japan, and we only fought for [our] very existence." This interpretation leaves out a great deal of information. However, it effectively communicated the threats Japan faced.[21]

In addition to their other concerns, Japanese commentators also focused on relations with China. Earlier in World War I, Japan had issued the so-called Twenty-One Demands to China for greater control over China's resources and political decision-making. Japan was rebuffed on the demands that it be allowed administrative advisement in the Chinese government, but it received many important leases and took formal control over the Shantung Peninsula in northern China from the Germans.

Yamato Ichihashi, a Japanese national who became a professor at Stanford University, wrote an article in 1919 for a moderate circulation American magazine *Asia* called "The Industrial Plight of Japan" in which he argued that Japan needed the resources of China but had blundered in its heavy-handed policy of the Twenty-One Demands. Japan needed a constructive policy in China because it was a small nation without any substantial natural resources and if it was to continue to industrialize, it would need the resources of China. Later, Yamato wrote a book on the Washington Conference that endorsed the Washington Conference outcomes and earned him the enmity of hardliners in the Japanese government.[22]

A Japanese foreign student at Columbia University, Kenkichi Mori expressed similar views. Mori identified Japan's minimal resource base and large population motivating its diplomacy in East Asia. "Japanese statesmen are wrestling with intricate problems arising out of Japan's insular position, limited resources, and rapidly increasing population." Mori concluded that these facts made it necessary for Japan to look outside its borders to survive as a nation. "Her movement is the movement of life itself." Later in the article, Mori suggested that "The Japan of today will not be the Japan of tomorrow. She must either progress or retrogress." These dramatic expressions were perhaps exaggerated but they accurately reflected a prominent Japanese view shared by supporters and detractors of the military that Japanese expansion was key to its survival and therefore Korea, Manchuria, and China were closely linked to Japan's destiny. Mori claimed that Americans misunderstood Japan's purpose in China. Japan had nothing but friendly intentions toward China, did not intend to make China into a protectorate, and wanted to counteract foreign influences damaging to China.[23]

Japanese who were more anti-Western also tried to influence the American public's view of Japan. In 1919, Nagai Ryutaro wrote an article for the American magazine *The Living Age* on U.S.-Japanese tensions and the recent Versailles Peace Conference. Nagai criticized the American delegation roundly for its biased approach, against Japan and in favor of China on East Asian questions before the conference. Control of the Shantung peninsula was on the table and American President Woodrow Wilson, the chair of the conference, was unwilling to confirm Japan's claim on Shantung. Only when the Italian Prime Minister Orlando left the conference in protest over Wilson's unwillingness to grant Italy territory it desired to control, Fiume, did the Anglo-American Alliance break. Arthur Balfour, the British foreign secretary, negotiated a confirmation of Japan's control over Shantung into the treaty.[24]

Nagai also criticized Wilson's rejection of the Japanese delegation's proposed Racial Equality Clause. This was a rare instance where the Japanese and the Chinese agreed at the conference. China's representative Wellington Koo supported the clause. Even though a majority of the committee considering the clause voted in favor of it, Wilson ruled that it could not proceed because the vote had not been unanimous. Wilson opposed the clause because it was politically unpalatable in the United States. It might have been interpreted to allow the League of Nations to interfere in the U.S. treatment of Japanese immigrants, which was characterized by inequality.

Nagai's response accused the United States and England of an "Anglo-American Combine" to dominate the world and limit Japan's influence. Nagai dismissed the Anglo-Japanese Alliance as an "empty carcass" and noted the rise in anti-Japanese feelings in the two countries. He claimed that William Hearst, the American newspaper magnate, had told his editors to portray Japan as the next great menace in the world like Germany before World War I. However, Nagai for all of his anti-Western vehemence, had no faith in the military and bureaucracy to manage these threats except to enrich themselves. Within Japan where discontent was already widespread, Nagai predicted "an upheaval far more serious than the rice riots of last year, and there may follow a second regeneration of the country, as it went through at the time of the Meiji Reformation in consequence of pressure from the outside."[25]

Uenoda Setsuo, a YMCA leader stationed at an overseas branch of the Japanese YMCA in Chicago, also criticized Wilson and his ideas, calling them a "colossal illusion." "It is significant that the principles of justice and humanity so nobly advocated by President Wilson not only collapsed at the Peace Conference but that they have driven the United States into a position both awkward and untenable."[26]

JAPANESE SKEPTICISM OF INTERNATIONALISM

Nagai and Uenoda's frustrations with the West represent a deep vein of thought in interwar Japan. With the end of World War I and the rise of an internationalist movement in the 1920s, there seemed to be two alternatives, either a new peace system or an old-style European war system that had led to World War I. Although many in Japan wanted to participate in the peace system there was grave suspicion that the war system was still in place in the West. This led to skepticism about professions of internationalism emanating from Western nations.

Japanese liberals were strongly affected by the carnage of World War I and President Wilson's internationalist ideas gave them hope. In 1919 Ozaki Yukio traveled to Europe with his son Ozaki Yukitero. He was shocked at the scene of battlefields littered with helmets and swords. At Verdun, brass shell casings were still visible. Ozaki wrote in his diary, "The battlefield was a vast opencast mine of iron, copper, and lead. The landscape was a scene of utter destruction."[27] As he left Europe, Ozaki pondered what he saw. He was disturbed by the fact that Europeans seemed to feel no remorse for the war. He believed that little had changed in the attitude of Europeans after the war but also noted that the world had changed greatly; it had become much more internationalized. He resolved to work for arms limitation and international peace and proposed arms reduction bills in the Japanese Diet after he returned to Japan.[28]

Along with his appreciation of the horrors of war, however, Ozaki expressed skepticism about the postwar trend toward internationalism. He addressed the issue of internationalism and the League of Nations in *Kokusai Chishiki* (International Understanding) a journal with an internationalist perspective sponsored by the Japanese League of Nations Association (LNA) begun in 1920. Ozaki found much to be discouraged by in the postwar environment. He wondered if the major powers would work in any way other than to enhance their own power and shut out other nations. The international environment was not to be trusted.

Ozaki then articulated his own nationalist version of internationalism. The European use of military force as in World War I was dangerous to internationalism, but the leadership of the Japanese Emperor supported internationalist efforts, according to Ozaki. "Speaking of the imperial way of Japan, the detail of the contradiction between it and internationalism is very small." The Japanese Emperor supported international justice, whereas European militarism and imperialism subverted it. Since the kingly or imperial way was better than European militarism, Japan should through its imperial system play a larger role in international political arrangements rather than military nations such as Germany or Russia. While Ozaki's skepticism of Western internationalism was understandable, his faith in the Japanese Emperor as a force for internationalism was myopic. He wanted to believe the best about the emperor. In reality, the emperor was Japan's commander in chief of the military, and given Japan's recent military incursions in Siberia and Korea, it was difficult to imagine the Japanese Emperor as a leader of the internationalist peace movement.[29]

Nitobe Inazô understood Japanese hesitance about the League and after his return to Japan from his post as assistant secretary-general of the League of Nations in 1927, he wrote several newspaper articles attempting to assuage the doubts of Japanese. However, Nitobe was said to harbor his own doubts, and other well-known Japanese Christian leaders Kozaki Hiromichi and Ebina Danjo were very critical of postwar internationalism and the League.[30]

One Japanese commentator, calling the ideas embodied in the League of Nations Covenant "pseudo-internationalism," stated, "Although there were fourteen points of internationalism, the Covenant, when it was finally drawn up, had quite another nature." The author went on to point out that the equality of races was denied, a regional doctrine of spheres of influence similar to the Monroe doctrine was confirmed by the League Mandates provisions, and the institution was weakened because it has no standing army.[31]

Anesaki Masaharu, internationalist and professor of religions at Tokyo Imperial University, took a philosophical approach in an article on internationalism and the League of Nations for *Kokusai Chishiki*.

> Humanity is neither entirely angelic or thoroughly evil. It follows that the people of the world are both good and evil. This is self-evident. In contrast to this, the people who belong to and believe in the aims of League of Nations are exceedingly hopeful and have the root of idealism. These people believe that they will start a great change directly in the world.
>
> However, from the start, this has been connected to excessive prospects and it has not penetrated very far. Also, impatience has been encouraged by hope and so this has essentially become for the internationalist a curse. The immaturity of this movement means that those who in reality disagree and stand in opposition to internationalism can work from various selfish motives inside these organizations. This indicates the weakness of these organizations. To give a general conclusion, the League of Nations is merely a puppet of various capitalist nations such as England.[32]

Japanese liberals wanted internationalism to work but were skeptical of the League and postwar internationalist rhetoric. Given the experiences of the Japanese with Western diplomacy such as the Triple Intervention in 1895, their hesitancy is understandable.

WAR TALK AND JOHN DEWEY: TENSIONS CONCERNING CHINA

> As to the chances of war between the United States and Japan, if you listen to
> the talk in the foreign clubs and circles of the Orient, especially wherever the
> banner of England flies, there is no chance about it. When I was in Shanghai
> they were betting even money that it would come in six months and three to
> two that it would come within a year.

THIS WAR PREDICTION, FROM CHARLES EDWARD RUSSELL, AN AMERICAN
journalist and socialist, was made not in 1941 but in 1921, twenty years
before the attack on Pearl Harbor.[1]

By that time, tensions between the United States and Japan had risen to
an all-time high. The countries had gone from friendly cooperation and
support before the Russo-Japanese War (1904–1905) to a position of great
rivalry in the Pacific. Each country saw the other as the single greatest threat
to itself and war-planned with the other in mind. This situation spawned
public discussions on both sides as to whether Japan and the United States
were going to war. In the United States books such as *Must We Fight Japan* by
Walter Pitkin indicated rising fear of war.

Japanese naval officer Captain Mizuno Hironori published *Our Next War*,
a fictional novel about Japan attacking the United States and several other
nonfiction articles, one of which concerned the strategic deployment of troops
and the protection of resources in case of war. Mizuno lost his job with the
navy after publishing an article on the psychology of Japanese soldiers and
sailors but he continued to publish on military affairs and became an outspoken critic of Japanese military planning. He noted presciently that Japan
planned to occupy China in case of war to secure China's resources and that

plans for a very large army could only mean that military planners were considering an attack on the Philippines. Both of these predictions came true.[2]

On the other side of the Pacific, Hector Bywater, a naval expert, wrote *The Great Pacific War* (1925), a bestselling novel that predicted a naval war between the United States and Japan would take place in 1931. Bywater, a Britisher transplanted to the United States, portrayed the Japanese as winning the first battles and then succumbing to the great American fleet, although he did not predict the Japanese surprise attack on Pearl Harbor as some have asserted. Bywater also wrote a nonfiction work called *Sea Power in the Pacific* (1921) and covered the Washington Conference (1921) with sharp insights. He gained the ear of influential Americans such as Franklin Delano Roosevelt, who had served as assistant secretary of the navy in World War I and eventually became president. Bywater died of alcoholism during the blitz of London in 1940, a year before the conflict he predicted came to pass.

Professor Kenneth Latourette of Columbia University and an East Asian expert created a syllabus of the history of Japan in 1921 that became so popular he updated it every couple of years through to a seventh edition in 1934. Latourette acknowledged the war talk in his syllabus and he took it seriously. He claimed that the Washington Conference's main purpose was to resolve the issues that threatened war between the United States and Japan in 1921. This interpretation is no longer prevalent in thinking about the goals of the Washington Conference. Perhaps with the perspective of the war that did take place, the Pacific War, we recognize that tensions between the United States and Japan were not at a point where war was a realistic option. After all, tensions worsened for another decade and a half afterward before war actually did take place. However, war talk was widespread and seemed serious at the time. *The New York Times*, the *Literary Digest*, the *Forum*, and *Collier's Weekly* all noted the prevalence of war talk in the United States. Even John Weekes, the American secretary of war, sought to ally fears of war in his speeches by announcing that war was not imminent.[3]

THE IMPORTANCE OF CHINA

Much of the war talk centered on conflicts over China. The main issue of contention in China was over the American policy of the Open Door. Created by Secretary of State John Hay in 1898–1899 in cooperation with the European powers, the Open Door policy declared that the foreign powers in China must observe a policy of free and open economic competition. China had been carved up into spheres of influence in the 1880s and 1890s allowing the European powers exclusive economic privileges in their particular spheres: The French in the south, the British in the middle along the Yangtze River and in the northern city of Tientsin in Shantung, the Germans also in the north in Shantung, and the Russians in Manchuria. Second, the powers agreed to work toward reform of China's government (read democratization) and enhancement of its sovereignty under terminology of "administrative reform."

The Open Door allowed the United States to gain a foothold in China through its economic power without a large navy as the other powers possessed. The United States had a large industrial base but not enough domestic markets to satisfy its surging industrial production. It was thought that the China market would relieve the American economy of this problem. The Open Door opened sectors of the China market that had been closed to the United States because unlike the European powers, it possessed no exclusive economic spheres in China. Finally, it stopped the European powers, especially the Russians, from gaining more influence in China. It should be noted that the Open Door policy was evolving and while the concrete economic and diplomatic interests of the United States were front and center in 1898, American policy in China was affected profoundly by the existence of a huge group of protestant missionaries in China, more than 2,000 strong. After the Chinese Republican Revolution in 1911, Americans began to see China, not Japan, as the country with the best chance in East Asia to become a democracy and follow the lead of the United States.[4]

American missionaries had gone into Japan in the 1870s–1900s, but by 1921, the number of converts there was still quite small, although many of them were well-educated samurai Christians who had become powerful leaders in Japanese society. The hope of American Protestant missionary leaders that Japan would become thoroughly Christianized faded.

The American missionary leadership turned to China as their next great hope for Christianization of the world. After all, China's population was (and still is) the largest in the world and Protestant Christianity had already made inroads there. With the election of President Woodrow Wilson, a devout Presbyterian, in 1912, hopes were raised further. Wilson offered the job of American ambassador to China to the famous YMCA missionary leader, John Mott. Mott declined saying that he could be more influential as missionary leader than as ambassador. Paul Reinsch, a scholar of East Asia but more importantly a close friend of the missionaries, took the job as American ambassador to China. In addition, American China policy was influenced by missionaries on the ground in China sending home circulars about conditions there. As a consequence, American China policy was driven not just by the hard requirements of geopolitics and economics but also by the soft feelings of affection for a country seen to be emerging from its long sleep of traditionalism and ripe for conversion to Christianity and democracy.[5]

The Japanese considered a stable China crucial to their own national security. Japan was security conscious in part because of the carve-up of China by the Western powers. Japanese soldier and statesman Yamagata Aritomo, architect of the modern Japanese Army, saw Japan's destiny in East Asia inextricably linked to China and Korea. He called Korea a dagger pointing at the heart of Japan. The United States and Japan actually agreed on the goal of a stable China outside of European dominance. It was the question of how to achieve this goal that created tensions.

The Americans wanted a China open to trade and strong enough in domestic government to resist further intrusions by the European powers. Japan wanted a China that served Japan's security and economic interests in East Asia. An unstable China threatened Japan's security and economic interests much more than it did the American interests. Japan's close proximity to China made this point clearly. In addition, some Japanese believed that Japan had a mission to create a progressive modernizing East Asia outside of Western domination.

Japanese attempts to create exclusive influence in Northeast China violated the spirit if not the letter of the Open Door and opened up a chasm between Japan and the United States. Several issues loomed large. The Japanese had penetrated ever further into the Manchurian economy since the Russo-Japanese War. Japanese officials also rebuffed American attempts to make investments in enterprises in Manchuria. This violated the Open Door policy but the Americans protested to no avail.

During the early stages of World War I, the Japanese took advantage of the wartime preoccupation of the Europeans, moved troops into areas occupied by the Germans before the war, and took over the Shantung peninsula. This also violated the spirit of the Open Door because the expectation was that China should regain its sovereignty as soon as possible and exclusive spheres should be given back to China. China's infant Republican government formed after the revolution of 1911 proved to be very unstable and Japan attempted to impose requirements upon China's government in 1915 in the form of the so-called Twenty-One Demands. In effect, Japan sought to exploit China's weakness to gain further influence in China.

The Twenty-One Demands consisted of several sets of requirements. Most of them gave Japan the same rights as the European powers in China. Japanese in Manchuria and Shantung in the north and Fukien province in the south gained rights to lease mineral wealth and to build railroads. The last set of demands would have allowed Japanese advisors to the Chinese government and joint policing. This was a direct infringement on China's sovereignty. The Americans were not yet in the war and protested vehemently against the Twenty-One Demands, especially the last set because it violated their commitment to China's sovereignty under the Open Door. Eventually Japan backed off of the last set of demands and China resolved the crisis itself by accepting the others. But the Twenty-One Demands and Japan's occupation of Shantung damaged Japan's credibility in the international arena. Especially in the eyes of Americans, Japan was seen as less trustworthy.

After World War I during the Paris Peace Conference, Japanese negotiators were asked to give up Shantung in the spirit of the Open Door and Woodrow Wilson's support of national self-determination worldwide. They adamantly refused and though the Chinese delegation at the conference under the leadership of the brilliant young Wellington Koo made a strong case for receiving Shantung back from Japan, the Allies relented and allowed Japan to retain German possessions in Shantung and Pacific islands while the Japanese quietly dropped their bid for the addition of the racial equality clause to the League of Nations Covenant. Though this satisfied the negotiators and governments involved, the Japanese public remembered only that the racial equality clause had been rejected by white men from Western nations and the American and Chinese public remembered only that Shantung which under Wilson's fourteen points should have gone back to China remained with Japan. Both issues contributed to rising tensions between the two nations.[6]

The May Fourth Movement of 1919 also contributed to tensions. This revolutionary movement presaged turbulent times for China as the younger generation sought to uncouple China from its traditions and drag it into modernity. A group of 3,000 Chinese college students marched through Beijing in protest of the Paris Peace Conference decision to allow Japan to continue to occupy the Shantung peninsula. Twenty students were arrested but when more sought arrest the government released all of the students and issued an apology. Later the students and a few of their professors issued a manifesto for change advocating morality in politics, democratic governance, social reform, political activism, a modern educational system, and women's rights. They were anti-Confucian and took their inspiration from Western philosophers and intellectuals. A Marxist political party was established in this time period as well.

Rodney Gilbert, the American vice consul in Hankow at the time, wrote of the movement, "This gathering inspired the local students to do something on their own account, and whatever one thinks of the action they eventually took they certainly deserve full credit for being the first in China to substitute action for talk." The American public saw this early attempt at revolution in China as akin to early battles in the American Revolution (the similarities are superficial; the differences are many and deep). Their sympathies were with the young students who fought against imperialism and for democracy and good government.[7]

JOHN DEWEY, JAPAN, AND CHINA

Between 1919 and 1921 John Dewey, the famous American philosopher and activist, traveled to Japan and China. He spent four months at the beginning of 1919 in Japan and then traveled to China where he intended to stay a couple of months but ended up staying for two years. When he compared the two nations shortly after arriving in China, his thoughts revealed his bias. "Japan was rather baffling and tantalizing. China is overpowering."[8] Ostensibly in China to teach and do research at Nanjing (Nanking) and Beijing Universities, he traveled around China as well. An activist and public intellectual, Dewey wrote to the American public about the political situation in East Asia and China. He took assiduous notes when he traveled and wrote almost forty articles, publishing many of them in the popular journal *The New Republic*. When he returned to the United States in 1921, he bundled some of the articles together and published them as a short book under the title *China, Japan and the U.S.A.* Altogether, Dewey's irrepressible energy and prolific writing on China amounted to a public relations campaign on behalf of China and against the Japanese presence there.

Part of the reason Dewey found China intoxicating is because he arrived at the founding moment of the May Fourth Movement. Three days after the Deweys arrived in Beijing, the students marched. Dewey felt the excitement of the moment and sensed the potential of the demonstrations, stating, "In another sense, it may be—though probably not—the beginning of an important active political movement, out of which anything may grow . . ."[9]

Given this revolutionary atmosphere, Dewey was himself treated as a revolutionary. Enamored of China, Dewey gave dozens of lectures, some of them impromptu, and as many as eight per week. Believing that the revolution was intellectual as well as social and political, some Chinese saw him as one of the leaders of the revolutionary movement and flocked to his talks. He also met some of his former students in China and one of them, Hu Shi, who eventually became Chinese ambassador to the United States in 1937, acted as interpreter for his lectures in Beijing.

Initially Dewey made the Orientalist assumption that the Chinese were conservative by nature, similar to George Knox and others' arguments about unchanging nature of the Orient. He told of new Chinese houses built the traditional way that flooded every time it rained, Chinese baths built without drains so that a house boy had to be hired to carry the water away after a bath was finished. However, the longer he stayed, Dewey became convinced that the Chinese refusal to change was "much more intellectual and deliberate and less mere routine clinging to custom than I used to suppose." He came to believe that China's crowded conditions had led to the "live and let live" approach to life there. He also noted that the Chinese resistance to modernization stemmed in part from skepticism of the benefits of Western industrial life.[10]

Dewey believed that China needed to change its way of thinking before it could have a successful political revolution. In the aftermath of the May Fourth Movement, Dewey analyzed the political failures of the protest but took comfort in what he saw as an "intellectual awakening in the young men and women who through their schooling had been aroused to the necessity of a new order of belief, a new method of thinking." He later stated that he had placed too much emphasis on the movement to save China. However there is no surprise that Dewey interpreted the May Fourth Movement as the beginning of the Chinese democratic movement. This after all was the focus of his philosophy and writings. And in a way Dewey was right. If not the beginning of Chinese democracy, the May Fourth Movement was a new stage in Chinese intellectual, cultural, and political revolutions that played out over the course of the twentieth century.[11]

Dewey took an evolutionary approach to change and recognized that because China had no experience of moderate liberal change, real change would come slowly and the demand and results of change could become radicalized. He spoke out strongly against Bolshevism and tried in other ways to moderate the radicalism of the young students he addressed. Dewey did arrange for British radical Bertram Russell to come to China while he was there sensing that Russell would be listened to more carefully because he had a more radical reputation. After Russell arrived, he became seriously ill and spent time in a hospital in Beijing—Dewey even took down Russell's last will and testament when it was thought he might die—and when he recovered, he left China immediately and eventually became a savage critic of Dewey's philosophy of pragmatism.[12]

While Russell wrote a book about China from his quite limited experience, Dewey, who spent more time in China, never did. It is a testament to his commitment to pragmatism that he understood that China was in the midst of a grand experiment and he simply did not know the outcome so he choose not to write a summation. It was Dewey's open method of reportage that attracted the praise of Americans interested in China. One American commentator noted that Dewey's reporting was hopeful with an air of freedom and expressed thanks for Dewey's honest appraisal of the Shantung situation.[13]

Dewey spent several weeks in North China in the Japanese controlled province of Shantung. Shantung was an attractive prize with coal deposits, factories, a railway, and a deepwater harbor at Kiaochow (Jiaozhou), in addition to access to Beijing and the interior of the country. The capital city of Tsingtao (Qingdao) had been modernized by the Germans with water and sewer, telephone lines, schools, hospitals, and even a German-funded brewery that continues to make beer to this day.[14]

Regarding the continuing Japanese presence in Shantung, Dewey rejected the Japanese claim that they would eventually give sovereignty back to the

Chinese while retaining economic rights. Dewey undermined the assumption that it was possible to separate out economic privileges and the all-important question of sovereignty for China.

> To one who knows the history of foreign aggression in China, especially the technique of conquest by railway and finance, the irony of promising to keep economic rights while returning sovereignty lies so on the surface that it is hardly irony. China might as well be offered Kant's Critique of Pure Reason on a silver platter as be offered sovereignty under such conditions. The latter is equally metaphysical.[15]

Dewey also commented on the anti-Japanese propaganda circulating through Shantung. Chinese student protests and a boycott of Japanese goods had begun. Dewey regarded the boycott and protests as completely understandable given Japanese repression there. He told tales of the arrest and torture of Chinese student protesters in Tsingtao. Dewey compared this treatment of the Chinese in Shantung to the recent uprising and brutal repression of it in Korea by Japanese authorities there.[16]

Pro-Japanese views told a different story than Dewey, especially of the anti-Japanese movement in Shantung. K.K. (Kiyoshi Karl) Kawakami, one of the founders of the Japanese Socialist Party and a Japanese journalist and author who had spent a number of years in the United States writing on American issues for various Japanese newspapers, claimed that the young Chinese students protesting the Japanese presence were being manipulated by opposition politicians in China in an attempt to embarrass the sitting Chinese government. The student demonstrations that took place in 1920, according to Kawakami's source, were financed to the tune of $200,000, paid for by the late president of China Feng Kuochang, who had a deep grudge against the sitting Premier Tun Chijui.[17] In another critique of the Chinese protests, the editor of *The Japan Review* commented on Chinese propaganda against Japan both in China and in the United States and listed several American magazines that were generally considered to be involved in anti-Japanese propaganda: the *China Review, Far Eastern Republic*, and *Chinese Student Monthly*.[18]

Beyond his sympathy for China, John Dewey expressed a very sophisticated understanding of the domestic political situation in Japan in support of its empire. Dewey had no special expertise on the Japanese situation. He did however come to embrace the Chinese perspective that saw through Japanese propaganda and instead assessed the results of Japanese imperialism. His view was far superior to either the missionaries who thought Japan was at the edge of democratization or those who distrusted Japanese modernization and put the blame on the military.

Dewey understood that support for the Japanese Empire was strong not just among Japanese conservatives and militarists but also among Japanese liberals and Japanese industrialists.

> While the western world supposes that the military and the industrial party in Japan have opposite ideas as to the best methods of securing Japanese supremacy in the East, it is the universal opinion in China that they are working in complete understanding with one another and the differences that sometimes occur between the Foreign Office of Tokyo and the Ministry of War (which is extra-constitutional in its status) are staged for effect.[19]

Then he returned to his theme of the force of propaganda and suggested that Japanese propaganda in the United States needed to be countered by American propaganda in Japan.

> Unfortunately the press of Japan treats every attempt as evidence that America, having tasted blood in the war, now has its eyes on Asia with the expectation later on in getting its hands on Asia. Consequently America is interested in trying to foster ill will between China and Japan. If the pro-American Japanese [sic] do not enlighten their fellow countrymen as to the facts, then America ought to return some of the propaganda that visits its shores. But every American who goes to Japan ought also to visit China—if only to complete his education.

When John Dewey added it all up, he agreed with the judgment that the seeds of war had been planted in the soil of China.[20]

John Dewey was well remembered for his support of China after his return to the United States. In 1938 he was awarded the Blue Grand Cordon of the Order of Jade by the Chinese government. Even after the Pacific War began, Dewey was believed to be so influential that the American State Department asked him to write a leaflet expressing American support to buoy the Chinese. The leaflet was dropped from airplanes by the thousands throughout China.[21]

Nathaniel Peffer, a young journalist and budding China expert, wrote of the war crisis for *The Century Magazine* in an article called "The Playground of the Spoilers: Would War with Japan Solve the Far Eastern Problem?" He called the war talk then proliferating "the inevitability complex." Peffer, like Dewey, had spent time in China (considerably more time than Dewey) and like Dewey he was more pro-Chinese than pro-Japanese. But Peffer took an historical perspective on the U.S.-Japanese conflicts rather than the philosophical and public activist approach of Dewey.[22]

Peffer laid out the concerns of the United States in China and acknowledged that Japanese imperialism especially in Shantung was rough and crude.

But if the American goal was to secure free and open trade and diplomacy with China, Peffer pointed out that even a triumph over the Japanese would not achieve this. For in China there was not one but several major imperialists and most of them were European. The British and the French stood in the way of the Open Door in China as much as Japan. So a war on that basis would not solve the problem. Peffer also pointed out that practical American interests in China such as trade and geopolitical strategy were relatively minor.

Peffer argued that if war must come, it should come out of rational policy concerns and not the rousing of public sentiment. "If America is convinced that its interests in China are sufficiently vital to be worth the price of war, which I maintain they now very clearly are not, let it at least be logical." Peffer also mentioned his belief that U.S. China policy could backfire on the United States. Like Dewey, he saw some Chinese looking to the United States to fulfill China's destiny instead of fighting for China's independence.[23]

Charles Edward Russell also visited Japan in this time period. Russell had a slightly different perspective on the cause of what he called the "Japanese scare" in the United States. Less inclined to blame the Japanese, Russell sympathized with them. "The clear impression remains that somehow Japan is our menace, that her methods are covert, treacherous, guileful and perilous to our national existence and some day we shall have to fight her." Russell did not share this view and criticized it, and he also pointed to the American misperception of Japanese peoples' quietness as hiding a deceitful nature. "They will never arouse much enthusiasm in the American breast—these shy, silent and painfully self-conscious people, whose silence is always mistaken for plotting and whose self-consciousness is supposed to cloak deep iniquity and guile . . ." Russell saw the China situation as central but also justifiable from the Japanese point of view. "Japan is driven into China not by mad purpose to annex everything in sight but because old Economic Necessity, demanding raw materials, has a pistol at her head."[24]

JAPAN, CHINA, AND KOREA

Influential Japanese recognized as did Dewey, Russell, and Peffer that China was at the center of U.S.-Japan tensions. Count Soyeshima Michimasa, one of the original founders of the Meiji state who served on the Privy Council alongside Kido, Okuma, and Okubo in the early years, wrote an article for American consumption in *The Japan Review* in 1921 examining the possibility of war between Japan and the United States. Soyeshima recognized that China was the most important of the troubles surrounding U.S.-Japanese relations.

When the United States comes to press upon Japan over this [China] question on the strength of her boundless wealth, the national destiny of this country

[Japan] will be menaced, and with all our regard for peace it will be impossible for us to remain inactive.

Willing to compromise, Soyeshima suggested that international administration of China along with the development of China's economy and reform of its government would prevent a U.S.-Japan war. Soyeshima also endorsed the American Open Door for all of China including Manchuria as a reasonable solution to some of the conflicts over China.[25] However, not all Japanese agreed with these suggestions.

Baron Sakatani Yoshiro in his article "Why War between Japan and the United States is Impossible" in the same issue of *The Japan Review* also endorsed the U.S. Open Door with regard to China and argued that a stronger and more stable China would immediately end talk of war between the United States and Japan.[26] Others suggested that the Open Door would be acceptable for China proper, but Japan had special interests that had been wrought with Japanese blood in Manchuria. The Open Door there was unacceptable. Nonetheless, here were some points of general agreement.

First, the American policy of the Open Door had more support than Americans thought. These commentators also suggested that Japan would like to have friendlier more cooperative relations with China and wanted to see China strengthened and stabilized through economic development and internal political reforms as the Americans wished. However, Americans did not understand that Japan viewed China through the lens of improving the security of a chaotic neighbor as often as it did through the lens of economic exploitation or hegemonic control.[27]

On the other hand, these Japanese did not hesitate to defend Japan's presence in China. Soyeshima stated, "Though Europe and America are in the habit of denouncing Japan as an aggressive Power, Japan has really been irreproachable in her international dealings . . ." Then he backtracked, excepting that the Twenty-One Demands in 1915 had been a bad approach and the Siberian campaign of 1918 had been expanded too much by Japanese militarists. "In fact there is nothing in the diplomatic history of the world that is so ill-considered as the Twenty-One Demands." His only justification of it was the Triple Intervention of 1895 in which the French, Russians, and Germans forced Japan to give back the Liaotung peninsula to China after Japan had won it in the Sino-Japanese War.

Soyeshima then made it clear that Japan regarded China as essential to her national destiny. Suggesting that if Japan had not agreed to the demands of the European powers in 1895, both Japanese and Chinese sovereignty would have been forfeited, Soyeshima interpreted the giveback of the Liaotung peninsula as a sacrifice. "For the sake of Japan and China, therefore, Japan submitted to the humiliation and sacrifice." How should we treat this slightly overblown language? Expressions that linked Japan and China's destinies were common parlance in the interwar period. But how seriously did the Japanese take these expressions? This is a difficult question to answer. Japan saw itself succeeding China as the new center of gravity in East Asia. Some Japanese believed that Japan had the responsibility for modernizing East Asia outside of Western imperialism. Others argued that China was integral to Japan's national security. The problem lies not in the ties between Japan and China but in language that portrayed them as inextricable and inviolable. This kind of language distorted the Japanese perception of the relationship and made the problems in China seem more threatening than they were. Even if most Japanese in 1921 did not believe Japan and China's destinies were so linked together, Soyeshima's comment eroded reasonable argument about the China issue. Over time this way of thinking about China grew so that by the time of the second Sino-Japanese War of 1937 the language of national survival linking China and Japan together had become a stumbling block to compromise on China.[28]

Soyeshima also defended Japan's policy in Korea by pointing out that the annexation of Korea was approved by all the great powers when it was accomplished in 1910 and suggested that Korea had been brought from ruination to general progress and improved welfare.[29] He also brought up the marriage of the offspring of Korean royalty to the Japanese royal family as a sign of rising Korean status in the world due to the beneficence of Japan. Soyeshima was perhaps too optimistic about this union of Japanese and Korean royal families. The truth is less attractive. The Japanese government initiated this marriage and it was made clear to the Korean royal family that the Japanese would not take no for an answer. Such a persistent suitor was not to be turned away although patriotic Koreans chafed at the experience. Like the Japanese presence in Korea generally the marriage was more representative of Japanese hegemony there than of any notion of union between Korea and Japan.

Soyeshima used the marriage to make unflattering comparisons to American actions against the royal family of Hawai'i after its annexation to the United States. The royals were forced off the throne after a coup d'état in 1893 when U.S. Marines participated in the sugar planters' revolt. Queen Liliuokalani wrote petition after petition asking that her authority be restored and traveled to Washington, DC to no avail. Soyeshima also discussed the treatment of Philippine rebel Emilio Aguinaldo by the American Army in the Philippines during the American-Philippine War of 1899–1906.

Soyeshima then condemned the justification by the comparison he had just engaged in.

In my opinion, it is unwise to defend excesses, great or small on the part of Japanese in Korea by referring to the situation in Ireland and the lynchings in

America . . . Just imagine how the Americans would feel, should active propaganda be started in Tokyo for the independence of the Philippines or Hawaii, or should a League of Negroes' friends be organized in Japan with the support of peers, professors, and priests.

The Japanese became very adept at pointing out the flaws of the Americans to justify their own actions in the interwar period.[30]

Soyeshima neglected to mention one event that had inflamed the Korean issue in the eyes of the American public: the Korean Independence Movement of March 1, 1919. However, Baron Sakatani mentioned it as a bone of contention in his article. The protests took place on the birthday of the Korean King Gojong, March 1, and were led by Korean nationalists and several thousand Korean Christians who wanted independence from Japan. The Japanese brutally repressed the protests by executing the agitators, including approximately 2,000 Korean Presbyterians. This action outraged American missionaries in Korea and American Protestant Christians back in the United States.[31]

Baron Sakatani, whether to try to minimize the harm or because he did not understand the extent of the damage done, dismissed a report of the Japanese repression of the Korean Movement as "inflammatory propaganda." Then he proclaimed the bottom line.

But the question is purely Japanese, with which no other nation is entitled to interfere. Since the insurrections in 1919, efforts have been made to reform the administration of Korea. In view of those facts, we cannot conceive that Korea will be the cause of an American-Japanese war.[32]

The real problem according to Soyeshima, Sakatani, and others was not Japanese actions but American misperceptions. The commentators concluded their comments by stating that the problems were perceptual, not geopolitical. Soyeshima stated:

In the eyes of the majority of Americans in China, however, the annexation of Korea is a serious crime and they show uncompromising hostility towards Japan. In fact many of them are laboring under considerable misunderstand-ings about this country. For instance the editor of a certain review under American management has said to me: "In the end Japan will convert China into a Korea. In that case we must fight Japan for the sake of justice and in self-defence." But this is an instance of misunderstanding and imaginary fear pushed to an extreme.

Soyeshima also pointed to four pro-Korean organizations in the United States that were creating anti-Japanese propaganda: The Korean National Association,

Korean Knights, New Korean Association, and the League of Korean Friends. He also noted several recent American book titles pointing to anti-Japanese propaganda: *The Rebirth of Korea, Korea's Fight for Freedom, The Germany of East Asia,* and *Japanese Atrocities in Korea,* and claimed that the books were full of "fabrications."[33]

Was Soyeshima and Sakatani's own counter propaganda effective in persuading Americans that Japanese intentions in East Asia were honorable? Since the publication in which the articles appeared, *The Japan Review* (continuation of *The Japanese Student Bulletin*), was a small circulation journal edited by Japanese foreign students and printed by the American YMCA, the article likely had more impact upon Japanese students in the United States reading it than on the American public. However, both illustrate the perspective of many Japanese that their intentions in East Asia were pure, but misrepresented by a small group of Koreans and Chinese who mobilized the American public against Japan. Certainly a pro-Korean movement existed in the United States as Soyeshima pointed out and later the pro-China campaign was organized and lobbied the American government, especially after the Manchurian Incident of 1931. According to Soyeshima, the Japanese government had more success in persuading Americans on the issue of the Japanese occupation of Shantung.

> American propaganda on the Shantung question is also very active. The American press was strongly denouncing Japan in this connection in 1919 when I was there, but the repeated statements issued by our Government succeeded in having this country's bona fides appreciated for a time at least.[34]

Baron Sakatani agreed with Soyeshima that misperceptions were at the root of the problem, not real issues. He stated,

> The truth is that the Americans suspect the aggressive policy of Japan, while the Japanese harbor the same suspicion against the Americans. Such suspicion ends in mutual fear and misapprehension of each other, but I cannot realize how this fear could be cleared away by war between the two nations.

After an extended discussion of the existing issues between Japan and the United States, Sakatani argued,

> Taking these facts into consideration, I hold there is no question pending between Japan and the United States which is impossible of peaceful solution. It is only the infernal influence of rumors which distort apparent facts and would rush both nations in preparation for fantastic war.[35]

FAR EASTERN OLYMPIC GAMES

The tensions between Japan, the United States, and China—this time with the United States in the middle—were also illustrated through sports. The Far Eastern Olympic Games originated in 1913 through the efforts of the Philippines YMCA. The YMCA became involved in sports and physical training as a part of their emphasis on the training of the body and the mind for Christian spirituality. In fact, James Naismith the renowned inventor of basketball in 1890, created the sport in a YMCA gymnasium in Springfield, Massachusetts and was YMCA physical director in Springfield and, later, in Denver.

YMCA leaders believed that the creation of the Far Eastern Games could strengthen the bonds of friendship between Asian countries.

> The plan to bring the races of the orient—the yellow man, the brown man, and the omnipresent white man—together in friendly athletic rivalry through recurring Oriental Olympics has not merely an athletic but also an ethical and international aspect.[36]

As relations between Japan and China deteriorated in the 1920s, the resulting tensions were exhibited in the planning and management of the Far Eastern Games. Control over the Games became a power struggle between Japan and China. And the Americans were stuck in the middle. Franklin Brown, an American YMCA missionary, took over the management of the Games as the newly appointed secretary of the Far Eastern Athletic Association (FEAA) in 1916. His office had been moved to Tokyo for the 1917 Games. The Japanese then put forward a motion in 1921 at the meetings before the Shanghai Games to create a permanent FEAA secretary and base the FEAA office in Tokyo. The Chinese responded unfavorably to the motion and eventually the Japanese dropped the idea altogether. The Chinese wanted the office to be moved to Shanghai for the Far Eastern Games in 1921. The office stayed in Tokyo, a temporary but increasingly long-term arrangement.[37]

The form of representation from each participating country also raised tensions at the meetings. Each country sent three representatives to the meetings. The Chinese sent two Americans and one Chinese representative to the meetings that irritated the Japanese who according to Brown "naturally looked with suspicion upon whatever looks like American domination of things Chinese."[38]

At the Games themselves, tension between the Chinese and Japanese was evident. No Chinese officials came to meet the Japanese athletes at the docks on their arrival. There was also a bitter row over the movie rights to the Games in Shanghai. Movie rights had been granted to a local Chinese firm to create a film, and the firm reserved all other rights in the film. The Japanese representatives protested when they recognized that the filming was a form of propaganda about East Asia and if they did not control it, they might end up suffering damage to their image.[39]

The Japanese believed that the local YMCA secretary in Shanghai, Dr. Gray, who organized the Games, was anti-Japanese. In addition, a story circulated among the Japanese that Gray was profiting unfairly from the Games by asking the crowd to sit closer together so that he could sell more seats.

The situation worsened once the Games started. They were very disorganized. There were not enough seats for the number of spectators who attended, not enough baseballs were brought to allow the teams to change balls during rainy games and during the track and field competition the cartridges were the wrong size for the starter's pistol. One judge, a Chinese man, made the wrong ruling on a Japanese competitor's throws in the discus trials. And he neglected to call another of the Japanese athletes' names and so the athlete missed his turns at the discus throw. In another incident, a Chinese judge, Mr. Hoh, asked that the coaches for the Japanese volleyball team leave the field while the Filipino team coaches whom they were playing were allowed to stay. The situation bordered on comedy, although the implications were more serious.[40]

Tensions between the Chinese and Japan spilled over into the American YMCA secretaries from those respective countries. Franklin Brown from Tokyo and Dr. Gray from Shanghai got into a verbal fight that almost came to blows over Brown's presence on the field for some of the events. Gray believed that Brown sided with the Japanese athletes and thought he would prejudice the Games by his presence. Predictably, the Chinese leaders backed up Gray and the Japanese leaders took Brown's side in the dispute. The Games turned into a replica of the tensions between Japanese and Chinese governments with the Americans in the middle, instead of an event that could bring the two sides together. The Games illustrate the point that cross-cultural contacts did not always strengthen connections but were subject to the tensions and problems that already existed in the relationship.

CONCLUSION

Concerns were raised that because of heightened tensions between the United States and Japan, smaller issues such as the Far Eastern Games, immigration problems, racial tensions, or some other peripheral issue could provide the spark to light a fire that could turn into a raging inferno of war. Charles Edward Russell, visiting Japan in 1921, spoke for many when he mentioned this possibility.

The point of danger then, is that if Japan pursues her present policy in China, if alarmed American interests continue to misunderstand and misrepresent it, if the minds of the Japanese people are at length angered by continuous and gratuitous insults from America, if outside influences are sufficiently or successfully irritating, then say the quarrel grows about wretched Yap or California race prejudice, the temptation to use these great fighting machines may be overwhelming when there will not be the slightest justification for their use.[41]

However, war did not come and war talk was just that, talk, in 1921. Unofficial diplomats countered the war talk by rejecting it and giving a positive evaluation of U.S.-Japanese relations. Even John Dewey who was more negative agreed that a war between the United States and Japan would be a foolish enterprise. The fact that these commentators were well respected meant that their comments carried some weight with their respective publics and also with those who made the decisions of state—official diplomats—although neither diplomats nor politicians were inclined to go to war at any rate. U.S.-Japanese relations seemed to improve a short time later with successful multilateral treaties that came out of the Washington Conference and American assistance to Japan in the aftermath of the Kanto earthquake.

But the war talk did more than simply foreshadow the future Pacific War. Although some Japanese tried to dismiss tensions over Japanese actions in China and Korea as a product of misperceptions, China troubles real and imagined were central to U.S.-Japanese tensions in the interwar period.

THE WASHINGTON CONFERENCE, THE KANTO EARTHQUAKE AND JAPANESE PUBLIC OPINION: VICTORIES FOR LIBERALS?

THE WASHINGTON CONFERENCE MARKED AN UPTURN IN U.S.-JAPANESE relations. War talk disappeared virtually overnight, replaced by optimism that the major point of tension, China, had been resolved at the negotiating table.

The Washington Conference took place between November 1921 and April 1922 in Washington, DC. The major powers all participated including Japan, the United States, Great Britain, France, and several other smaller nations. Organized by the American secretary of state Charles Hughes, the conference was designed to promote interregional stability, especially in the Pacific. It also showcased new American leadership in world politics. Hughes and others envisioned that the Washington Conference would replace the older European system that had broken down amidst a European arms race and secret alliance system that had led to World War I. The new system would create conditions for peace in the Pacific, where the tensions between Japan and the United States had created worrisome discussions about the possibility of war.

The Washington Conference was designed to swing the diplomatic initiative back to the United States, to do it outside of the League of Nations, which both Americans and Japanese suspected of simply furthering the goals of European powers, and to press forward with the ideals of Woodrow

Wilson, especially sovereignty, free trade, democracy, and disarmament in the Pacific region. It was also an official response to the postwar atmosphere that saw the expansion of internationalist ideas.

RISE OF INTERNATIONALISM

As Akira Iriye remarks in his book, *Cultural Internationalism and World Order*, "Cultural internationalism came of age in the aftermath of World War I." The rise of internationalism after World War I was made possible largely by a reaction against the war itself and President Woodrow Wilson's push for peace during and after the war.[1] Wilson, who has been described as a secular missionary, believed that the basic conditions of the world order had created World War I and that those conditions could be changed to lay the groundwork for world peace and prosperity.[2] Wilson's father was a Presbyterian minister and Wilson exemplified the fervency of a true believer. Constitutional scholar turned politician, Wilson admired the British constitutional system greatly.

After World War I began (1914), Wilson began to envision a new world order consisting of collective security, free trade, national sovereignty, and democratic governments throughout the world. Diplomatic conflicts would be solved in open session instead of behind closed doors, arms would be limited by multilateral treaties, and collective security would alleviate the need to create strategic alliances of the kind that also led to World War I in Europe.

Even though Wilson failed in his goal of creating a new world order, he succeeded in laying the groundwork for a new order that took shape in the Washington Conference and eventually came to fruition after World War II in the United Nations. In addition, Wilson inspired a generation of internationalists to work for the end of wars like World War I, cooperation between nations, world peace, and fair adjudication of international disputes.

Internationalists saw themselves as working to replace the old European "war system" with a new "peace system," in the words of Sherwood Eddy, YMCA missionary leader and scholar and writer of East Asia. Eddy toured Europe and Asia after World War I and advocated for the principles of internationalism: open diplomacy and peaceful means to settle disputes instead of the old European system of secret pacts and large armies engaging in warfare.[3] He and Sidney Gulick as well as many others supported the new internationalist movement in the United States.

The YMCA, Eddy's employer, also supported these new ideas. Other new organizations sprang up in the United States such as the National Council for the Prevention of War (NCPW), the Women's International League for Peace and Freedom (WIL), The Foreign Policy Association (FPA), and the League of Nations Association (LNA). All these organizations and others represented the internationalist vision.

The Japanese also supported Wilson's internationalist ideas enthusiastically. They formed Japan branches of the same organizations such as a Japanese LNA and studied Wilson's ideas. For them it held the promise of escape from the European-centered war system they deeply distrusted. Although the Japanese supported the rise of internationalism, they had doubts about its authenticity and wondered whether it would benefit Japan.

THE WASHINGTON CONFERENCE

While the Japanese delegates planned the conference in the spring and summer of 1921, the Japanese diplomats, official and unofficial, discussed the issue of cooperation with the West. In the public arena, some Japanese magazine and newspaper articles expressed distrust in the United States and criticized the agenda of the Washington Conference. Although this should not be surprising given the amount of distrust, tension, and talk of war within the U.S.-Japanese relationship in 1921, historians have generally interpreted the Washington Conference as a win-win situation for both the United States and Japan. Walter Lafeber's award-winning book, *The Clash*, argues that Japan went away from the conference strengthened by its agreements. "Everyone except China went home with reasons to be satisfied. With their naval superiority in East Asia and the U.S. pledge not to fortify further western Pacific holdings, the Japanese were safe from American attack across the central Pacific."[4]

But the Japanese public, in general, was not as impressed with the outcome. One commentator believed the Washington Treaties, far from creating a new, more peaceful world order, maintained the status quo. He quoted Bismarck as saying "the satiated states wish to maintain their present supremacy and possessions."[5]

In the end the Japanese probably gave up more than they wanted. The Americans convinced the Japanese to give back Shantung peninsula to China, with the reservation of railroad leases. And Japan had to live with a smaller naval ship tonnage ratio than either the British or Americans. Negative Japanese perceptions clung to this part of the treaty in spite of the reality of continued Japanese naval supremacy—the Americans and British were not interested in building up to their tonnage limits and this left Japan in a superior position—because it seemed that the Japanese once again had been placed in inferior status vis-à-vis the Western powers. The Japanese inserted special language of "propinquity" into the treaty to confirm their exclusive interests in Manchuria. However they agreed to live with the American "Open Door" everywhere else in China. This fact, instead of appearing to level the playing field in China, seemed to disadvantage Japan because of its concerns over the instability of China that the Open Door seemed to aid and abet. As a result, the Japanese view of the Washington Conference needs a closer examination.

The official Japanese view of the pre-conference situation came from Count Uchida, the Japanese foreign minister, in an address to the Japanese Diet in January 1921. Uchida identified several areas of concern in foreign affairs: disarmament, League of Nations, Anglo-Japanese Alliance, China, and tensions between the United States and Japan. The overall tenor of the speech though positive was also cautious and skeptical. Uchida paid lip service to disarmament while commenting on U.S.-Japanese relations obliquely by stating that disarmament would only work if "all nations acted in harmony and in good faith."[6]

Uchida also mentioned the Anglo-Japanese Alliance. The Alliance had been formed in 1902 and renewed in 1911. The British had used the Alliance to block the Russian advance in the Far East. The Japanese had cooperated admirably by defeating the Russians in the Russo-Japanese War of 1904–1905. The main impetus to abandon the Alliance came from the British who no longer needed it. The Russians had allied themselves with the British in World War I and then went onto the October Revolution, and were no longer able to challenge British influence in East Asia. The Japanese had benefited tremendously from the protection of the British and Uchida stated that many in Japan wanted to see the Alliance continue if not in letter then in spirit.[7]

The Anglo-Japanese Alliance brings up an intriguing question. Why did the Japanese give up the treaty with so little fuss? Why did they not fight harder to maintain their bilateral relationship with Great Britain. Uchida put forward the official Japanese line that the League of Nations superseded the Anglo-Japanese Treaty. But the Japanese had little faith in the League to protect Japan's interests the same way the British had.

It is possible that Japan now looked to the United States for leadership and the Washington Conference and its treaties was the logical outcome of faith in this newfound powerful friend. The problem with this argument is that the United States and Japan were no longer friends by the 1920s. Maybe the Japanese assumed the breach with the United States was temporary and reparable. It turned out to be neither.

The Japanese did have the promise of the huge American economy before them and so enhanced trade with the United States might result from cooperation and closer diplomatic ties with the Americans. Ambassador to the United States Shidehara Kijuro (later the foreign minister), who was the lead negotiator of the conference took the view that cooperation with the United States could only strengthen Japan's economy.

Roger Dingman points out that the Japanese leadership had domestic reasons for supporting the Washington Treaties. Hara Kei, under whose leadership the Washington Treaties were negotiated, wanted to reduce the power of the military in general within Japanese politics. He also desired to support the navy and reduce the power of the army. The navy supported negotiation with the Western powers while the army wanted a more hard-line approach. The treaties emphasized diplomacy over force and focused on the naval affairs and therefore met Hara's goals.[8]

In any case, the demise of the Anglo-Japanese Alliance was a major turning point for Japan in international affairs. American historians have tended to downplay this because the Washington system designed by the Washington Conference replaced it. It will become clear however that the Washington Treaty did not satisfy Japan like it was assumed.

Uchida's comments on China were standard fare. Japan was sympathetic to China's plight and "peculiarly interested, that complete and peaceful unification of China is not yet in sight." This strangely phrased statement nonetheless indicated very clearly the importance of Japan's strategic and economic interests in China.[9]

Finally Uchida came to the U.S.-Japan relationship. Sounding like an estranged lover, Uchida marveled at the tradition of friendship while at the same time taking the United States to task over the treatment of Japanese immigrants in California. The prominent place given in the speech by the foreign minister to the issue of Japanese immigrants in the United States indicates the importance the Japanese placed on it. If Uchida had addressed the American Congress, not the Japanese Parliament, the issue would scarcely have been mentioned, but the Japanese public felt very strongly the injustice of the ongoing immigration restrictions against Japanese in the United States.[10]

One month before the conference began, Kawashima Saijiro, editor of *Dai Nihon*, echoed Uchida and others' skepticism tempered by hopeful optimism. Kawashima wrote directly to the American public:

> True, an idea is advanced by some, not without some speciousness, that the conference is part of a scheme to assert a new-born principle in America, which is in substance the same as the old Germanism, "might is right," by transferring the theatre of its operation from Europe to the Far East and the Pacific. But there are not a few Americans, in whose veins still runs the Puritan blood and who make it their ideal to serve the cause of the world's peace with justice, righteousness and liberty. Before these American lovers and defenders of true peace and justice, I wish to lay bare the Japanese ideals and aspirations in their native honest light and invite them to speak out their mind.[11]

Then in a more ominous vein, he wrote

> There would surely be a Japanese outburst of indignation at the outcome of the conference if it be such as would bring pressure to bear upon Japan,

unwarrantably and perfidiously, for purposes of unjustifiable coercion—an out burst which will not fail to make itself felt by the world.

These seem unnecessarily strong words before a conference whose avowed purpose was to repair the tensions of the last several years and open a new paradigm of disarmament and peace in the Pacific. The best way to explain this attitude is to see the tensions of the pre-conference atmosphere in Japan as very serious. All the more serious because Kawashima as editor of *Dai Nihon*, one of the more influential monthly magazines in Japan, was embedded in Japanese media and had a strong feeling for the pulse of Japanese popular opinion.

Some in Japan believed that it had been blockaded from expansion into China by the West. Others believed that Japan was accursed by the bad luck of having developed a bad image in the West. Kawashima addressed the negativity head-on. Japan had become one of the world's great powers at the end of World War I. Therefore others would examine Japan closely and critically. Kawashima did not think this was a reason for pessimism. He rejected the old Japanese proverb of the tall tree that is lashed by the wind bent this way and that way.

Winds strike tall trees hard; but that furnishes no reason to call the tall trees accursed . . . The fact that the wind strikes a full-grown tree is no reason to condemn the tree for its height. Nor should, for that reason, a high tower be hermetically closed. Let Japan be a great tree, a great tower open on all sides. Let there be no talk of accursedness and blockade, which is possible only when Japan fails to observe and get up to the principle of justice and righteousness.

Kawashima argued for openness to the international world, a willingness to negotiate and adjust to the outside world. Japan needed to embrace its new role in the world and not carp and whine about criticism and unfair treatment. Kawashima balanced Japanese concerns with an argument for engagement. Kawashima's article is persuasive in tone. He was attempting to convince a skeptical Japanese public that good things could come from Japanese participation in the Washington Conference.[12]

Were the Japanese really so distrustful of U.S. motives in the Washington Conference? Public feeling in Japan immediately before the conference was mixed overall. On the one hand, Kawashima expressed an unease that resonated through Japan that other nations could not be trusted to deal fairly with it. On the other hand, Ozaki Yukio, the famous Japanese parliamentarian, favored negotiation and mounted a powerful campaign for arms limitation ahead of the conference that had support among others in Japan including liberals such as the Christian Yoshino Sakuzo. Reports that over 90 percent of the population supported some form of disarmament appeared in the liberal press although there is no evidence that this is a credible figure.[13]

More evidence of skepticism appeared in the *North China Standard*, a Japanese-owned newspaper in the Shantung area of China.

> When the idea of the Washington Conference was first mooted, apprehension was almost universal in Japan that it was intended to open up the way for occidental intervention in the affairs of the Far East . . . The inclusion of the Pacific and Far East problems in the coming conference appealed to the public as only another form of American intervention in Japan's national rights and interests.

Later the article indicated that suspicion surrounding the conference had been removed by pre-conference discussions. Although there was support for the idea of disarmament among the Japanese public, there was also concern that the Washington Conference could end up as another Western intervention in the Far East at the expense of Japan.[14]

As delegates gathered for the conference in November 1921, one of the Japanese delegates, Baron Kanda Naibu, a Japanese MP, gave a talk at the Cosmos Club in Washington, DC about Japanese intentions and concerns. Here in front of American journalists, politicians, and diplomats, Kanda outlined Japan's rationale for its position. The British and Americans had proposed that their own navies be limited to 500,000 tons of ships in the Pacific while Japan's limit would be set at 300,000 tons. Japan proposed to modify this by increasing the Japanese limit to 350,000 tons. In the end, Japan accepted 300,000 tons, a position interpreted by Japanese Westernizers as a legitimate compromise and by Japanese conservatives as one more instance of appeasement by the Japanese to the demands of the West. But for the negotiators, this issue was straightforward and resolvable. Baron Kanda stated, "It is an example of frank consultation of sincere minds coming together." Kanda was less sanguine about U.S.-Japanese relations and the China issue at the conference. Kanda expressed weariness at the war talk swirling about US-Japanese relations and was just as tired of reiterating Japan's friendship with the United States.

> Let me touch in this connection, upon the talks of war between the two countries. War talks necessitate talks of friendships, which I confess I too have often indulged in, but frankly I am tired of both. "What's the use," as one of my friends said the other day, "of repeated assurances of friendship when we are in fact already friends."

An apparent secondary consequence of the war talk was a kind of weariness among those who were most vigilant in trying to keep U.S.-Japanese relations on the right course.[15]

Kanda spent most of his speech defending Japan's China policy, arguing that Japan could not survive without access to China's resources. He expressed "deepest interest and sympathy" for China, accepting the notion of the Open Door in China, arguing that all Japan wanted was "a prosperous and stable China as her neighbor and customer, well organized and able to buy and produce, and an equal opportunity there with all nations for commerce and industry to meet her vital necessity."[16] This harmless sounding rhetoric of course did not acknowledge that Japan had already rejected the idea of the Open Door in Manchuria by rejecting attempts at American investment there and instead forced the Americans to funnel money through Japanese enterprises.[17] Kanda's approach in the speech was smart; he was blunt when discussing U.S.-Japanese tensions, molding his words to an American audience that appreciated this kind of undiplomatic (and un-Oriental) frankness and analytic and careful on China, again recognizing his audience's tendencies.

China was the focus of much Japanese commentary. In addition to a defense of Japan's policies there, the chaotic situation in China was also mentioned. Because China's government was weak and unstable in the aftermath of the Republican Revolution, powerful men in the regions of China took control in the 1920s. These warlords recruited and coerced Chinese peasants into large armies that controlled the country from the regions. The central government was powerless to stop them. They fought one another for territory and spoils, they ruthlessly exploited the peasants, and their wars produced forced migrations of millions of Chinese. It is estimated that up to 20 million Chinese were killed in the Warlord Period that lasted from 1916 to 1927. The Japanese looked at China nervously in this period. China's relative proximity, huge population, and great resources made it attractive but also very dangerous for Japan's own security.

At the conference the Chinese negotiator Dr. Sao Ke Alfred Sze put forward an official statement of China's goals, written with help from Robert Lansing, secretary of state in the Wilson administration and Paul Reinsch, former ambassador to China. The goals—territorial integrity, no exclusive spheres of trade or control, and abolition of extraterritoriality—reflected the Open Door policy of the United States.[18] Though the close alignment of the United States and China made the Japanese uncomfortable, the Japanese delegation issued a positive statement in basic agreement with China's goals. Beyond the official statement, however, there remained skepticism of China's intentions and goodwill.

Off the record, one Japanese representative denounced the corruption of Chinese provincial bureaucrats and anti-Japanese propaganda coming out of China.

Japan hopes to add to her international prestige the liberality, sincerity and correctness of her course in this conference. China can do likewise by adopting a safe and sane course, based upon facts instead of suspicion, distrust and misrepresentations . . .

Kato Katsuji, editor of *The Japan Review*, evaluated the goals and agreed with them. However, he noted that China was so chaotic that there was little hope that the nation could actually develop the independence and strength needed to implement its goals. Kato also mentioned Chinese propaganda against Japan and noted that the propaganda took place both in China and in some newspapers and magazines within the United States, and called it the "moral perversion of China . . ." In truth, though Japan was concerned about China's lack of stability, the Japanese government used the chaos to further its own ends, gaining more control in Manchuria.[19]

At its conclusion, the conference participants reached several important agreements on China. The Open Door policy was confirmed, including expressions of China's territorial integrity and sovereignty. The Americans convinced Japan to leave the Shantung peninsula that they had occupied since World War I. In return, the United States allowed special language to be inserted describing Japan's interests in Manchuria in a way that left little doubt that these interests were exclusive and inviolable. The Open Door was closed in Manchuria. On the whole, all participants came away with something. Japan's rights were guaranteed in Manchuria and it gained a commitment from the Americans that they would not fortify their Pacific bases, China got back Shantung and the Open Door was confirmed there, the United States and Great Britain got a naval treaty limiting Japan's fleet at levels well below the American and British tonnage. But of all the participants the Japanese gave up the most. The Japanese gave up Shantung, the Anglo-Japanese Alliance, and had to settle for junior status in naval limitations.[20]

JAPANESE RESPONSE

Although the Americans could point to the success of the Washington Conference in creating a more peaceful and stable Far East and the Japanese delegation left the Washington Conference with some achievements, there were in fact many reasons for the Japanese to be uneasy with the results. China was still in chaos even though Manchuria had been formally secured. No longer protected by the Anglo-Japanese Alliance, the Japanese now had an uncertain future in a larger weaker alliance of the Americans, British, and French on East Asian issues. The Americans and British limited Japanese naval tonnage ratios at the conference and pressured the Japanese to return Shantung so there was some concern that what Japan really faced was an Anglo-American combination against the nation.

Cooperation and accommodation was perhaps the best the Japanese delegation could do under such circumstances.[21] One commentator argued just this course in an article for the *Japan Advertiser* in February 1922 as the conference wound down. He criticized the Japanese delegates heavily for not resisting American and British demands more vigorously. On the other hand, he pointed out that with the end of the Anglo-Japanese Treaty, the Japanese had very few friends in case of a war with the United States, and therefore a policy of conciliation was the only rational approach.[22]

The Japanese press at home criticized the outcome vigorously. The moderate *Tokyo Asahi* questioned the Japanese delegation's agreement to a lower naval tonnage limit.

Was the 70 percent ratio [350,000 tons] asked by the Japanese delegates really the minimum which the defense of Japan could accept? It has, at any rate been represented that this is the case. Why have the delegates then accepted the 60 percent ratio?

The conservative *Kokumin* also discussed the naval agreements and accused the United States of being a tyrant by insisting that it be able to build two new battleships so that Japan did not have to scrap its battleship, the *Mutsu*.

Such being the case America has daringly played at politics and it is most regrettable that what should have marked a new epoch of permanent peace with reduced armament, has gone no further than adhering to the same old naval rivalry.

The *Kokumin* went on to state that the Americans mistakenly believed that the Japanese had received benefits at the conference. The more liberal *Jiji* was more positive about the outcome, especially the naval reductions that it saw as the first step toward a more permanent world peace and offered congratulations to the government authorities who engineered the treaty.[23]

The Japanese media were less dissatisfied with the resolution of Shantung issues. The Japanese attempted to negotiate with China directly over the issue and China refused. The negotiations under American guidance became mutually agreeable and the Japanese press expressed general satisfaction with the outcome.

The mild press response concerning Shantung is somewhat surprising given that only a few months before, the Japanese government had refused to negotiate on the basis of joint involvement with the Chinese in managing the assets of Shantung, especially the major railway that had been built originally by the Germans. The Japanese now agreed to give back Shantung with some few strings attached. While this might have been the wise thing to do, one might have guessed that conservative newspapers would howl about it. The truth is that Shantung had become a bit of an albatross around Japan's neck. The strong anti-Japanese sentiment among the local population and the great pressure brought to bear by the Americans and the British had turned Japanese public and its diplomats against consolidation of Shantung into the Japanese Empire and allowed it to be negotiated back to China without much fanfare.[24] It is undeniable however, that when Japan gave up Shantung, nothing was forthcoming for the Japanese in return. The remaining great powers in China continued their spheres of influence apace. The groundwork for future resentment had been laid.

The Japanese press was also generally satisfied with the end of the Anglo-Japanese Alliance and the beginning of a new Alliance with the United States, Great Britain and France, although the more conservative Japanese newspapers such as the *Hochi* and the *Chugai Shogyo* pointed out that the United States was a newcomer to leadership in international diplomacy and therefore the future of relations still remained a question mark.

The conservative Tokyo daily *Yorodzu* summed up its view of the United States and the work of the conference this way. Accusing the Americans of being "hateful and haughty," the paper claimed

When America issued the invitation to the Washington Conference, our foolishly honest Government replied by acceptance of the invitation and sent our delegates to far-away Washington. When the Conference was opened, America introduced her selfish proposals and forced our country to accept the proposals blindly. If our delegates had valued the dignity of the Empire and the honor as an independent nation, they should at once have refused to accept the proposals and left the Conference. Yet they did otherwise. They simply accepted the proposals as America wanted them to do. Can our people who have a glorious history of 3,000 years endure this indignity?[25]

Another publication in Japan, the *Diplomatic Review* responded to the treaties by arguing that since the United States and Great Britain were joining forces against Japan, the Japanese had no choice but to ally itself with others against them.

The world is not to be expected to tolerate forever the monopolistic action of the same influence. If the Anglo-Saxons—more especially the Americans—continue on their arbitrary and arrogant course in defiance of international ethics and moral conceptions common to all nations, the other nations will be driven to unite their forces to oppose them. If Japan, China, Russia and Germany should unite against them, it will not be of their own choice and initiative, but only through incitement or compulsion by the Anglo-Saxons.[26]

While the rhetoric of this article and some of the others above was overblown, one can clearly sense the anger and outrage in it.

Two new organizations, the National Young Men's Association and the National Federation both held mass meetings in Tokyo denouncing the results of the Washington Conference. Composed of journalists, scholars, Diet members, and military men, these organizations represented a more conservative slice of the Japanese body politic. While it was claimed that these groups did not represent a majority of the Japanese population, the fact that conservative forces such as these were mobilized by the agreements was a disturbing sign.[27]

The U.S. media prominently represented a more positive view of Japanese opinion in Dr. Iyenaga's "How Japan Views the Arms Conference" in the *New York Times Current History Magazine*. Iyenaga, who had been a lecturer at the University of Chicago the decade before the conference, expressed great optimism that the conference had ushered in a new era of relations between the United States and Japan. Here as well, though, Iyenaga acknowledged the criticisms of the Japanese public against the treaties. Iyenaga's article was well balanced in argument and made a strong case that Japan received concrete benefits from the conference. The problem here is that his article was in the English language directed at an American audience that already approved of the outcome. Japanese public opinion needed this kind of argument in the Japanese language in a prominent publication to refute the criticisms being leveled against the agreements.[28]

Later in the decade, Shantung as well as the naval issues would emerge as rallying cries for the political right in Japan. They pointed back at the Washington Conference, accusing the negotiators of appeasement.

Adding insult to injury, it was revealed to the world later on that the Japanese secret code used to send messages between the government and its negotiators had been broken by Herbert Yardley. In his book *The Black Chamber* (1931), Yardley, who had become the U.S. government's chief code breaker in World War I, revealed that he had decoded Japanese plans for the conference. Yardley claimed the secrets revealed had helped American negotiators win the diplomatic battle and gain substantial Japanese concessions at the conference. He worked from a house in New York City that became known as the Black Chamber. By 1931 Yardley's operation was closed down by Washington and he made his living writing books about his code-breaking past. According one source, many university and higher schools in Japan had copies of *The Black Chamber* in their libraries.[29]

AMERICAN VIEWS AND JAPANESE LIBERALS

The Americans found themselves in the driver's seat at the Washington Conference, a relatively new position for them. American leadership had brought the conference together and American leadership pushed the agenda forward. Interestingly, sitting in the driver's seat made Americans suddenly more sensitive to what the Japanese were thinking and perhaps more importantly what the Japanese thought about the Americans. Several articles appeared before, during, and after the Washington Conference with titles like "What the Orient Thinks of Us," and "Oh Hateful Haughty America." In reality, this new sensitivity spurred Americans to attend more closely to Japan, but writing on Japan often did not reveal what the Japanese actually thought about the United States rather what Americans thought about them.

Lucian Kirtland was a New York writer and a World War I veteran with direct experience of Japan. He had traveled there as a young man, hiking with friends along the Tokaido Road. His account of the trip was recorded in an artful narrative called *Samurai Trails: A Chronicle of Wanderings on the Japanese High Road* (1918). The book demonstrated the positive side of American Orientalist thought. Kirtland was enchanted by the trappings of old Japan: the Japanese Inn maid, the equivalent of a low-class Geisha, who entertained travelers, the practice of gift giving, the samurai distain for money, the hot baths the Japanese took at the end of the day, the paper umbrellas, and the jin-rickshas of Kyoto.[30]

Kirtland analyzed the results of the Washington Conference in an article called "What Japan Thinks of Us."

> Her [Japan's] fear of us has been the chief card of the military clique for two decades and when that ace ceased to be trump, Nipponese liberal opinion—which has always recognized the worthwhileness of friendship and understanding with America—was able to come into its own. It consolidated its strength and took over the direction of internal and foreign affairs. This doesn't mean that the liberal party's grip is invincible nor that it has brought in the millennium of the angels, but it does mean that Japan is more than anxious to co-operate with us in giving a quietus to the distrust business.[31]

Claiming that the objections of Japanese public opinion had stopped the militarists in Japan from staying in Shantung and Siberia and thus laid the groundwork for the Washington Conference outcome, Kirtland asserted,

> We may sometime realize that the proposals of the Washington Conference were not forced upon an unwilling Japan but instead granted Japanese liberalism a face-saving chance to extricate the country's foreign policy from inherited shackles. It unscrambled the eggs, as it were.[32]

While Kirtland accurately estimated the opposition to the Siberia and Shantung expeditions, he made the mistake of overestimating the strength of the liberal camp in Japan.

Arthur Jorgensen went to Japan in 1914 as a YMCA missionary. He ended up staying for twenty-eight years, repatriated to the United States in the summer of 1942 in a citizen exchange between the United States and Japan after the outbreak of the Pacific War. Jorgensen distinguished himself in his time in Japan with his intellectual talents, leading a study of racism among missionaries in Japan in 1924 and writing many analytical articles about Japan for the American audience. His understanding of Japan was deep and wide. However, he, like Kirtland, overestimated the power of liberalism within Japan in 1922. Jorgensen wrote of the Washington Conference,

> . . . I believe that the steady pressure of public opinion in this country has been in the right direction. Were it not for this fact, it would have been easy for the jingoists to have gotten in their oar . . . In other words the temper of public opinion in this country is such that the Japanese delegation will have the nation as a whole back of them if they take a liberal attitude toward the problems up for consideration. This conclusion is supported, I believe, by an examination of the press opinions as well as those expressed by a large majority of influential public men.[33]

Another YMCA missionary in Japan, Russell Durgin, commented on Japanese public reaction to the Washington Conference outcome. He was perhaps more realistic about the reaction of the Japanese press than Jorgensen or Kirtland but still found ample reasons to be optimistic.

> The past few months have, I feel, seen quite a change of attitude on the part of Japan toward America. The change also has been noted on the part of many people and the press from one of more or less pessimism toward world affairs and the Washington Conference in particular to one of great optimism and hope. There are of course as in every country a number of newspapers which are always ready to find fault with anything and everything, which at this time are loudly proclaiming that Japan has been unfairly dealt with at the hands of the Anglo-American combination, but in general the outcome seems to be quite favorably looked upon, especially perhaps the disarmament part of the agreements. The Japanese delegates, exactly as was the case in the settlement of the Russo-Japanese war at Portsmouth, N.H., are getting more than their share of censure and blame for all that happened at the Conference, but this is to be expected in view of the proverbial attitude which the newspapers and many of the people seem to take toward their delegates to any such conference of international scope.[34]

Even though Durgin acknowledged the existence of fairly widespread criticism of the conference results, he believed the response was very positive overall. Durgin made the mistake of dismissing the opposition. In the end he saw what he wanted and his conclusions matched his preferences.

The commentary also illustrates Durgin's somewhat condescending attitude toward what he saw as the provincialism of Japanese public opinion.

How can we explain the disconnect between a substantial segment of Japanese public opinion concerned about the outcome of the Washington Conference and Americans in Japan interpreting the outcome as a victory for the Japanese? First, the outcome was in fact a victory for liberals in Japan. The liberal outlook dominated the delegation and the decision to compromise. The mistake lay in interpreting this liberal victory as something the Japanese commoner supported unequivocally. And Americans, even those who understood the Japanese viewpoint, saw the Washington Treaty through an American lens that hailed Japanese cooperation and therefore did not see the inordinate cost of the treaty to the Japanese.

In addition, Jorgensen, Durgin, and other missionaries in Japan spent more time with Japanese of like mind while there. Jorgensen was friendly with Nitobe Inazô. Shibusawa Eiichi, a participant in the Washington Conference, sat on a YMCA committee in Tokyo, and was considered a friend by John Mott, the head of the American YMCA, who had dinner with Shibusawa when he came to Japan. Shibusawa's home was a must-stop for prominent Americans visiting Japan. But most Americans did not make contact with conservatives or militarists. Americans saw a small slice of the Japanese body politic and that slice shared the liberal internationalist view of many Americans supportive of Japan.

They missed the much larger segment of Japanese society that was not necessarily liberal or internationalist in outlook. Of course we have the benefit of historical hindsight. But there was enough evidence available before, during, and after the conference of opposition to the liberal approach to awaken Americans interpreting Japan to a more cautious conclusion about the situation on the ground in Japan. Americans found the answers they were looking for in the Washington Conference and stuck with those answers even later in the 1930s when it became much more apparent that liberalism in Japan was in trouble.

John Dewey returned to the United States in late 1921 shortly before the Washington Conference and published a survey of his thoughts on Japan and China in *The New Republic*. Dewey did not make the mistakes of those who were overly optimistic about the prospects of Japanese liberalism in the wake of the Washington Conference although he did acknowledge that the liberal outlook had been strengthened there. Instead he took a more balanced approach. Even though he had only a brief direct experience of Japan, Dewey's sharp intellect gave him important insights into the state of Japanese liberalism.

Dewey argued that liberal opinion within Japan had been bolstered by several important events in recent years: the effects of World War I, the failed

Siberian expedition, the protests and boycotts in Shantung, the strength of progressive thought in China (Dewey is singular in giving China some credit for impacting liberal Japan positively), the rise of a scientific consciousness, the problem of labor unrest and class consciousness, and the raising of taxes to support a large army and navy.[35]

Then Dewey tempered his positive assessment by explaining that even though liberalism had grown, support for the emperor proved a unifying factor and the Japanese were also united in their support of Japan's Empire in the Far East. Japanese of every stripe saw it as the only way to combat the threat of Western imperialism in East Asia.

> Add to these positive facts the outstanding fact that even a Japanese liberal has good reason to believe that in the predatory expansion of modern imperialistic Europe, her army and navy have alone saved Japan from becoming another India or China, and one begins to sense why in any crisis public opinion moves to the side of the military party.[36]

In the article, Dewey described a conversation he heard in Tokyo between two liberals, one Japanese and one Chinese. The Chinese accused Japan of meddling in China's internal affairs and told the Japanese to mind his own business. The Japanese gentlemen responded that Japan had no choice but to be concerned about China and be involved China's welfare because of the proximity of China to Japan and China's great importance to Japan's destiny.

Another prominent scholar who was a colleague of Dewey's at Columbia University for a time, Charles Beard, commented directly on the Washington Conference. Beard, the dean of American historians, had resigned his position at Columbia in the midst of a fight over the firing of two professors who opposed American involvement in World War I. It was a decision of personal conscience and it brought Beard much sympathy among liberals and did not damage his reputation as the leading American historian in the least.

Beard, like Dewey, took a more realistic view of Japan and American interests there. In a lecture given at Dartmouth College and published as *Cross-Currents in Europe Today* (1922), Beard argued that the Americans had effectively checked the rise of Japanese power in the Pacific by abrogating the Anglo-Japanese Alliance, by lowering the ceiling of naval tonnage, and by limiting Japanese expansion in China. But Beard wondered if this policy was wise in its long-term consequences because it would create a strong rivalry between the United States and Japan and could fuel conflict with the Japanese.[37]

Even Franklin Delano Roosevelt weighed in on the conference outcome. Roosevelt, who served as the assistant secretary of the navy under Wilson during World War I, had been greatly influenced by Wilsonian internationalism.

He wrote an article called "Shall We Trust Japan" for *Asia* in 1923 endorsing Japanese participation in the Washington Conference. Emphasizing cooperation and partnership with Japan, Roosevelt noted that a war between the United States and Japan would be a catastrophe for both countries.[38]

Overall, the outcome of the conference strengthened the view that Japan was moving in the direction of liberal modernity. Missionaries and others believed Japan to be in concert with the United States and Great Britain moving toward greater cooperation and away from a feudal past. The truth was more complex.

Japanese liberalism was rising, the militaristic group was powerful, and the two sides did political battle in the 1920s. But both respected the imperial system including both the Japanese Emperor and Empire. This unified them with the vast majority of Japanese public opinion and put them at odds with American liberals. Most American commentators did not understand this essential fact. And they overestimated the value of the Washington Conference for Japanese liberals. In the short run liberals were strengthened. But the negative reaction of Japanese public opinion to the Washington agreements meant the victory for liberals was bittersweet.

THE KANTO EARTHQUAKE

One year after the Washington Conference, the Kanto earthquake of 1923 shook the foundations of Japan, literally and figuratively. In Tokyo, the morning of Saturday, September 1, 1923 was very hot with downpours of rain followed by blasts of wind. At 11:58 a.m. just as the city-dwellers were about to take their noontime meal, the tremors began. The first movement was weak but it was followed by a very large shock that grew and grew in intensity. In nearby Yokohama, Otis Manchester Poole who was the manager of Dodwell & Co. Ltd. described the shock that shook the entire southern Kanto region. "The ground could scarcely be said to shake; it heaved, it tossed and leapt under one. The walls bulged as if made of cardboard and the din became awful . . ."[39]

After the quake came the fires. Tokyo had installed gas lines to many houses and fires were lit in most homes preparing for the noon meal. The fires began immediately afterwards and spread rapidly throughout the city. By 4:00 p.m. great cyclones of fire and wind roared through the city. Some 40,000 people had gathered in an open space in Sumida district away from the damaged and dangerous buildings elsewhere, bringing their belongings and sleeping futons with them. The wind came up creating a cyclone which brought the fire into the open space. A mass immolation of the 40,000 resulted. One of the survivors Morita Bensaku recently described his memories of the scene.

It was searingly hot, but the wind was so strong that breathing was difficult . . . people were blowing through the air like leaves. Tin plates and pebbles rained down from the sky. People were constantly buffeted by scorching wind gusts coming from different directions.[40]

After two hours lying prone, Morita awoke and found himself buried underneath a mass of charred corpses. Not surprisingly, he wonders to this day why he was allowed to survive. Tanizaki Junichiro, the famous Japanese writer, lived in Tokyo but was vacationing in the mountain resort Hakone to the north. Obsessed with quakes from his childhood, Tanizaki fled Tokyo for Kyoto with his wife and children after the quake and returned only in old age to live in Tokyo once again.

The quake and fires together destroyed the cities of Tokyo and Yokohama. 162,000 people were killed and millions left homeless. In the aftermath rumor spread that Koreans in living in Japan as conscripted laborers, intent on overthrowing the Japanese government, had set fires and poisoned wells. Though completely false, the rumors created strong anti-Korean feelings. Japanese went on killing rampages through Korean neighborhoods massacring an estimated 6,000 Koreans. One woman Mun Mu Son described how her father's friend went to seek out the police to file a complaint against those committing abuses against Koreans. The next day the severed head of this friend was carried through the streets past Mu on top of a bamboo pike.[41]

In the mayhem, vigilantes also attacked leftist activists. Osugi Sakae, well-known Japanese rebel and anarchist, was murdered along with his lover Ito Noe and a nephew by police lieutenant Amakasu Masahiko and his troops. Osugi was a leading socialist writer who had captured the public imagination with his autobiography. Amakasu received a ten year prison sentence. The government eventually declared martial law, and in an attempt to stop the vigilante killings, warned that only police officials could stop citizens and check for documents. These incidents of violence were rarely reported in American newspapers at the time.

Several American warships such as the USS *Huron* stationed in Dairien (Port Arthur) and USS *Preble* steamed to Japan to aid in relief efforts. American naval personnel observed the Japanese Navy's reaction to the disaster to measure the efficiency of a potential adversary. It seemed that they had little to be concerned about. The Japanese Navy got poor marks. Ships stayed offshore while Japanese in both Tokyo and Yokohama were in desperate need of transport and food and other supplies. When the ships finally landed, they had no extra supplies to offer the victims. Naval attachés from the American embassy concluded that either the Japanese Navy was simply witless, did not have the authority to act, or was suspicious of foreign help. In truth all three of these issues were in evidence in the relief effort.

Even though the Japanese had long experience in earthquake relief efforts (Japan is located on a major earthquake fault), it had little experience in the use of the military to help in these situations. There was a considerable amount of bumbling in the relief effort attempted by the Japanese Navy. Ships without supplies, ships without orders; these issues could have been avoided and in fact hampered the effort. The deck officers were also hesitant to act without direct orders of the navy department and this was well noted in the narrative reports of the American observers.

The Japanese also obstructed American efforts at times and exhibited a general suspicion of having American ships in her waters. The American ships were shadowed by Japanese naval vessels. The Japanese at one point tried to jam American radio transmissions. And the Americans had difficulty in getting reliable information about the damage and casualties. Some of this stopped once the American commander explained that his ships were there simply to offer help and not to interfere in any way with the Japanese relief effort.

American naval attachés in Japan explained the Japanese response in several ways. However, while drawing conclusions from the very limited experience of a few weeks of relief work with the Japanese, some did not hesitate to broaden their conclusions into generalized cultural critiques of Japanese society. Speaking of the relief operations, the commander of the USS *Black Hawk* stated, "Thus was there evident everywhere the outstanding fact that the Japanese have adopted, but have not absorbed our civilization." He claimed that in the emergency of the Kanto earthquake the Japanese had reverted "to their natural state of civilization and re-act to their native tendencies or will await the dictum of authority before acting at all."[42]

Japanese hesitance to act alone, which certainly sacrificed lives in this case, was explained in another report as simply the Japanese etiquette and custom of consensus decision-making.[43] It could become, however, a symptom of the Japanese veneer of modernity, and evidence that the Japanese while having modernized had not changed at all underneath. "But it has not been a change by absorption of Western ideas, as is occurring with ponderous slowness in China to-day, but largely by government edict."[44]

The American reports also noted that the Japanese relief effort on the ground, especially in Tokyo—not withstanding the blunders of the Japanese Navy—had proceeded with efficiency and dispatch. And many Japanese showed kindness and generosity, meeting relief trains with food and other supplies. However, even here an American observer interpreted the help as only "timid individualism" tempered by "fatalistic acceptance." A different interpretation could have concluded that long experience with deadly earthquakes had induced the Japanese to be patient and remain calm in the face of disaster. Another plausible interpretation might have concluded that the magnitude of the damage (the two largest and most important cities in Japan were leveled, 146,000 people were killed, 447,128 homes were burned, untold lives were shattered, and economic crisis ensued) paralyzed the Japanese and this explained their behavior. Certainly this helps to explain the nativist attacks on Koreans and leftists, which the Americans' reports rightly condemned.

The Japanese response, fear and paralysis, hatred and nativism, mixed with many acts of bravery and kindness was unsurprising given the magnitude (literally 8.2) of the Kanto earthquake. Gauging the impact on U.S.-Japanese relations is more difficult. Official diplomats spoke of the gratitude of the Japanese people for the relief efforts of the American Navy and American nongovernmental organizations such as the YMCA. They conveniently left out any explanation of the harassment the Americans had to endure to help out. American YMCA leaders expressed pride even years later at their efforts to help rebuild Tokyo and Yokohama.[45] They certainly thought that their efforts had helped improve relations between the two countries. Others reported the event had relieved tension and improved relations between the two countries. Charles Reifsnider, an Episcopal priest in Tokyo, argued that not only had relations improved but the earthquake also had stopped Japan's plans for external aggression and militarism.[46]

There was another view in Japan, however. Tsurumi Yusuke, a young liberal politician and an important public figure, had a different interpretation. Tsurumi, one of the brightest of the younger generation of Japanese liberals, graduated from Tokyo Imperial University in 1910. Liberal in political inclination, Tsurumi was a canny politician. He was elected five times to Parliament. He married the daughter of Baron Goto Shimpei, who was more conservative but very well connected in Japanese politics having served as director of the South Manchurian Railway (SMR), as mayor of Tokyo and at the time of the Kanto earthquake as home minister in the Japanese cabinet. Baron Goto was responsible for the reconstruction of Tokyo after the earthquake.[47]

Tsurumi wrote an article for *The Outlook* in September, 1924. In it he expressed the view that Japanese liberalism had been hurt, not helped, by the Kanto earthquake. Tsurumi told of a close friend, who with his wife and children had survived the quake in Tokyo but lived in fear for two days afterward because of the chaos that reigned afterward. The friend had been a lifelong liberal compatriot. People swarmed to Tokyo from the surrounding countryside and the Korean rumors provoked vigilante groups to action. On September 3, when the army took control of the city and the government declared martial law his friend was greatly relieved.

> Distracted for the safety of his wife and little children, the sight of those brown uniforms and shining bayonets meant for him safety, salvation. He said repeatedly, "It is all very well to talk in abstract terms when things are calm, *but we need an army—I tell you we need an army.*" [emphasis in original] And this was

the same man who only a few months before, had been agitating for drastic curtailment of army expenses.

The symbolism of military strength in fearful times rang true in that time as it does in our own time. Tsurumi along with other liberals in Japan had his hopes raised after the Washington Conference but seemed to be more concerned about the future of Japanese liberalism after the earthquake.[48]

CONCLUSION

One must not place too much weight on Tsurumi's conclusions. Elsewhere, he expressed the conviction that liberalism was on the rise in Japan. However, his conclusion that the army had been strengthened by its role in calming the chaos in the aftermath of the earthquake and stabilizing the situation coupled with the distrust generated by the Washington Conference agreements suggests more conservative strength than many have traditionally attributed to Japan in the mid 1920s. A few singular voices have recognized this reality. Historian Leonard Humphreys states "The desperate conditions after the great Kanto earthquake of 1923 and the changes in the international atmosphere after the Washington Naval Conference reversed the liberal trend and reestablished the good standing of the armed forces . . ."[49]

The backlash from these events was like a fire bell tolling in the night. It should have awakened the United States to the dangers in the U.S.-Japan relationship. Instead, they were interpreted as liberal victories in Japan. The rise of an anti-Japanese movement in the United States and the Japanese reaction to immigration exclusion finally got the attention of American liberals.

CHAPTER 5

IMMIGRATION
EXCLUSION

ON THE NIGHT OF FEBRUARY 23, FOUR YOUNG MEN FOLLOWED A MEXICAN
leader across the Rio Grande near El Paso, Texas. They made their way to a
hotel in El Paso and from there took the Sante Fe night train to Denver,
Colorado. Unexpectedly the men were pulled off the train at Albuquerque,
New Mexico and arrested as aliens illegally entering the United States. The
arrests did not stop there. Two American immigration officers, Dodd and
Pruett, in charge of the El Paso and Juarez Mexico district were also arrested,
having been accused of aiding their illegal entrance.

This incident appears on its surface to be a contemporary account. The
current state of illegal border crossings of aliens from Mexico to the United
States and the problem of corruption among border patrol officers both ring
true today. However, this incident actually took place in 1908. And the
young men involved were not Mexican nationals but Japanese immigrants
attempting to cross into the United States. A year earlier, the Japanese and
American governments had come to a Gentlemen's Agreement—a series of
six diplomatic notes—to stop Japanese immigration to the United States with
the exception of the families of immigrants already there and picture brides.
As a consequence, illegal immigration from Mexico into the United States
by Japanese commenced. Concerns over Japanese immigrants fueled an
anti-Japanese movement that culminated in the Immigration Act of 1924
that stopped all Japanese immigration to the United States. The immigration
situation became a major source of tension between the United States and
Japan in the 1920s.

The Gentleman's Agreement of 1907 arose out of the tensions in California
over Japanese issei and nisei (first and second generation) immigrants.
Between 50,000–75,000 Japanese lived in California.

For several years before 1907, a campaign of anti-Japanese feeling penetrated public opinion in California. Resentment built against Japanese farmers. They had purchased poor land and through fertilization and irrigation converted it into highly productive farmland. It was also felt that Japanese workers took jobs away from Caucasians living in California. In 1906 after the Great San Francisco earthquake destroyed many of the city schools, school board officials used the quake as a pretext for segregating all Asians into one school. The event provoked President Roosevelt to get involved in mediating the anti-Japanese dispute. Roosevelt had gained strong credentials with the Japanese government by negotiating the settlement of the Russo-Japanese War in 1905. He initiated contact with the school board telling them that the federal government would negotiate directly with the Japanese and asking them to rescind the segregation order. The Japanese government agreed to stop issuing visas to Japanese laborers with the exception of those who already owned land in California or had families there and eventually to the so-called picture brides who were chosen by male immigrants already in the United States and then were allowed visas to join them there. The ban was extended to Japanese picture brides in 1920.

The picture bride issue created some heated rhetoric. A naval intelligence report from California claimed that the sole purpose of the picture bride industry was to propagate the Japanese race and expand the Japanese Empire abroad.

> The primary object of Japanese emigration, not only from the viewpoint of the government, but of the emigrants themselves, is not the economic benefit of the emigrants, as in the case of European emigrants—but the political development of the Japanese Empire. [underlines in original][1]

Studying a newspaper article in the Seattle based Japanese-American *North American Times*, the writer, B. Haworth became suspicious after a comment by a Japanese-American association encouraging its members to petition the Japanese Army to allow young Japanese-Americans to go back to Japan and take brides without being immediately drafted into the Japanese Army (Japanese immigrants retained Japanese citizenship and military obligations even after emigration). Haworth saw the petition as a dangerous link between the immigrants and the Japanese Army. Not quite a plot to overthrow the United States or to establish a beachhead for the empire, the association was interested in protecting its members and knew that the Japanese government took an interest in its emigrants in all parts of the Americas.

Similar concerns about Japanese picture brides, propagation, and domination appeared in a report of an immigration officer in Hawai'i. The situation in Hawai'i was different because there, the Japanese-American population had increased dramatically to a numerical majority (150,000) and it looked as though they would dominate the population of the islands shortly. The officer, Richard L. Halsey, quoted a member of the Japanese parliament visiting Hawai'i as saying that Japan would dominate Hawai'i in ten years. In a theme that would recur as an American nightmare all the way up to Pearl Harbor, Halsey, the inspector in charge of the Honolulu immigration office, declared that the Japanese government was intent on taking over Hawai'i and population domination was the opening wedge in this effort. Halsey then turned ethereal,

> Even as the eyes of the Roman colonists were turned toward the eternal city beyond the sea, so the eyes of Japanese colonists here are turned toward the Sunrise Kingdom and her representatives here are doing their part to see to it that they do not avert their gaze.[2]

Even though the Japanese government had been interested in expanding to Hawai'i in the 1890s, by the 1920s the Japanese had no plan to takeover Hawai'i or California through immigrant infiltration. The paranoid responses of Haworth and Halsey did not brighten prospects for increased understanding on the immigration issue. Instead, an anti-Japanese campaign, born in 1905 as the Japanese and Korean Exclusion League and led by V.S. McClatchy, a prominent newspaper man in Sacramento, grew over the next two decades into a formidable political force in the Pacific region.

Later in 1913, California became the first state in the nation to pass an Anti-Alien Land Law that restricted Japanese immigrant property ownership. The law was strengthened in 1920. Ren Hirao a Japanese exchange student studying in the United States at Stanford University recognized the far-reaching consequences of the Anti-Alien Land Law, "But ever since the passage of the Anti-Alien Land Law, the relation between the two countries has not been as it ought to be."[3]

Instead of a menace, Japanese farmers were a boon to the California economy. They farmed land that was otherwise unproductive. One Japanese commentator estimated that Japanese farmers produced $45 million worth of agricultural produce in 1917, a substantial part of the California economy, on only 25,000 acres. They were mostly hardworking, sober, law-abiding people, who would make solid American patriots.[4]

California was not the only state that discriminated against Japanese-Americans. Japanese provided a labor pool for the workers needed in the hard conditions of the western mining industry. The mining camps of Magna, Garfield, and Bingham surrounding Salt Lake City were not very inviting to say the least. Japanese workers, unlike other laborers who lived in small cabins on the grounds, were herded into large crowded bunkhouses. There were not enough beds so the men slept in the same beds in different shifts. When Japanese workers went to Salt Lake City for entertainment, they were either refused entrance into theaters or had to sit in the gallery (balcony). In the American South, a similar practice forced African-Americans to sit in the balcony, so-called nigger heaven.[5]

Japanese immigrant workers did make more money than they could back in Japan. But the discrimination they suffered made their lives a misery, a kind of "well-paid slavery." Writing in *The Japanese Student*, the author communicated the plight of these workers to Japanese students studying in the United States, who were the cream of Japan's crop and likely knew little of lower-class Japanese immigrants in America.[6]

A Japanese-American community had grown up in Salt Lake City. Many mine workers had left the grueling mining conditions for the city. There they could find work as farmhands or start a business catering to the Japanese-American population. Restaurants, small shops, barbers, all Japanese-owned, took up two full blocks of the poorer part of Salt Lake City. Most Japanese eked out a living. And the discrimination held them down not only economically but also socially.

> Even the few professional men with secure positions and respectable income live far below that standard that should be properly their own. Being shut out from the better American society, they have little inclination to adopt its standard. There are married men in the city. But the home is not the center of social activities . . .

This situation discouraged assimilation and tempted Japanese men to visit geisha bars.[7]

This concern was echoed in many other commentaries of the time. In 1918, Kasai Juiji, editor of the *Pacific Press*, a Japanese-American newspaper, wrote in *The Japanese Student* that since implementation of the Gentleman's Agreement in 1907, more Japanese had departed from the United States than had been admitted. Stating that Japan sought no special privileges, Kasai emphasized that what Japan objected to was the outright and blatant discrimination that he and others had experienced and witnessed in the United States. The Japanese accepted immigration restriction as official policy but rejected outright discrimination. Not an unreasonable concern, the issue of discrimination was very clear to the Japanese.[8]

Baron Shidehara Kijuro, Japanese ambassador to the United States and later Japanese foreign minister, addressed the immigration dispute in the spring of 1921, giving a speech before the Cleveland Chamber of Commerce. He tried to make light of the problem. "So I said to myself: What do these Ohio men want of men? Don't they know that I am a Japanese—the representative in this country of the 'Yellow Peril,' and a very dangerous character." One suspects that Shidehara's tone here was received more with grinding of teeth than genuine laughter. After all he was mocking the Americans and the audience had to know. He recovered from this faux pas to praise Ohioans' wisdom and democracy. Shidehara explained the immigration problem as a misunderstanding without substance, fueled by American yellow journalism. Noting that assimilation would be more easily done "in the balmy air of friendliness than under the stress of ostracism and discrimination," Shidehara claimed that Japanese immigrants would assimilate very well into American life and so the charge of inability to assimilate was a canard.[9]

The well-known intellectual and Christian socialist Abe Isoo also wrote on the immigration dispute in *The Japan Review* with a frank and self-critical explanation, unlike Shidehara's defensive posture. He had visited Hawai'i several years earlier and witnessed the tensions there surrounding the issue. Abe was more critical of the Japanese side than any other commentator. His explanation for the tensions was threefold: first, Japanese were educated not only at American public schools but also at Japanese language schools in Hawai'i and this dual education system prevented Japanese from integrating to American life completely and more importantly aroused the suspicions of white Americans. To Abe's mind, the lack of assimilation on the part of Japanese-Americans was a legitimate concern. Second, Japanese-Americans retained Japanese citizenship even if they were born in the United States and were liable to be conscripted into the Japanese Army. Abe believed this policy to be against Japanese customs and traditions and was not surprised in the least that it aroused fears of divided loyalty among Americans. He also accused the Japanese of being very intolerant of foreigners themselves and mistreating both Chinese and Koreans. This comment, made even before the attacks on Koreans that took place after the Kanto earthquake, expressed an opinion not many Japanese were willing to admit publicly, but of course this did not justify American discrimination.[10]

Abe insightfully identified some of the problems in Hawai'i. After Abe's visit, the American territorial legislature passed laws to restrict and eventually close down the Japanese language schools. Some Japanese responded by initiating a lawsuit against the territory. In a major victory for Japanese in Hawai'i and elsewhere, the lawsuit was upheld by the Supreme Court in 1927. In response to the issue of nisei holding both American and Japanese citizenship, the Japanese government implemented a law in 1924 that allowed nisei to voluntarily give up their Japanese citizenship. Not many nisei went through the process of giving up Japanese citizenship but they now had that option.[11]

Japanese plantation workers were very involved in the labor movement in Hawai'i that concerned both white and Japanese elites. They led a successful strike against Oahu plantations in 1909 and again in 1920. The Japanese Foreign Ministry was concerned enough about this potentially negative impact on U.S.-Japanese relations that they hired a Japanese-Christian pastor Okumura Takie through the Japanese consulate in Hawai'i to help Japanese plantation workers assimilate. For several years, Okumura traveled around the territory to plantations giving lectures to workers stating rather ironically that it was their duty as loyal Japanese to cooperate, learn English, and be patriotic Americans while keeping traditional Japanese culture.[12]

In the same journal, Anesaki Masaharu, another well-known intellectual, discussed the immigration problem through the lens of history and an innovative concept of race. He used historical examples of the consistent amalgamation of races when they came into contact to assert that "Pure race is a fiction and an uncontaminated nationality or civilization is merely an idea or ideal." Anesaki noted however that few contemporary nations or peoples recognized this fact; most still operated on the idea of racial purity.[13]

A truly white West Coast and Hawai'i was also a fiction since people of various shades already lived there. In fact Anesaki pointed out that the conception of a white race based upon European origins was also problematic since Europeans themselves had mixed with Asians over a very long time period. "Their conception of the 'white' race is based on a mythico-geographical denomination called Europe, which contains a respectable amount of mixture in the blood with peoples from another mythico-geographical area, called Asia." Anesaki balanced his argument by including Japan and also pointed out that historically racial conflict many times ended in "bloody combat" and even extermination as in the case of the Incas or the Huns eliminating their enemies. All in all it was a remarkable statement about race in general and the danger of the immigration tensions besetting the United States and Japan.[14]

The Japanese view was more than a political defense of Japanese immigrants, and even though it was this as well, it accepted immigration restriction, and allowed that the immigrants own particular cultural habits had caused ill-feeling among Americans, whether this was justifiable or not. This was a generous stance overall. Without this wider reading, one might come to the conclusion that the Japanese damaged their case through a bellicose response. Instead, the Japanese staked out a complex position that was not just critical but took responsibility for educating Japanese immigrants to assimilate them to their new status in America.

In 1919–1920, Dr. Harada Tasuku, a University of Hawai'i political science professor, was hired by the Japanese-American Relations Committee of Japan to study the anti-Japanese campaign in the United States. Hawai'i was an incubator of Japanese immigrant identity and the perfect place to draw outside expertise on the Japanese immigrant issue in the Western United States. There race relations while still tense at times did not suffer from an exclusive focus on Japanese immigrants and less open discrimination took place there than in California. Part of the reason for this difference is that in Hawai'i Japanese immigrants did not become landowners but worked the sugar and pineapple plantations and therefore seemed less threatening. Harada asked the kind of questions that Japanese wanted to know the answers to and so his report contained a Japanese perspective. However, Harada was a kind of cultural broker who hobnobbed with the white American elite in Hawai'i and had friends among the powerful in Japan. His survey examined attitudes among white Americans toward Japanese immigrants. The overall response indicated that "the primary prerequisite of the American-Japanese friendship is the absolute restriction of Japanese immigration into the United States." In addition, assimilation of those Japanese already in the United States must be encouraged for white Americans to be satisfied, according to the survey results.[15]

Americans, according to the survey, were split on whether or not Japanese immigrants intended to stay permanently or go back to Japan. Harada's report placed the onus for negative perceptions of Japanese immigrants on those who were short-termers, calling them "parasites" at one point and suggesting that they deserved the discrimination they were getting from Americans.[16]

The intensity of feeling Harada found against Japanese immigrants also existed in the Americanization campaign that reached peak intensity during and immediately after World War I in the United States. Immigrants from eastern and southern Europe came to the United States before World War I in great numbers. Around 40 million immigrants reached American shores between 1880 and 1940. In Chicago by 1900, one-third of the population had been born in a different country. Because these immigrants held values seemingly incompatible with Anglo-Americans, who had represented a majority up to that point in time, an "Americanization" campaign began to assimilate them to dominant Anglo-American culture. Fear and tension generated by World War I ratcheted up the Americanization movement to a fever pitch. German-Americans were openly discriminated against. In Iowa, speaking German in public and over phones lines was made illegal. Henry Ford made his employees take a loyalty oath to the U.S. government. And in the small hamlet of New Ulm, Minnesota, a German-American community, the mayor and town council had their powers revoked and the town was run from the Governor's office for the duration of the war. All of this poisoned the atmosphere for immigrants including Japanese immigrants, and made immigration restriction into a major political movement.[17]

YELLOW PERIL

The root of discrimination was the yellow peril sentiment. It was a strong feeling that Japanese immigrants were incompatible with American life and were poised to dominate white Americans economically and politically. The anti-Japanese movement churned out propaganda against Japanese-Americans and encouraged discrimination against them. There were others however who felt that the outright discrimination in property ownership, schooling, and other areas in the Western states was unfair and needed to be turned around.

Those who cried of a "yellow peril" were led in California by V.S. McClatchy, retired newspaper owner of the *Sacramento Bee* in Sacramento as well as a prominent member of the Japanese Exclusion League of California and one of its main financial supporters. Izumi Hirobe comments that McClatchy and others such as Senator James D. Phelan of California, whose families were both immigrants from Ireland, could have been more sympathetic to these new Japanese immigrants.[18] However, by this time the Irish had fully integrated themselves into American society and had aligned themselves with "white America," in contrast to their arrival in the 1840s and 1850s when they were likened to apes in cartoons and were considered closer to African-Americans than white Americans.[19]

Ironically, the McClatchy newspaper, the *Bee*, claims today to have been at the forefront of human rights in the 1920s, when they outed Sacramento's Ku Klux Klan members by publishing their names in the newspaper in 1922. Regardless, McClatchy and his newspaper were staunchly anti-Japanese and believed immigration exclusion was the only option to stem the tide of yellow sweeping across California. McClatchy wrote a legal brief for the U.S. State Department in 1921 outlining the rationale for excluding future Japanese immigrants. In a demonstration of the paranoia fueling the anti-Japanese movement, McClatchy argued

> the Japanese have determined to colonize favorably sections of the United States, and permanently establish their race in this country; that they openly preach their plans of peaceful penetration, "get more land and beget many children," as the most certain method of accomplishing this purpose; that in so doing they do not contemplate assimilating as American citizens, loyal to the country of their birth or adoption, but plan to serve the ambition of Japan in world subjection as taught in her religion and schools . . .[20]

James Phelan expressed much the same sentiments.[21]

Hiram Johnson, U.S. senator from California became another leader of the anti-Japanese movement. Johnson, an imposing florid-faced former prosecutor who had also served as governor of California, was a progressive

Republican who attacked corporations and political corruption in California. But this record did not stop him from being a nativist and an isolationist. He is perhaps best known for having opposed approval of the Treaty of Versailles as one of the "irreconcilables." He was also the driving force behind the anti-Japanese laws in California when he was governor from 1911 to 1917.

The whirlwind of anti-Japanese activities in California did not mean that other parts of the country were isolated from this issue. A recent study has argued that the concentration of historical analysis on California has meant a neglect of other parts of the West where there were similar movements, propaganda, and campaigns.[22] In addition to the Pacific Northwest and other areas in the West, there were many proponents of immigration exclusion and Americanization in the rest of the country.[23]

The Supreme Court also weighed in on the yellow peril in 1923, confirming as constitutional the California laws denying citizenship to Japanese who were not already citizens and preventing them from owning land or sharecropping. The justices' explanation, not based upon sound law, but apparently upon their gut feelings about the Japanese race, was circular rather than logical. They used the decision to deny citizenship to Japanese immigrants to in turn argue that as these Japanese were not fit for citizenship, they could not own land because they would not work for the best interest of the state. The connecting tissue was that of race and nationalism. Only those of European descent obtained eligibility for citizenship since they were white. And only white Europeans would serve the nation well through their private dealings such as in land ownership.[24]

Calling the decision "common sense" and "incontestable" newspapers throughout the country praised the ruling and expressed admiration for the political abilities of Californians who succeeded in getting constitutional approval for their anti-Japanese agenda. The only hesitance expressed among them was the concern that now Japanese-Americans would begin to migrate out of California and into Eastern states. Western newspapers noted that the last step on the path of limiting Japanese-Americans was to tighten up what they saw as the failed Gentlemen's Agreement by passing an exclusion law through the Congress. And indeed the Supreme Court's decision had given the anti-Japanese movement the momentum they needed to finish the job.[25]

ANTI-EXCLUSION MOVEMENT

A small number of newspapers questioned or rejected the Supreme Court decision. Expressions of concern over further strains in Japanese-American diplomatic ties were scattered among opponents' explanations. One newspaper, the *Brooklyn Eagle*, even condemned the ruling as unfair to Japanese whose children were citizens by birth but the parents of whom could now not become citizens and were excluded from owning land. However, it was increasingly difficult to oppose the rising tide of anti-immigrant sentiment in the United States.[26]

Sidney Gulick, perhaps best known of those who opposed immigration restriction, represented the most open and progressive approach to the issue. Gulick, born into a missionary family, had spent twenty-six years in Japan as a Congregational missionary. He was sympathetic to the plight of the Japanese and understood how the political fallout of the anti-Japanese movement worked back in Japan. He returned to the United States in 1913, just in time to witness a surge in the anti-Japanese campaign, as California's new Alien Land Law had just been passed. Both an activist and an intellectual, Gulick churned out several books in the period of the anti-Japanese movement and also headed up several church-related and other organizations opposing the anti-Japanese movement.

Given his strong background and knowledge of the Japanese, it is a little surprising that Gulick did not mount a stronger defense of Japanese immigrant community. Certainly he worked hard to forward his view. But he did not disagree at all with the view that immigration was a dangerous trend and should be restricted. Gulick in fact argued that the United States should restrict immigration to a quota system but not exclude any groups altogether. Historian Sandra Taylor has portrayed Gulick in a sympathetic manner in her biography of him. She endorsed his work to try to stop the total exclusion of Japanese immigrants. And she critiqued the exclusionists. But one wonders if at a deeper level a critique of Gulick and other anti-exclusionists' stance is not also warranted.[27]

In 1917 Gulick wrote an article in *Asia*, a popular American magazine concerned with politics and current events in Asia. In it, he condemned discrimination but noted that Japanese immigrants had to be willing to be "Americanized." By using the same term Americanization used by those who sought to curb immigration and mold the immigrants, Gulick demonstrated how difficult it was to carve out a position outside of the powerful Americanization movement.[28]

Others involved in mission work came to the same conclusion as Gulick. Arthur Judson Brown, whose *Mastery of the East* (1919) was considered an authoritative account of the rise of the Japanese to world power, was a prominent missionary leader who served as secretary of the Presbyterian Board of Foreign Missions. Brown viewed unrestricted immigration as unacceptable.

Unrestricted immigration of large numbers of peoples of different racial types is clearly objectionable, in every land, whether the immigration be Japanese in America, or Americans in Japan. It is not a question of equality, but of national traditions and economic and social adjustments. Differences in race, language, customs and industrial competition and scale of living are not conducive to sympathetic personal relations anywhere.

Brown saw California Japanese-Americans as low-class and unworthy representatives of their nation. ". . . the majority of the Japanese on the Pacific Coast are of a type which high-class Japanese do not care to have considered as representative of their people." Lower-class immigrants were convenient scapegoats for pro-Japanese Americans and Japanese liberals.[29]

Not all who were pro-Japanese made cultural or racial distinctions the centerpiece of their arguments. Colonel John P. Irish, a retired farmer from the Sacramento area, organized the American Committee of Justice. Irish was motivated to speak out because of his contact with hardworking Japanese farmers he thought were being treated unfairly. He knew of and admired Sidney Gulick's work on behalf of Japanese immigrants.[30] Irish traveled to parts of the West giving speeches denouncing the anti-Japanese movement. Irish's forthright approach probably made him as many enemies as friends but makes for enjoyable reading.

In Idaho in 1921, Irish attacked the anti-Japanese movement with vigor, pointing out that their stated statistics about the menace of Japanese domination in California did not add up. McClatchy of the *Sacramento Bee* had stated that because Japanese birthrates were so high, eventually the Japanese would dominate the population of California. "When has it occurred in the history of the world that 2 percent of a population could outdo 98 percent of it in biological production? You see how absolutely ridiculous it is, absolutely ridiculous!" Irish called him "Malthus McClatchy" and declared that McClatchy used "ouija board mathematics" to show that the Japanese would take over the state.[31]

Irish was outraged that a provision of the 1913 Anti-Alien Land Law allowed Japanese children to be placed in the guardianship of a public administrator. He blamed the laws on "the falsehoods and the appeals and the defamation and the nagging of our venal press and politicians."[32] Then he turned to a defense of Japanese farmers who had according to him taken land that appeared to not be farmable—other Americans had lost their life's savings trying to farm it—and turned it into productive land through grit and genius. He ended with a visceral condemnation of discrimination.[33]

In spite of Irish's strong rhetoric, the Idaho chapter of the American Committee of Justice could muster only a restrictionist declaration. After Irish's speech, a resolution passed unanimously by the 1,200 people attending advising the restriction of further immigration, although it did support giving citizenship to all Japanese already living in the United States if they met the other requirements for citizenship and a plea that Japanese-Americans get fair treatment. In reality, the restrictionist position was the most progressive response available to liberals in this anti-immigrant atmosphere.[34]

Other organizations also fought the anti-Japanese movement. The Northern California Peace Society issued a pamphlet on anti-Japanese legislation in 1915. The organization had very influential patrons including Chancellor David Starr Jordan of Stanford University, President Benjamin Wheeler of the University of California, and several other prominent clergy and educators in the San Francisco area. The pamphlet consisted of press reports on the introduction of a bill in the California assembly to roll back Japanese immigrants' land-leasing rights that had been retained in the first Alien Land Law of 1913. The pamphlet indicated that no newspaper report could be found which had responded positively to the introduction of the bill. Unfortunately, this wishful thinking did not hold and five years later a law was passed in California banning Japanese immigrant leaseholds.[35] As the movement to ban immigration completely gained force other organizations were formed to oppose it: the Pacific American League was founded, a group of professors from Stanford organized against the laws, some powerful corporate executives in San Francisco joined together to denounce the anti-Japanese laws, but all of this was not enough to prevent the strengthening of the anti-Japanese laws in California in 1920 and the eventual passage of the federal Immigration Act that included an Asian exclusion clause in April 1924.

Controversy has surrounded the Immigration Act ever since its inception. Historians are divided about whether the Act itself was the culmination of years of work and represented the will of the American people or was simply an overheated response to the Japanese ambassador's highly charged letter to the American secretary of state Charles Hughes that was leaked to the press. The letter, which was actually solicited by Secretary of State Hughes to try to clarify the Gentlemen's Agreement of 1907 claimed that passage of the Exclusion Act would have "grave consequences," for US-Japanese Relations. Henry Cabot Lodge, influential senior senator from Massachusetts and head of the Senate Foreign Relations Committee, called the tone of the letter a "veiled threat." Lodge, who had in 1919 turned against the Versailles Treaty dooming it in the Senate, used the letter to justify his support of exclusion.

Crediting the role of Washington politics and especially the Hanihara letter, these historians have tended to minimize popular support for exclusion throughout the country. The implication is that save for an unfortunate turn of phrase, immigration exclusion would have never come to the United States, when in reality the trend of Americanization and the anti-Japanese movement was strengthening. The evidence presented above paints a different picture: a powerful anti-Japanese movement with many statewide legal successes in California linked to a strong Americanization movement that supported exclusion and forced even those opposing the anti-Japanese movement to adopt its language and accept at the very least immigration restriction (an immigration restriction law imposing strict quotas had been passed by Congress in 1921). Even before the letter became public, a majority of a joint congressional committee studying immigration issues supported exclusion.[36]

DAMAGE TO U.S.-JAPANESE RELATIONS

In the aftermath of the law's passage, the damage to US-Japanese relations was extensive. Both ambassadors, American and Japanese, resigned in protest. Cyrus Woods, the American ambassador to Japan, called the law an "international disaster of the first magnitude . . ."[37] Newspapers throughout Japan denounced it as well.

The traditional argument is that American newspapers generally condemned the law. However, a closer examination of newspaper opinions points to as many newspapers siding with the law as against the law. One question was whether the United States could unilaterally change its immigration policy toward Japan because the Gentlemen's Agreement had addressed the issue as a treaty between the two nations. How could the U.S. Congress undo the agreements without the approval of the Japanese? On this point many newspapers proclaimed that an act of simple national sovereignty to exclude Japanese immigrants was perfectly legitimate in itself and clearly in the American national interest. Even the *New York Times*, which elsewhere expressed distaste for the law, stated that on technical and legal grounds the Japanese did not have a case. *The Washington Post* went further, stating that

> The United States has acted in obedience to the national will in excluding Japanese immigrants. However unfortunate the method employed, it is an act that can not be undone, and it is a policy that will not be modified, no matter how serious may be the interruption of good relations between the two countries. The continued influx of Japanese into the United States would be intolerable and would lead to grave consequences.[38]

Even Sidney Gulick in his private correspondence with his sons did not think the law was so bad except for the complete exclusion of the Japanese. With the inclusion of a small quota for Japanese picture brides and children of parents already in the United States, Gulick apparently would have fully endorsed the law.[39] Gulick himself seems to have not taken notice of the possibility that immigration restriction and the anti-Japanese movement came from the same root, a fundamental antipathy toward "Orientals" on the part of many Americans. Gulick shared this antipathy toward the nature of Oriental culture and society. His writings on the differences between Oriental and Occidental cultures bear this out. His hope lay in Westernizing Japanese society and politics in Japan and Americanizing those Japanese immigrants already in the United States. Although Gulick's greatest fear was that the exclusion law would cut off Japan's source of westernization, cross-cultural exchange with the West, his responses were timid and politically correct for that time.

The new law, instead of creating a profound movement to change it and attitudes toward the Japanese in the United States, propelled Gulick and others to propose amendments that invariably failed. The law enhanced already prevailing attitudes against the Japanese and did what official diplomats feared it would do: drove another wedge between Japan and the United States.

Gulick used various platforms between 1924 and 1927 to raise consciousness of the situation and convince Americans that a quota system was preferable to outright exclusion. The campaign lacked the vigor from the beginning to properly attack the law. Instead the campaign inadvertently reenergized the anti-Japanese movement in California, so much so that by 1927 Gulick abandoned the open quota campaign in favor of quieter work to simply educate Americans about the Japanese immigrant situation and its impact on U.S.-Japanese relations.[40]

Immigration exclusion and the anti-Japanese movement exposed a frightening mean streak in American society. Colonel John P. Irish understood this best when he said to the crowd in Boise,

> why it gives me the most unpleasant possible feeling. I begin to wonder why Sodom and Gomorrah were destroyed and a place permitted to live and bloom and blossom and its peoples to riot in pleasure when they will eat the bread and sleep on the pillow of a charitable and kind neighbor and then stab the donor in the back . . .[41]

George Swan, a YMCA missionary stationed in Tokyo, claimed that exclusion was a part of the economic control the West exerted over resources of the world. "Those abundant resources of the earth which are now held by western nations to provide the means whereby their own people far into the future can enjoy high standards of living are clearly not to be shared with the races now occupying this part of the world." Swan then did a shocking about-face, endorsing exclusion on a racial basis. "And yet I am in favor of exclusion, for it seems certain that worse evils would befall humanity, as it is now constituted, in the event of promiscuous interracial mingling . . ."[42]

Another missionary V.S. Peeke of the Reformed Church was more broad-minded, but probably far ahead of his time in his thinking. Peeke had been a missionary in Japan for over two decades and had a great deal of wisdom about the state of U.S.-Japanese relations. He wrote a quarterly circular letter that went out to supporters back in the United States. He looked forward to the day when the races of the world would mix together. He also sounded a concerned note about the dangers of the current state of racial antagonism and with some prescience predicted the conflict that later took place.

For myself I prefer a world in which there is more or less interpenetration of races, with the wise and good in league, than a world in which the yellow are by the white to keep apart by themselves and the black by themselves. It looks to me very much as tho [sic] there is bound to be a collision some day if one race seeks to insist on another race's keeping on its own side of the street.[43]

JAPANESE RESPONSE

The Japanese responded very negatively to the law, staging protests in all their major cities. July 1, the day President Calvin Coolidge signed the bill into law became known as National Humiliation Day in Japan and Japanese thereafter mourned the event annually, worshiping at shrines and saying prayers for the protection of Japan from this "insult." The American flag was stolen from the ruins of the American Embassy, destroyed in the recent Kanto earthquake. One man committed hara-kiri or ritual suicide in front of the ruins. A poster read

Japanese must never forget July 1, when America inflicted an intolerable insult on Japan. Always remember the date. Prepare for such steps as are demanded by the honor of the Fatherland when the occasion comes. Every Japanese must remember the following rules: 1-Alter your mode of living so as to impress the date lastingly upon your mind, 2-Hate everything American, but remain kind to American individuals. 3-Deny yourself all luxury. 4-Never forget national honor for private gain. 5-Never enter a church supported or guided by American or United States missionaries.[44]

This strongly nationalist response was common. The right wing came out in force to sponsor protests. The Amur River Society (Kokuryu Kai) a major right-wing organization held forums in Tokyo. At their national convention in June, attended by 30,000 people, rightists declared that the United States could not be forgiven because of the insult to Japanese national honor. Speeches focused on strengthening the East against the West, on uniting Asians and fusing East and West into one world culture. One rightist Shinkichi Uesugi, a professor from Tokyo Imperial University, stated that the situation had gone beyond diplomacy and into the realm of individual heroic action. He referred to the assassinations that took place before and after the Meiji Restoration committed by men of spirit (Shishi). He also claimed that since war with the United States was unavoidable, Japan should act first and lead Asians into war against whites in the West.[45]

The bands of young men that had been active in the nationalist resurgence of the 1890s were becoming active once again. The journal *Kokusai Chishiki* (International Understanding) that was the publication of the LNA of Japan, a liberal internationalist group, changed its English-language Table of Contents to Italian to spite the Americans. The change did not last but it demonstrated the depth of feeling.[46]

Japanese liberal intellectuals, shocked at what they saw as a betrayal of American values, reacted strongly. Nitobe Inazô declared that he would not return to the United States until the exclusion law was lifted. Shibusawa sent a sorrowful cable to the American YMCA. "Senates action regarding Japanese immigration has been painful shock to Japan who had reposed firm trust in senatorial justice and fair-mindedness." Anna Louise Strong, American radical feminist who had close ties in Soviet Russia and later moved to Communist China permanently, did an interview with Shibusawa in which he seemed "broken-hearted" in her words.[47]

Liberals also suffered public condemnations from the political right. Publisher of the *Kokumin Shimbun*, Tokutomi Soho, who was famous for his attacks on Westernization in Japan, claimed that Japanese liberals saw the United States, not Japan as their "spiritual mother country."[48] Liberals themselves recognized that the political situation in Japan shifted once again with the response of exclusion. Tsurumi Yusuke argued in the *Saturday Evening Post*, one of the most popular magazines in the United States, that the issue

> . . . affected the internal conflict of social forces in Japan more than the diplomacy of Japan towards America. It was decidedly a great setback for the forces of democracy and liberalism in Japan. It gave a great plea to conservatives and nationalists in their fight for a stronger government with less individual liberty.
>
> It was a terrific blow to the Japanese who had been patiently and courageously fighting for international amity and cooperation. Basing their theory on peace and not on war, they had fought for the reduction of the navy and the army and the recasting of policy toward China and Korea. In the rising tide of democracy and liberalism, they had been making a steady advance upon the citadels of conservatives who stood for vigorous foreign policies. Then abruptly there came this blow from the hand of their traditional friend, who had opened their country to foreign intercourse, had helped them to go through the dangerous channels of diplomacy in early days and had sent Christian missionaries to teach them the spirit of international brotherhood and peace.[49]

Later Tsurumi claimed that exclusion "naturally tended to turn them [the Japanese] back to Asia."[50]

Newspapers in Japan responded with outrage, the *NichiNichi* and the *Osaka Asahi* both accusing the Americans of crude racism. The editors also worried that it would further damage U.S.-Japanese relations. The *Asahi* went further, pointing out that while in the past Japan owed a debt of gratitude to the United States for help in its modernization, the editors stated that this feeling of gratitude had disappeared completely during the immigration dispute. Then the commentary turned ominous.

> The seed of racial hatred has been sown in the bosom of the Japanese. When the agony of surplus population becomes acute, this seed will begin to germinate which, it is feared, will grow into a fierce anti-American boycott. If this proves to be the case, the anti-Japanese immigration under discussion is solely responsible.[51]

The Tokyo *Asahi* pointed out that the yellow peril in California was unjustified since Japanese population was tiny there compared to the white population, 75,000 to 3,264,000. A more nationalist response was to be expected from the *Kokumin*. Calling the law a "masterpiece of jingoism," the newspaper encouraged public demonstrations to show that Japan would not accept this humiliation without protest. Apparently quite concerned about how the rest of the world and especially the rest of East Asia would respond, the editors imagined the dire consequences if the Japanese people simply accepted the law with head bowed.

> Once Japan is coerced into disgrace, her neighboring peoples will begin to disdain her, she will lose influence in the Far East and her independence will be endangered. Even worse the illustrious achievement of the late Emperor will be utterly swept away from Japan.[52]

Although the rhetoric was overblown, the reality is that some Japanese were persuaded that their nation was imperiled by the law.

The *Kokumin* also expressed concern about the future of relations between the United States and Japan. Perhaps the most telling feature of the *Kokumin* response came in its list of recent grievances with the United States. Starting with the rejection of the racial equality clause at Versailles, the editorial mentioned the lowered ship tonnage ratio at the Washington Conference and the loans Japan was forced to take out from Western banks after the Kanto earthquake to pay for reconstruction. This accumulation of resentment did not bode well for U.S.-Japanese relations.[53]

The Tokyo *Hochi* also invoked the West versus East equation, claiming that English-speaking nations were persecuting Asiatics and that immigration exclusion would help to unite Asians. "In this sense the anti-Japanese measure adopted by the Congress is an epoch-making incident."[54]

An article in the Japanese journal *Kokusai Chishiki* defended Ambassador Hanihara's letter and explained that the American people simply misinterpreted the words "grave consequences." Apparently there was not a totally accurate or true translation of the ambassador's Japanese words, *judainaru kekka*. The author concluded there was no better translation than "grave consequences." He wondered if it would not have been better to leave the words untranslated. Possibly the language differences did produce a problem here. The Japanese could have been translated in a number of ways that might have softened the language a bit: weighty matter or problem, serious effect, serious issue, these all would have been ways to communicate concern without raising alarms as loudly as did the original translation. But as we have already seen, the immigration exclusion issue was about much more than a language misunderstanding.[55]

The magnitude of the immediate Japanese public response to the exclusion law was powerful, and perhaps an overreaction given that the concrete impact of exclusion was small. But this does not negate the enormous impact that exclusion had on U.S.-Japanese relations. What it does imply is that immigration exclusion was a culmination point in the erosion of U.S.-Japanese relations in the interwar period. Elsewhere this was confirmed by press statements afterward and by a speech former ambassador Hanihara made at a farewell party for William Castle, ambassador to Japan, who left this post to become Assistant secretary of state in 1930.

> Naturally the Japanese Government deeply resented this and the resentment is felt now as it was then, nor will it ever die out so long as the wound inflicted remains unhealed. A friendship once marred in this manner can with difficulty resume its wholesome growth unless some effective remedy is administered.

The July 1 commemoration of immigration exclusion as National Humiliation Day continued up to World War II.[56]

K.K. Kawakami wrote extensively about the exclusion act and its impact on U.S.-Japanese relations. At the time of the immigration restriction law, Kawakami was foreign correspondent in the United States for the *Tokyo NichiNichi* and *Osaka Mainichi*.

When Kawakami looked back upon recent relations with the United States his analysis was an index of Japanese frustrations: the dropping of the Anglo-Japanese Treaty with Britain in favor of the Washington Accords, the recurring war talk that had begun earlier, American "imperialism" in China at which point the Japanese "right of existence" could become threatened, and finally the humiliation of the Immigration Act.[57]

Kawakami also pointed the way out. If the Americans would only revise the immigration law to a quota system, this would put it in line with the law's approach to Europe and put Japan on equal footing with Europe. Kawakami also suggested that the United States and Japan work together in China, using the example of building radio stations and transmitting towers in China and Manchuria, where Japan proposed this cooperative venture and the United States had so far rejected the idea.[58]

Kawakami also interviewed the new ambassador to the United States, Matsudaira Tsuneo for *The Outlook* magazine. Descended from a powerful Japanese clan that ruled Japan in the Tokugawa period, Matsudaira, when asked about exclusion, invoked a speech by Shidehara Kijuro, the Japanese foreign minister, in which Shidehara expressed the hope that the American love of justice that ignited independence from the British so long ago would reemerge to correct the injustice of exclusion.[59]

It was in the realm of public opinion and unofficial diplomacy where the repercussions were the strongest and the most damage done. The fundamental respect of the average Japanese for the United States disappeared. The right wing had been strengthened at the expense of liberals in Japan, who were best positioned to work toward improving relations through unofficial diplomacy. The illusions of an American democracy that ensured fair treatment had been shattered and were replaced by suspicion and distrust. And the result for U.S.-Japanese relations was ominous: more tensions, more distrust, and a longer more difficult path to better relations.

A well-known Japanese-Christian Tagawa Daikichiro communicated directly and with an objectivity generally lacking on both sides to Americans in an article in *The Living Age*. Tagawa was a member of the Japanese Diet for many years and also served as president of Meiji Gakuin University. He became an intense critic of the Japanese government and was arrested in 1940. After World War II, he was released from jail and participated in public life by supporting Japanese calls for more freedom of speech under the American occupation.

Tagawa first suggested that the exclusion law had not damaged U.S.-Japanese official relations or economic ties very much. However, he noted a very sharp rise in anti-American feeling in Japan. Although he thought the talk of war between the two countries exaggerated, Tagawa also acknowledged that many Japanese now saw the United States as its greatest threat: "but it is only necessary to say that if Japan were to consider any nation her enemy it would be the United States." The causes of this sentiment were: the Monroe Doctrine, U.S. unwillingness to join the League of Nations, the American attitude toward China, American militarism, the Gentlemen's Agreement, and the naval limitations agreement of the Washington Conference. Tagawa concluded that American Christian ideals though often expressed were in reality not as widespread or well practiced.

The average Japanese might not know exactly what the Monroe Doctrine or League of Nations were, but had a clear sense that they both contributed to "selfish and deceitful" American actions and American hegemony in the world, in Tagawa's analysis. He saw the American refusal to join the League of Nations after their own president had proposed the idea as an unfaithful about-face. In addition, Tagawa claimed that many Japanese saw the Washington Conference as another selfish act on the part of the United States, to strengthen its own navy and simultaneously weaken the Japanese, creating the perception that the "Americans are always trying to injure Japan's interests, and to prevent her from increasing her national power. Such is the prevailing sentiment among the Japanese public."[60]

Tagawa, like other Japanese, prescribed the cure for ill relations. The Immigration Act would have to be revised as well as the U.S. Naturalization Law (this law prevented issei from becoming citizens through naturalization). The goal here was to allow Japanese in America to live productive and happy lives. He thought these two changes would improve U.S.-Japanese diplomatic relations. Tagawa was the first Japanese commentator to bring up the issue of the U.S. exclusion of Chinese laborers in 1882. He condemned it, stating, "the United States is not fair in giving a discriminative treatment to a certain nation or race as such . . ."[61]

In official diplomacy, both sides tried to limit the damage. Shidehara denounced exclusion although his denunciation was clearly for domestic consumption and he also made it clear that it would not affect diplomatic ties with the United States. After both the American and Japanese ambassadors resigned in protest, both sides moved on. The American government treated exclusion as a closed matter.

The Japanese government split their response to immigration exclusion. The official response was muted. But in unofficial organizations and journals such as the *Kokusai Chishiki* (LNA journal) and *Gaiko Jiho* (a semiofficial journal of foreign affairs), the tone was much harsher. According to historian Izumi Hirobe, this split response typified the approach of the Japanese government in interwar diplomacy.[62]

Several months after the immigration law passed, the American Navy planned to do their war games in the Pacific for the first time in many years in spring 1925. To some Japanese, it seemed a provocative act. Once again in the streets of Tokyo and other large cities there were protests. The Japanese public and conservative opinion-makers responded with outcry against the maneuvers and the ensuing controversy added fuel to the fire created by exclusion.

In Tokyo, B.W. Fleisher, editor and publisher of *The Japan Advertiser*, noted the renewed protests in a December 1924 editorial provocatively called "Who Owns the Pacific?"

During the past fortnight virtually every organ [newspaper] of liberal opinion in this country has shown that the present recurrent wave of narrow-visioned nationalism and anti-Americanism has blinded it to a tolerant, unprejudiced and more truly patriotic view of naval and military affairs.

Fleisher, an American citizen, stated that the Japanese protest against the naval maneuvers were "ridiculous" and said of the Hawaiian Islands, "they are American—not Japanese—territory. There is no more reason why the United States should not be fully prepared to defend those islands any more than to defend any other inch of American soil as long as they remain American; and American they will remain." Fleisher criticized Japanese patriotism but then did an about-face, unleashing his own strong patriotic feelings in threatening language.[63]

Fleisher then cited a British MP's statement from the previous year to the effect that Japanese militarists, especially the navy, were using anti-Americanism to wave the flag, fueling patriotism and gaining support for a larger naval budget and building program and keeping the liberals, some of whom occupied cabinet positions, in check.

George Swan, an American YMCA missionary stationed in Kyoto, commented obliquely on Japanese conservatives in the government fomenting hatred for the Americans.

> The leaders are practical enough psychologists to know that the most effective means of creating group solidarity is to have the people feel that they are threatened from the outside. It is very interesting in this connection to note the assiduity of the high government officials in declaring that they are sure America has no bellicose intentions in carrying out the naval maneuvers in the Pacific while on the other hand a large section of the press and a number of organizations are ranting furiously on the subject. These latter are of course under the direct control of the government, and it is very likely that they are being inspired from the top in the line that they are following. This sort of thing has happened in the past. Unfortunately it is an exceedingly dangerous game to play. Violent language on this side of begets the same sort of thing at home, and feelings grow increasingly exacerbated on both sides. International relations become dynamic and a very small affair may take on huge proportions.[64]

Then Swan inadvertently revealed how his own view contributed to the problem.

> And then the mercurial temperament of the Japanese makes such absurd incidents as the one reported in the paper today, in which the son of a priest is supposed to have tried to get at ambassador Bancroft and knife him if the latter did not satisfactorily answer certain questions, very likely. Regarding the temperament of the Japanese, they suffer from such severe repressions psychologically

because of the nature of the family system and the policy of the government that they are peculiarly liable to emotional outbursts.

Theories of Japanese "repressions" and accompanying irrationality attained strong legitimacy among American academics and policy makers by World War II.[65] Another source, a newspaper editorial from the *Japan Advertiser* a business-oriented English-language newspaper published in Tokyo, claimed that the Japanese were "blinded," by anti-Americanism and not able to do "sane reasoning," on the issue of control over the Pacific Ocean. The belief that the Japanese were irrational contributed to increasing suspicions about them in the ratchetting up of tensions.

CONCLUSION

Even though it was easier to point the finger of irrationality at the Japanese, the Americans suffered from this same spell of ill-reason in their treatment of Japanese-Americans and in their discriminatory laws. As the rhetoric of patriotism increased, words and actions became more irrational on both sides. The Japanese held the Immigration Act as a major insult to their national pride. The issue stuck in the hearts and minds of Japanese like nothing else up to that point. Open discrimination against Japanese in the United States linked to the Americanization movement culminated in the internment of Japanese-Americans in 1942. For a problem that had begun on a small scale on the Rio Grande and on the farms of California, the result was a devastating blow to U.S.-Japanese relations and one more seed sown in favor of war.

CHAPTER 6

THE LIBERAL
CHALLENGE:
RESPONSES TO
IMMIGRATION
EXCLUSION

THE IMMIGRATION ACT AFFECTED U.S.-JAPANESE RELATIONS IN SEVERAL AREAS. Anti-Americanism began to mirror already existing anti-Japanese sentiment in the United States. In addition, Japanese conservatives were emboldened by immigration exclusion and other recent events such as the Washington Conference and the Kanto earthquake.

Although Japanese cooperation at the Washington Conference had given American liberals confidence that Japan was continuing down the path of liberal modernity and American cooperation in the aftermath of the Kanto earthquake had suggested that U.S.-Japanese relations were improving, the furor over the immigration law left liberals on both sides with a lump in their throats, a feeling that their cause had been damaged by events beyond their control. Disturbed by both the crudity of the new law and the anti-Japanese campaign in the United States, they argued in writings that Japanese democracy was going through growing pains and needed American support, not hostility. Seeing the Japanese response to immigration exclusion as part of the larger question of Japan's modernity, other American commentators renewed their questions about whether Japan was modern or trapped in its past.

Beset by internal and external challenges liberals sought solace in activity. The creation of the IPR in Hawai'i, the speeches of Tsurumi Yusuke in the United States, and articles by high profile Japan-watchers such as Charles and Mary Beard and William Eliot Griffis indicate that the problems that beset

U.S.-Japanese relations had gotten the attention of high-powered shapers of American public opinion.

JAPAN'S CONSERVATIVE TURN

Immigration exclusion was not the only issue affecting Japan dramatically in this period. The mid and late 1920s marked a period of great uncertainty in Japan. Japanese liberals had been able to gain the passage of a Universal Manhood Suffrage Law in 1924 that seemed to indicate that Japan was becoming more liberal. On the other hand, another law passed at the same time, called the Peace Preservation Law indicated the continuing strength of conservatives in Japan. The law outlawed organizations that called for the abolition of the Imperial Throne or were critical of the emperor. It was clearly aimed at the growing Marxist movement that advocated the abolition of the Japanese throne. Economic prosperity during World War I had turned into economic stagnation in cities and tough times for tenant farmers in the Japanese countryside. The rise of ideologies on both the right and the left provided new channels for the rising discontent and added to the chaos of the situation. On the left, the Communist Party became very active in Japan in the mid 1920s, as well as a variety of Japanese socialist organizations.

Japanese conservatives became more active in the aftermath of immigration exclusion. Right-wing ideologist Kita Ikki characterized the situation in Japan as a crisis and called for the mobilization of a union of "national opinion" emphasizing loyalty to the emperor that would tolerate no dissent. Baron Goto Shimpei began a lecture campaign to restore traditional morality in Japan in 1926. Concerned over the rising acceptance of Western values such as individualism and the radical ideas of Marxists, Goto preached patriotism, loyalty to the emperor, and duty. He recruited one million Japanese youths to his "Moralization Campaign." In the countryside, others started a "Save the Village!" Campaign. Focusing on agrarianism, Shintoism, and loyalty to the emperor, they were able to recruit 300,000 Japanese youths to go to Manchuria and Mongolia to become farmers. They were opposed by left-wing farmers' organizations such as the Farmers Union.[1]

Liberals were negatively impacted by the more repressive policies put in place after passage of the Peace Preservation Law. Intellectuals, educators, laborers, and artists all had their rights of assembly and speech infringed upon in the late 1920s. One official pronouncement from the Ministry of Education read, "Any society or association in which dangerous thoughts are either to be read or studied is absolutely prohibited irrespective of whatever form or name taken." Even if not enforced completely, this broad decree probably had a dampening effect on liberal organizations. The Education Ministry had compiled a blacklist of 1,500 students suspected of left-wing tendencies in 1925. One right-wing newspaper the *Chugai Shogyo* urged the Ministry of Education to investigate university professors. "We think students are involuntarily captivated by radicalism because of the influence of their lecturers. Not a few professors advocate radical principles. Let the fountain-head be purified and the stream will become pure."[2]

In addition to the growth of rightist movements in Japan, the suppression of leftists, and rising anti-Americanism, the foreign policy of the Japanese government began almost imperceptibly to turn away from reliance solely on Western alliances and pursued closer relations with several Asian countries. After losing the Anglo-Japanese Alliance at the Washington Conference, Japan looked for partners closer to home. In fairly innocuous moves, Japan concluded treaties of trade with Persia (Iran) and Turkey and then in a more dramatic move, officially recognized the Bolshevik government of the Soviet Union in 1925. Diplomats on the American side took little note in the aftermath of Japan's concessions at the Washington Conference. Although this did not yet mean that Japan was abandoning its Western allies, some Japanese saw this as a step turning away from the West and strengthening ties in the East.[3]

K.K. Kawakami reported in *Current History*,

> Forsaken by her Western friends, as Japan saw at the Washington Conference, she made up her mind then and there to alter her diplomatic orientation with a view to seeking new friends among her immediate neighbors, that is, those on the Asian continent.

Kawakami's report included a glowing account of Japan's kindliness toward China. Tsurumi said much the same in his American lectures. In truth, Japan was creating the means for its own future prosperity through the exploitation of North China and Manchuria. Kawakami's article can also be seen as persuasion directed at Americans to induce their diplomats to save the U.S.-Japanese relationship.[4]

The magnitude of the change should not be overstated. At this time the Foreign Ministry under the leadership of Shidehara Kijuro, wanted to continue cooperative relations with the Western powers to insure Japanese trade with the West. However, Japan did begin to turn its gaze from the West to the Asian continent closer to home. Tsurumi Yusuke noted that the popularity of translations of Western texts had declined in the 1920s. Japan wanted to read its own thinkers, demonstrate its patriotism and loyalty and make its own way in foreign policy. By the late 1930s, the ideas of Pan-Asianism and the

Japanese announcement of a Greater East Asia Co-Prosperity Sphere made this turn more concrete and one of the causes of the Pacific War in 1941.[5] In 1925 Inoue Junnosuke was at the height of his career. Inoue, who was a major politician and financier in Japan, had just finished two years as the finance minister of Japan after having served in the private sector as president of Yokohama Specie Bank and governor of the Bank of Japan. He was considered somewhat liberal and Westernizing in his political inclinations. He accurately expressed the situation and temperament of Japan.

Japan today floats on a sea of doubt in all directions and does not know what to do. The conditions obtaining in Japan at this hour are not those that prevailed half a century ago when our predecessors could without restraint import and imitate in a body the civilization and institutions of the advanced nations of the world. Times have changed. Europe and America have nothing more to offer Japan. The multitude of problems which are left to us to solve admit of no assistance from outside nations in the way of their successful solution, as they should be attacked only from the angle represented by the Japanese standpoint.[6]

INSTITUTE OF PACIFIC RELATIONS

While many Japanese looked to the nation for solution, other Japanese and Americans sought solutions in the new internationalist atmosphere of the 1920s. Organizations such as the YMCA and others were galvanized into action. Japanese and Americans committed to improving U.S.-Japanese relations founded a new organization called the IPR in 1925. While the IPR arose as a result of the immigration problem, the vision of its founders was to build cooperation among Pacific Rim countries to encourage peace in the region. The Pacific would be a harmonious contrast to the Atlantic region that was dominated by aggression. The IPR came to be the foremost organization for unofficial diplomacy in the U.S.-Japan relationship and its rise and fall marks the limits and failings of unofficial diplomacy in the U.S.-Japanese relationship.

The founders of the IPR met in Honolulu, Hawai'i in 1925 for their first conference. They look like a Who's Who of missionaries. J. Merle Davis, the first secretary general of the IPR, Galen M. Fisher, one of the founders of the IPR, and George Sidney Phelps, who attended the first meeting, all had worked for the YMCA in Japan as missionaries. John Mott, the head of the YMCA, was also involved in the founding.

The Japanese founders of the IPR, Christians Nitobe Inazô, Yoshino Sakuzo, Ibuka Kajinosuke, Niwa Seijiro, were even more influential than their Americans counterparts. Zumoto Motosada, who was presently editor of the *Herald of Asia* and had spent time in Korea as a journalist, attended the conference. Several Japanese scholars from Tokyo Imperial University participated in the conference or expressed their support for the enterprise: Professor Yanaihara Tadao, a student of Nitobe and a pacifist Christian who studied colonial policy and was harassed by the government during World War II for his pacifist stance, Professor Anesaki Masaharu, who studied religion, Professor Takagi Yasaka another student of Nitobe who studied American history and politics, and Professor Abe Isoo from Waseda University, a legendary Christian Socialist and political leader, also attended. Sawayanagi Masataro, a leader in the educational establishment and a member of the House of Peers, led the delegation to Honolulu. Tsurumi Yusuke attended from the United States where he was on a lecture tour. In addition, Shibusawa Eiichi, Baron Goto Shimpei, and Matsuoka Yosuke, a young ambitious politician and diplomat, supported the founding of the IPR.

The list of leaders indicates a couple of trends. First, it confirms religious groups such as the YMCA were at the forefront of unofficial diplomacy in the interwar period. Second, not all of the Japanese involved were liberals. Goto Shimpei and Zumoto Motosada were more moderate in their political leanings. Goto and others were interested in the nationalist potential of the IPR in Japan as a tool to aid formal diplomacy and to project Japan's presence onto an international stage. The distance between moderate and liberal in Japan was small. They found the common ground of emperor and empire to work together.

The founding meeting in Honolulu was successful. The discussions were wide-ranging and focused on the major problems of the Pacific including the immigration issue. The meeting had plenary and smaller roundtable sessions and was a model of unofficial diplomacy, engaging person-to-person dialogues and exploring solutions that official diplomats could not consider.

However, underneath the success of the meeting there lay some problems. First, the IPR was organized upon a national model. Each nation of the Pacific that joined the IPR organized its own member unit. This fact tended to emphasize national power and interests. Increasingly national interests came to dominate the IPR proceedings and proved a major source of tension, especially in the 1930s as U.S.-Japanese relations declined.

Second, while the IPR sought to cut through the irrationality of politics by sponsoring research in the Pacific that would answer controversial questions with rational science instead of politics, politics reared its ugly head within the research initiative. The research questions were devised by each national group and the questions formulated aggravated the rivalries that beset U.S.-Japanese relations.

For instance, the Japanese council molded their questions not only to meet their own national interests but also to discredit the United States. The Japanese Council suggested a study of American foreign policy in Latin

America in places like Nicaragua and Mexico, where the United States had recently sent troops to protect its interests. Without missing a beat they also suggested that a study of "the American Monroe doctrine in relation to the Pacific area" would be appropriate. The questions caused J. Merle Davis, the American secretary general of the IPR, considerable consternation.[7]

A careful study of the American Monroe Doctrine in the Pacific would have shown American influence in the Pacific to be what it really was, not a moral-minded impartial attempt at arbitration and fairness through the Open Door but an ever creeping growth of power in the Pacific achieved through moral suasion, diplomatic gambits, and brute military force, as in the case of the Philippines. It would have looked like the same kind of control the United States exercised in Latin America and the Japanese were developing in Manchuria.

The influence of the United States in Latin America was often cited by the Japanese as justification of their involvement in Manchuria. When Americans expressed outrage at Japanese ambitions, the Japanese often suggested to them that just as the United States had its sphere of unfettered sway in Latin America, Japan should be allowed to have its own Monroe Doctrine in northeast Asia.

Far from objectivity, the IPR research proposals are remarkable for their almost mischievous attempts to bring to light issues which would make the Americans uncomfortable. Of course none of these proposals were implemented. But finger-pointing contributed nothing to a calmer atmosphere in the Pacific.[8]

Finally, the links between the Japanese government and the Japanese Council of the IPR (JCIPR) were very close. So close in fact as to raise the question of how "unofficial" the JCIPR really was in its status. The Japanese government through the Foreign Ministry decided that the founding of the IPR offered an opportunity to improve U.S.-Japanese relations without the strictures of official government policy. As a consequence, the Foreign Ministry put up 12,000 yen or one-third of the total cost of the delegates' expenses for the founding conference in 1925.[9] The Foreign Ministry continued to fund JCIPR activities and kept close ties with it, eventually encouraging the consolidation of the JCIPR with the Japan International Association (JIA) which was a semiofficial arm of the Foreign Ministry in 1935.

TSURUMI YUSUKE, CHARLES BEARD, AND AMERICAN LIBERALS

In the wake of the immigration fiasco, Tsurumi Yusuke, an important prewar liberal who was involved the JCIPR, sought to restore U.S.-Japanese relations by traveling to the United States at his own initiative to give a series of lectures across the United States. While speaking at over thirty universities and 100 clubs, Tsurumi spent fourteen months in the United States between 1924 and 1925. His task was to convince the American public that the Japanese were still friends of the United States. He emphasized the great influence the United States had exerted over Japan in its formative years in the Meiji period (1868–1912).

Tsurumi had made the acquaintance of Charles and Mary Beard, well-known historians, when the Beards and their children traveled to Japan in 1922–1923 at the request of Baron Goto Shimpei, then mayor of Tokyo, to consult on city planning issues. Tsurumi who married Goto's daughter met the Beards through Goto. The Beards gave speeches and were feted as famous people. They met officials and intellectuals and made several friends including Tsurumi. Deeply impacted by his trip to Japan, Charles Beard stated that he "became a changed person. I have never been the same again." Commenting frequently on American foreign policy and U.S.-Japanese relations in his speeches and bestselling books, Beard, like John Dewey, used his trip to the Far East to influence American public opinion. He communicated his conviction the United States had pushed Japan too far at the Washington Conference and while the concessions gave the United States an advantage, it fueled a rivalry that could end in war.[10]

When Tsurumi came to the United States one of his first stops was New York City. Beard supported Tsurumi's trip and organized lectures for Tsurumi at Columbia University and Dartmouth College. Tsurumi also lectured at Brown and Yale. He later gave Tsurumi a ringing endorsement in Tsurumi's publicity materials.

Letters from Charles Beard to Tsurumi document a close friendship. Beard invited Tsurumi to come and stay at the Beard farm in New Haven, Connecticut while he was in New York. In the letters Beard referred to Tsurumi as Jeff and himself as Mutt, after the famous comic strip of the time, Mutt and Jeff. Beard (Mutt) offered to come and get Tsurumi (Jeff) at Penn Station if Tsurumi did not know the way. The friendship illustrates the strength of informal connections between Americans and Japanese in this time period.[11]

However, as tensions between the United States and Japan increased, and especially after the Manchurian Incident in 1931, the friendship faded. In the last letter that he wrote to Tsurumi in November 1933, Beard called the decline of U.S.-Japanese relations a great tragedy for the world and the death of Nitobe Inazô a great tragedy for U.S.-Japanese relations. Beard put the blame for the decline of relations on tensions over the immigration debacle, and he claimed that the IPR would cease to be effective because it had abandoned person-to-person diplomacy for a research orientation. The letters ceased after this point and we can assume the relationship did as well.

Tsurumi sought to illustrate the plight of liberals in Japan in his speeches, describing their uphill battle against conservatives to bring democratization to Japan and explaining how the Immigration Act had hurt their cause. He pointed out that liberals in Japan in the late nineteenth century worked under a serious handicap: the Western imperialist threat. Liberals had to contend with the irony that Western actions in East Asia had turned Japanese against liberals and Westernizers.

> So from the very beginning the potential Russells, Gladstones and Morleys of Japan, have had to work under the thundering guns of the Western powers blowing their way to new territories, new empires of trade, new spheres of influence. It is not surprising that they made little headway.[12]

Thus, Japan built its military and its empire rather than an internationalist and democratic political system, according to Tsurumi. In wars with China and later Russia, Japan won great victories, expanded its empire abroad, and strengthened conservative militaristic forces at home. Ironically Tsurumi gave credit for these interventions to an obscure American, General LeGendre, who had fought in the Civil War and later traveled to Japan as a diplomat. LeGendre told Count Soyeshima, Japan's foreign minister in the 1870s, that Japan had to act aggressively to protect its flank in Korea and China. Tsurumi claimed that LeGendre was very influential and that even Saigo Takamori, the great Satsuma general of the Meiji Restoration, sent an advisor to be briefed by Soyeshima on LeGendre's advice. Tsurumi's account suggests that this is where Saigo got his idea for an invasion of Korea. While this is an interesting account, Japan had a long history of picking on Korea. Most historians credit soldier and statesman Yamagata Aritomo, not LeGendre or even Count Soyeshima for the Japan's continental security policy after the Meiji Restoration. Tsurumi played to his American audience in handing the credit to an American for Japanese foreign policy. It also allowed him to lay part of the blame for Japan's militarism on the United States.

American influence continued with the visit to Japan in 1878 of Ulysses S. Grant, civil war hero and recently retired U.S. president. Grant apparently told the Japanese to avoid war with Korea for the moment and concentrate on internal development in the early 1870s. Japanese historians normally credit Okubo Toshimichi with this insight. Grant also was asked by the Japanese government to mediate a dispute with China over control of the Ryukyuu Islands (Okinawa) and ruled in favor of the Japanese.

Tsurumi also discussed American influence on Mori Arinori's Meiji educational policy and on post–World War I internationalist ideas. He argued that American president Woodrow Wilson's internationalism inspired liberals in Japan. Tsurumi's narrative was a history of American influence; Americans had nothing to fear in a nation they had influenced profoundly. However, the United States would lose the power to sway Japan if the Immigration Act was not repealed. In 1924–1925, as Tsurumi gave these speeches, he saw liberalism threatened in Japan but also perceived it as a major force for positive change.[13]

It is difficult to tell what impact Tsurumi's speeches had on his American audience. His speeches reached a fairly large audience. His tour garnered some newspaper coverage although certainly not daily headlines. Tsurumi's speeches were later put together along with some articles he wrote for the *Saturday Evening Post* and published as a book in English by *The Japan Times*, an English-language newspaper located in Japan. Probably, Tsurumi's impact was greatest on liberals such as Charles Beard and others who were alarmed by the turn U.S.-Japanese relations had taken.

In 1925, the popular liberal magazine *The Nation* devoted an issue to Japan, presumably because of the furor surrounding the immigration law. The editors stated bluntly:

> We are not interested in pretty stories of cherry blossoms and lovely Buddhist temples, but we should like to help make Americans aware of the essential humanness of Japan—as of all the other picturesque far-away nations—a nation of people very much like ourselves, with militarists and imperialists in positions of power and a liberal movement struggling for expression, with labor and capital in bitter conflict—as in Pittsburgh and Glasgow and St. Etienne and the Ruhr. We should like to help the American people to understand the subtle propaganda which is poisoning their minds and building up here a conviction of inevitable hostility.[14]

The editorial acknowledged that the negative perceptions of both sides about the other created a situation in the United States where policies were being created out of suspicion and distrust and which unnecessarily risked war through misunderstanding. "If, instead of drifting along in such fatal policies, we shape our minds for the preservation of an historic friendship, we may remake the future of the Pacific."[15]

Other articles in the issue included a piece about the rise of the Japanese labor movement, a diplomacy article about the United States, Japan, and Russia by Louis Fischer who would later become famous for his biography of Gandhi, and another by Miriam Beard—daughter of historians Charles and Mary Beard—called "Our War Advertising Campaign." Miriam Beard asserted that the "yellow press" of *Hearst* newspapers in recent months deliberately stirred anti-Japanese propaganda for war with Japan. Why? To support the U.S. Navy Department's arguments for an expanded navy, according to Beard. "The main hope for peace is not in human decency but in the terrific power of the latest fighting machine" in the words of one of the Hearst newspaper's bylines. Others included the claim by Naval Rear Admiral Fiske that Japan was aiming to take over the Philippines and yet another charged that Japan had elevated its battleship guns to gain greater range in the coming war with the United States. War talk, in fashion since 1919, continued strongly through this period and proved useful on both sides to those committed to militarization.[16]

Beard also pointed out that dangerous misperceptions had been created in American popular culture about the Japanese. A recent movie called "Shadows of the West" portrayed Orientals as abductors of white girls and American Legion boys as their rescuers. Two new novels in the mid 1920s, *Kimono* and *Broken Butterflies* depicted Japanese males as villains and Japanese women as sensuous and immoral. Beard noted that Harry Franck in his travelogue about Japan and Formosa (Taiwan) noted that Tokyo had an inordinate number of underground tunnels that seemed to suggest sinister plans. Beard later wrote a book on Japan.[17]

Charles Beard also wrote an article for *The Nation* on the Japan situation. Beard believed China loomed large as a problem for U.S.-Japanese relations.[18] In another article concerning Japan and China, Charles and Mary Beard criticized other American liberals as too softhearted on China and not hard enough on American policies in Latin America, ". . . if any American is bent on freeing the downtrodden from the yoke of power, he can more easily begin in Haiti . . ."[19]

INTERPRETING JAPAN: MODERNIZATION
OR INESCAPABLE PAST

In the mid-1920s developments within Japan held more hopeful signs of expanding democratization, but these American hopes were mixed with questions about the basic nature of Japan's modernity.

The American perceptual window on Japan was framed by Japan's rapid modernization and the constant puzzle of the existence of traditional culture within Japan's modern society. Journalist Margaret Deforest Hicks saw Japan at a turning point, forced to choose between the old political conservatism and the new mass political participation allowed by the universal male suffrage law, which she viewed as the most dramatic political innovation in Japan since the beginning of the Meiji period, comparable in her mind to the Magna Carta of England. Although this comparison overstated the importance of the suffrage law, Hicks' analysis in the popular magazine *American Century* once again shows us how Americans thought about Japan. Japan was at the edge of Western democracy and the rough and tumble political world that came with it and Hicks openly wondered if Japan could hack it.

She noted that along with universal male suffrage came the Peace and Preservation Law and a crackdown on Marxists and other radicals which threatened to extinguish Japan's newly developing political consciousness.[20]

The editors of *The Japan Advertiser*, an American-owned English-language newspaper in Tokyo agreed that the suffrage law in Japan represented a major achievement and preached patience, comparing the development of the Japanese democracy to the development of Japanese baseball.

> When an American baseball team visits Japan nowadays it finds that the game is well understood and as well played here as on its home fields. Ten years ago the case was different. The Japanese played poorly; they disappointed themselves and their supporters; and there were critics who said they would never make good players, they lacked team spirit, the game was not suited to Orientals, etc, etc.

In other words Japan simply needed time to make progress in democracy.[21]

At about the same time, several other articles appeared in a related vein chronicling Japan's rapid Americanization. They told of how the Japanese were developing a taste for Western items such as cars, clothing and even Western food. There was ample evidence that Japan was becoming just like us. American films became very popular, the Western sports of baseball, tennis, and golf were taken up. Young women wore Western dresses instead of kimonos and donned American bathing suits at the beach. Many young people learned English, and they loved American jazz.[22] The *Literary Digest* pointed out that the Japanese were very enamored of many foreign songs including the American favorite, "My Blue Heaven."[23] *Collier's*, a popular American magazine, commented on Americanization in Japan with the title "The White Peril," a play on the words "yellow peril."[24]

Another commentator told a story of how a young Japanese flapper girl quarreled with her foreign lover and ended up shooting him. She dressed in a provocative short skirt and went about Tokyo with this foreign man. Every part of the story indicated how Americanized this young Japanese woman had become. She even used an American revolver to shoot her lover. However, the Japanese press used the incident as an opportunity to rail against the corruption of Japan's youth by Western habits and ideas.[25]

Not everyone agreed that Japan was becoming Americanized. In 1930, a travel group consisting of Samuel McClune Lindsay, a sociologist at Columbia University, Ellery Sedgewick, editor at the *Atlantic Monthly*, Sarah M. Lockwood, a New York City decorator, photographer, and author, and several others spent time in Japan as a part of a world tour. They all wrote articles on their views of Japan. Lockwood saw the modern and ancient side by side, most strikingly in the contrast of cities where modern railroad

Pullman cars whisked passengers along and the Japanese countryside where farmers clad in blue cotton work pants drove buffalo through drenched rice fields using wooden plows.

> Japan seems to wear her modern progress like an outer garment, much as her men wear Western dress and for the same reason—convenience in business . . . One feels that she is much more comfortable in her old kimono and that she gets into it every chance she gets. It is Japan in her native dress that one dearly loves and she is not difficult to meet in her old clothes if she knows that she is appreciated and admired in them.[26]

Other articles appeared with similar themes but less positive views than Lockwood. Titles like, "What is Wrong with Japan?" or "Japan Returns to Feudalism" appeared in *The Living Age* and *The Nation* in 1926. Statements such as "The shackles of tradition are extraordinarily strong and universal" and "The most striking feature of this Orientalism is a lingering acceptance of the dictates of authority" indicated the Japanese simply had not overcome the "habit of subservience" that had been cultivated for centuries. One article suggested that the resentment against Americans was not in fact connected to immigration, but a holdover from the days of foreigner exclusion in the Tokugawa period. The American public was being exposed to the argument that Japan had not escaped its past.[27]

The notion that Japan was a great political and military power was also challenged. In an article in *Current History*, Roderick Matheson, editor of *The Japan Times*, wrote that this myth was the greatest of all.

Matheson identified several issues at the core of Japanese culture which contributed to inefficiency. His subheadings reveal these: "A People Without Initiative"—the Japanese could not take the initiative because they had no original thoughts; "Overmanned Services"—because they had no original thoughts and were so group oriented, the people of Japan had to create so many rules to live by that their bureaucracy was overmanned and inefficient; "Literate But Unthinking"—Matheson stated that over 99 percent of the Japanese population were literate but were not allowed to think for themselves because the government so tightly controlled information.[28]

Because the Japanese in reality were quite inefficient, according to Matheson, the assumption that Japan was one of the great powers was a myth as well as "a hollow bubble, blown almost to the bursting point." Japan did not deserve the label because her army and navy were not as powerful as befitted a great power. (Never mind that the American Army in this time period was the smallest of all the so-called great powers, much smaller than Japan's.) Matheson concluded that in a potential war with a Western nation, the Japanese, because of their lack of originality and inability to think for themselves would fight textbook style and would lose because the commander of a Western nation's military, original thinker that he was, would innovate and crush the Japanese.[29]

These perceptions of Japan in their appalling ethnocentrism had an impact on military views of Japan. The Japanese military was not taken seriously. An American military manual described Japanese pilots as myopic suffering from inner ear weakness and therefore unable to fly airplanes effectively at night. The Japanese infantry could not run because of the imbalance the wearing of the *geta* had created in their gait by dividing their big and middle toes. These crass and silly assumptions seem unbelievable but historian John Dower demonstrates that military advisors took them seriously. At the beginning of the Pacific War, this lack of respect gave the Japanese a huge edge they exploited very well with a rapid and efficient invasion of Southeast Asia.[30]

In a view that confirmed Matheson's assumptions, a Western military analyst assessed the Japanese army's abilities during the Sino-Japanese War in 1937.

> Assuming that American, British, French and German armies are equivalent to mature 25-year-old men, China's army at its present stage of training and equipment is equivalent to a 10 year old boy, while Japan's army, which is supposedly equivalent to a 21-year-old young man, has proved itself only equal to a 14-year-old boy.

This article published in *The New York Times* added that this assessment was considered by foreign military experts to be accurate. Regardless of how "old" the Japanese army really was, it is clear that at least some Westerners believed that East Asians existed in a childlike state that prevented them from being considered grown rational adults.[31]

The editors of *Current History* recognized that Matheson's argument might provoke controversy so they allowed a Japanese national to provide a rejoinder. K.K. Kawakami wrote the response. Rejecting the argument that others had to model themselves on the United States, Kawakami criticized Matheson's view that the Japanese were inefficient. "Japan is efficient in her own way, not in the American way. It is wrong to argue that, because we do not do things in the same way as the Americans do, we are inefficient." Kawakami also used examples of political corruption in Chicago and the bootleg liquor traffic that flooded into the United States in the aftermath of the passage of prohibition to point out inefficiencies in the United States.[32]

William Elliot Griffis responded to this Orientalist writing on Japan with his own modernizing argument in 1928. Griffis had traveled to Japan shortly after the end of the Japanese Meiji Restoration and took a job teaching at

Tokyo Imperial University, eventually writing *The Mikado*. He returned to Japan for a visit in 1927 and summarized his views. It was straightforward story of the success of Japan's modernization along Western lines, a classic tale of the West as the wellspring of Japan's progress. Griffis understood that some Americans rejected this account of Japan and he sought to address them directly.

> Let me say respectfully to those writers on Japan who insist that this Oriental nation has but a thin veneer of Western civilization, and that "beneath the surface" the Asiatic attitude of culture and temperament will be found unchanged by contact with the West, that in my profoundest belief, they are mistaken.[33]

It was not that Griffis believed that these writers had misinterpreted the nature of Oriental culture. Griffis simply believed that Japan had torn itself away from the "Orient," while other commentators believed that Japan was still fundamentally Oriental in nature. Griffis claimed to have seen with his own eyes the death of Oriental feudalism in a ceremony held in Fukui in Echizen prefecture in 1871. As Griffis looked on, the Samurai gave up their oaths to their daimyo and swords in a dramatic and solemn ritual. Writing of the changes that he had seen in Japan since 1870, Griffis sought to balance his argument, "Our own distant ancestors passed through similar stages of progress. I do not mean to say that Occidental persons or things borrowed from the West have exclusively made the 'beautiful New Japan.'" But he believed that the West had largely shaped Japan's modern destiny. In advanced age, Griffis died shortly after he wrote these articles.[34]

V.S. Peeke, a veteran Reformed Church missionary in Japan who had met with Griffis on his 1927 trip agreed with many of Griffis's views. Peeke was very skeptical of the Orientalist views many of his fellow Americans held about Japan. In a letter back to supporters in the United States, Peeke told a story of traveling on a river to Minobe. The boat which took him there was equipped with an airplane engine and prop at the stern and Peeke thought this very ingenious and up-to-date. He commented sarcastically,

> Here back in the heart of the mountains of Japan, were two such boats [airboats] making two fifteen mile journeys, up and down the river each day, and all on a commercial basis. It made me rub my eyes. Whatever the Japanese may be,—deceitful, cunning, blood-thirsty, war-like, and all the rest,—they certainly are not back numbers.[35]

CONCLUSION

The aftermath of immigration exclusion marked a new atmosphere in U.S.-Japanese relations. Liberals concerned about the relationship on the both sides of the Pacific understood that immigration exclusion had changed the relationship irrevocably. They worked to overcome the skepticism and distrust that now pervaded the relationship. But they were hampered by widespread misperceptions, superpatriotic language, and the relative success of more conservative forces in the battle to shape public opinion on both sides of the Pacific. Notwithstanding attempts to argue otherwise, more often now Americans saw Japan as deeply traditional nation with a veneer of modernity. The accession of a new emperor in 1928 added weight to this view. It was an opportunity to highlight that most ancient and mysterious of Japanese institutions, the Japanese imperial house.

CHAPTER 7

NEW EMPEROR, NEW TENSIONS IN MANCHURIA

THE LATE 1920S BROUGHT INTERESTING AND DISTURBING CHANGES TO THE landscape of U.S.-Japanese relations. The accession of Hirohito in 1928 shined a spotlight on the Japanese monarchy and the myths surrounding it, bringing once again to the fore the question of whether Japan was a modern nation. Japan's expanding influence in Manchuria also attracted attention, though unwanted, to its empire.

American observers were fascinated with the pageantry and ritual of the accession of Emperor Hirohito in 1928. As outsiders who did not have a monarchy, Americans were interested in the enthronement ceremonies and the emperor himself. By this time the rituals involved in enthronement were minutely prescribed.[1]

A procession from Tokyo to Kyoto started the spectacle. Then the emperor took possession of the imperial regalia: a sword, a jewel, and a mirror. Later, there was an even more elaborate ritual performed in the dead of night to confirm the emperor's divinity. On the grounds of the Kyoto Imperial Palace a series of wooden huts were specially constructed for the ceremony. The ceremony that transformed Hirohito from human to deity enacted his ritual descent from heaven. The ritual involved the emperor laying in the fetal position wrapped in a quilt supposedly performing his figurative marriage with Amaterasu. While most rituals were open to the public, this private ceremony had a very small elite audience including the major political leaders of Japan. The press encouraged the public to suspend rational judgment about this ritual.[2]

Hugh Byas reported Hirohito's accession in the pages of the *New York Times*. A Scotsman, Byas spent thirty-six years covering events in Japan for

The New York Times and *The Times* of London. His reports had as much credibility as any news emanating from Japan in the interwar period. Byas, himself a subject of the British Crown, became the foremost interpreter of Hirohito's accession to the American public. He emphasized the ancientness of the throne and the exotic rituals involved in the accession ceremonies. "His Majesty's worship before the Sun Goddess's sanctuary was an awe-inspiring rite that carried the imagination back to a world in which human institutions were young and primitive." He reported every detail of the ceremonies at the Kyoto Palace. For the first time in the history of Japanese enthronements, press reporters were allowed to witness the ceremonies, although they were required to remain outside the south gate of the palace for the Kyoto ritual, where they could see it from a distance without disturbing it. Focusing on the exotic aspects of the celebrations, Byas's reports fed the Orientalism of his American audience.[3]

If one reads between the lines of Byas's coverage, however, one can see the power and modernity of the Japanese throne. Byas reported that the ceremonies cost 12 million dollars, more than had ever been spent on an enthronement anywhere in the world. Byas noted in other reports that Hirohito displayed openness to commoners in Japan that would have provoked a scandal in an earlier time.[4] The young emperor rode through Tokyo in an open carriage and shook the hand of a plain commoner, a golf course manager. In addition, the Showa Emperor traveled to Europe in 1921 and met with other monarchs. This was tacit admission that the Japanese throne was equal to other thrones. These facts were a subtle but significant sign of Japan's modern monarchy.[5]

Elsie Weil, the editor of the magazine *Asia*, also analyzed the ancient/modern structure of the Japanese monarchy.[6] Weil had heard that many Japanese worshipped the emperor as a god and mentioned the well-known example of General Nogi, a war hero, and his wife, who committed seppuku together in front of a portrait of the Meiji Emperor at the time of his death. Then Weil traced the evolution of the emperor from hidden deity to a more modern monarch accessible to the public, meeting foreign dignitaries, and traveling abroad. Meiji was the first emperor to appear in public. His meeting with General U.S. Grant in 1879 caused a stir for this was the first time the emperor had met another head of state as an equal. Meiji even shook hands with Grant and took advice from him.[7]

The emperor worship of previous times had evolved with the emperorship.

To the new Emperor, who is twenty-five years old, the Japanese turn with an adoration and hope approaching the feeling they had for his imperial grandfather [Meiji] during the last years of his reign, but perhaps with not quite the same attitude of blind worship; for since the Meiji era, two generations of Japanese have been educated abroad and have seen other countries and other customs.

She asked her friends in Japan whether they believed in the Sun Goddess story. They responded that they treated it as myth, not as historical fact. While the enthronement ceremonies appear to have been designed to bolster the divine image of the Japanese Emperor among his subjects, there were many Japanese who, though they went along with the ceremonies and cooperated with enthronement, did not see the emperor as a deity.[8]

The average Japanese person still believed in another imperial artifact, the unbroken imperial line, according to Weil. This story was taught in public schools in Japan, but we do not know if many Japanese actually believed it as historical fact. The veracity of it is questionable since at one point in Japan's history there were two claimants to the throne, one from the north and one from the south. Wars were fought over which emperor was legitimate and the northern Imperial House won.

Americans with a special interest in Japan such as missionary Georgene Esther Brown were also captivated by the spectacle of the Imperial Throne. Brown worked for the Unitarian Universalist Women's National Missionary Association at an orphanage/school called Blackmer Home in Tokyo.[9]

Georgene took a night class focusing on the Imperial House. Coming into the course Georgene understood that the widely circulated idea that the Imperial House represented an unbroken line from ancient times was a myth. When her Japanese friends asserted the unbroken line, Georgene exclaimed,

> it made me mad. Especially when I knew that until the late Emperor Taisho's time the Emperor's children were borne by women other than the Empress. At least their idea of an unbroken line was my idea of a badly bent one!

But when Georgene studied the Imperial House she was told that the Japanese Imperial House did indeed represent an unbroken line of lineage from at least 711 AD and maybe as far back as 660 BC. And in spite of her earlier skepticism, this time she believed it. Apparently, the Japanese were not only ones in Japan affected by imperial propaganda.

Georgene also had occasion to see the empress and emperor in person and this experience enhanced her appreciation for the imperial institution. She learned the concept of imperial *kokutai* that linked the emperor with the Japanese people and was the most widely accepted conceptual basis for the emperor system in the 1930s. Instructed that all Japanese elected the emperor by common consent every day through their approval of the imperial institution, Georgene made the connection that *kokutai* meant that the Imperial House was strongly identified with the people.

> It [the Imperial House] is not a family of individuals but a symbol. It is an idea that is so much a part of life, education, religion, government, blood relationship to the people that it is the people. Fathom that if you can! [underlines in original]

She also learned of the terrible treatment of the Imperial House over the centuries at the hands of the shoguns and felt sympathy over it. Apparently overcome with excitement, Georgene embraced the Imperial House. "It's all just thrilling,—and more so because it's true." There were not many Americans as enthusiastic about the Japanese Emperor as Georgene was, but her great interest intimates the curiosity of Americans concerning the Imperial House.[10]

The accession of the new emperor also caught the attention of the American military intelligence community. In a military intelligence summary of 1929, the history, mythology, and even the philology of the Japanese Emperor were analyzed.[11] The report focused on the response of the public conception of the emperor as a living god who led and fully represented the nation. The conclusion was clear. With a timeless emperor in place, the Japanese people, regardless of their modernization campaign, had not changed at all.

> Superficial observers are prone to regard the political and social events subsequent to the Meiji Restoration as a complete revolution and to marvel at the extraordinary adaptability of the Japanese. As a matter of fact, age-old customs cannot be changed in a day . . . to interpret the modifications which have occurred in Japan as a complete revolution is to exaggerate greatly. It is true that Japan now has a constitution which would have been impossible in her feudal days; but on keen analysis it will inevitably be concluded that this constitution merely replaced the old feudal military despotism by a military bureaucracy whose power is firmly consolidated and held by the leaders and protégés of the Choshu and Satsuma clans.[12]

Was one forced to conclude as did this report that therefore the Japanese hadn't changed much at all? While the rituals of emperorship emphasized the emperor's ancient divinity, some, perhaps many within Japan viewed the Japanese Emperor as the utmost symbol of Japan, not as a living deity. The unprecedented, huge propaganda campaign to solidify the position of the emperor in the late 1920s–1930s indicates concern among ruling elites that many Japanese did not comprehend the importance of the emperor. Historian Fujitani Takashi argues in *Splendid Monarchy* that many Japanese in nineteenth century Japan had little sense of the role of the emperor.

He outlines the invention of the modern Japanese monarchy in a mass media campaign, made possible with modern media implements such as mass circulation newspapers and magazines.[13]

The Japanese correspondent, K.K. Kawakami, set forward the view that accompanying the rest of the Japan's modernization, the emperorship in the hands of young Hirohito had become modernized as well. No longer was the emperor held behind a veil of secrecy. Hirohito went to school with subjects of the realm, albeit the sons of wealthy noblemen. He traveled the world and met many monarchs and dignitaries. He studied science and retained a strong interest in zoology and botany. He played sports such as golf and became an excellent horseman. He seemed to be quite worldly to many Japanese. Some Japanese approved, others were shocked by the commonness of Hirohito's approach. In a period where the voting franchise in Japan expanded, this common touch should not be as surprising as it was to many Japanese. Hirohito and his advisors had a modern grasp of the duties of emperorship and one of them was to mobilize the people through his example and spirit.[14]

Kawakami also commented on the seeming contradiction between the ancient institution and the very modern approach.

> In the present Emperor, Japan sees a ruler progressive and forward-looking, yet cherishing the memory of what has gone before him—a ruler who believes respect for the past essential to the conservation of what is best in the nation.[15]

For most Japanese, the monarchy was a practical form of stability and leadership within Japan and its empire, according to Royama Masamichi, a professor of Politics at Tokyo Imperial University. While admitting that rituals had been used to sustain the population's loyalty to the emperor, he rejected the notion that the main thrust of the monarchy was its ritual association with an immutable past of imperial deities.

> The shadowy aspirations and historical loyalties of earlier mention have been utilized to sustain the monarchical movement and have been to a certain extent satisfied by the person of the monarch and by the political philosophy associated with the monarchy. But when this has been said, the establishment of the Empire has had, from an internal point of view, an essentially practical inspiration.[16]

In fact, the myths of the Japanese Emperor system bear similarities to other nations' attempts to mobilize its people before World War II. Herbert Bix claims that Hirohito used the model of the British monarch George V to design a modern ceremonial monarch. One can identify a similar process of mythmaking and connecting the nation to its past in the rise of Nazism in Germany in the 1930s. The emperor myths were a part of a nationalist system of loyalty and patriotism used by many modern states to bind its citizens to the nation. With new technologies for communication and a mass education system, the Japanese Imperial House became the chief mythmaker of modern Japan.[17]

Even more attention might have been focused upon the new emperor if Chinese-Japanese relations in Manchuria had not begun to unravel in 1928. One normally thinks of the Manchurian Incident (1931) as a shocking turn in Japanese policy in China. However, if we look more closely at the period immediately preceding the Manchurian Incident, it became a pattern of escalating tensions between Japan and China in the late 1920s and early 1930s.

MANCHURIA UNRAVELS

Although the U.S.-Japan relationship was strained by fallout from American-centered issues such as immigration exclusion, the most dogged problems for the relationship lay in continental East Asia in Manchuria and China. Japan's close proximity to Korea and China and its historic ties to these places created the perception of a special relationship between Japan and continental East Asia. Americans had no business attempting to dictate or intervene in the affairs of the Japanese in East Asia, according to this view. The Japanese government and increasingly the Japanese military believed that Korea, Manchuria, and North China were the lifelines of Japan. They provided Japan with the raw materials for industry and held the potential to attract Japanese emigrants from the overcrowded home islands. As Japan's dependence on its "lifeline" increased in the 1920s, tensions worsened between Japan and the United States.

In the late 1920s, Japanese policy in China began to unravel when the warlord of Manchuria, Chang Tsolin, who until that point had been a cooperative partner of the Japanese in Manchuria, took control of North China by moving his troops to Peking in 1924. Chinese politics was a swamp of untrustworthy regional warlords who shifted alliances by the minute and a weak and ineffectual central government that exercised little control in the countryside. Chiang Kaishek (Jiang Jieshi), leader of the Guomindong (Nationalist Party), aimed to reunify China by marching his army north and signing alliances with warlords to back him.

The Japanese government recognized that if Chang was displaced in North China, this would mean more instability in Manchuria and possibly control by the Guomindong which was becoming antagonistic to Japan. Late in 1927, Chiang Kaishek's nationalist army began it's northern expedition, entering the southern capital of Nanjing. Amidst a massacre of Chinese communists carried out by the Guomindong, there were reports of attacks on Japanese civilians and the Japanese consul nearly lost his life. The Japanese sent in a small protective force there and another in Shantung in spring 1928 to protect Japanese civilians. The Japanese force actually clashed with Chiang's army. Chiang claimed that more than 1,000 Chinese were killed, and it looked for a moment as though the next war would break out between Japan and China in Shantung. Other European powers with concessions in China used force to protect their civilians as well. But the stakes were higher for the Japanese; they fought to retain control over Manchuria and their extensive investments and to protect their population throughout eastern China.[18]

The new Japanese prime minister, former army general Tanaka Giichi, promised to be more aggressive in protecting Japan's interests in China. Tanaka had worked actively toward the expansion of Japanese hegemony in China during World War I when he was army general. Tanaka now gave Chang an ultimatum about his presence in Peking: withdraw and maintain the support of Japan within Manchuria, or Japan would withdraw its support from Chang. However, when Chang decided to leave Peking and return to Manchuria, Japanese policy in Manchuria spun out of control. In a major blow to Tanaka's policy of working with Chang, junior officers in the Kwantung Army assassinated Chang as he returned to Mukden.[19]

The Japanese Kwantung Army in Manchuria, there ostensibly to protect the SMR and other Japanese property and people, was greatly influenced by right-wing ideologues in their junior officer corp. These young soldiers believed that Japan was far too soft in handling the Western powers and China. Taking matters into their own hands, they blew up Chang Tsolin's train as he traveled back to Manchuria on June 4, 1928 without Tokyo government approval. The explosion had far-reaching consequences. It destabilized the political situation in Manchuria and also in Tokyo. Chang's son, who was thought to be more malleable, took power in Manchuria but turned out to be less cooperative than the Japanese had hoped and eventually he became a sworn enemy of Japan. Because Prime Minister Tanaka had failed to restrain the Kwantung Army's activism, the emperor fired him but issued only administrative punishment to the assassins. The emperor unwittingly gave the Kwantung Army the impetus to take over policymaking for North China through the barrel of a gun. And this led directly to the Manchurian Incident.[20]

• The assassination of Chang was little reported in the American press because the Kwantung Army attempted to cover it up. It was a moment in retrospect when the American policymaking establishment and the public alike would have benefited from more information and the right kind of information. And yet little was forthcoming. There were no American intelligence reports covering the matter. And the press had slight coverage. The incident was completely covered up in Tokyo so the media there never knew the truth at least officially. Unofficially, everyone knew the Kwantung Army was responsible by the end of 1928.

American newspapers commented on the rising tensions in Manchuria generally. Suspicions were aired. *The St. Paul Pioneer Press* stated "it need cause no surprise if the world awakes one of these mornings to find that Japan has swept Manchuria into its imperial bag." *The Philadelphia Record* remarked "As a potential storm center, Manchuria might be considered the Balkans of Asia." *The Washington Post* reported that the American government had come to oppose Japanese aggression there and wanted reunion between China and Manchuria. *The Washington News* asserted that aggressive Japanese action in Manchuria would turn public opinion against them.[21]

As the Kwantung Army became more aggressive in Manchuria and China policy in Japan spun out of the hands of civilian politicians, the Japanese and American publics had little glimpse of this reality. Instead, the words and images coming out of Tokyo for American consumption were focused on party politics, the growth of liberalism, the influence of radicalism, the challenges presented by a depressed economy, and the positive impact of Japan upon its chaotic neighbor China. The popular Tokyo magazine *Chuo Koron* (The Center) pointed out that the Japanese wanted for China exactly what the Chinese wanted for themselves: political freedom, independence, and modernity. "To achieve her freedom and independence, China must first of all bring about the peaceful unification of herself. She must establish her domestic government, organize herself into a modern state. To this end Japan sympathizes with the nationalist revolution as an inevitable move, and gives to it her moral support." The article, which was picked up by the *Literary Digest*, had strong propaganda value in the United States where Americans concerned with East Asia supported independence for China.[22]

Japanese YMCA leaders, who had YMCA stations in China, Manchuria, and Korea, also expressed support in the aftermath of the assassination. Ibuka Kajinosuke and Kakehi Mitsuaki sent a letter to David Z.T. Yui, the secretary of the Chinese YMCA, expressing their view that Japan and China were intimately connected.

> First of all, let us assure you of the profound joy we feel in the knowledge that after these years of severe testing, China stands at last on the threshold of national unity . . . We of Japan have abundant reason to be grateful for the inspiration which the civilization of China has afforded us in ages past . . .[23]

Other points of view were in evidence in Japan, including suspicion of U.S. intentions in China and skepticism of China's intentions concerning

Japan and the United States. The comment of Secretary of State Kellogg in 1928 that the United States regarded Manchuria as Chinese territory and rejected the idea of special interests there aroused much press indignation in Tokyo. The *Asahi*, the *Yamato*, and the *NichiNichi* all attacked the secretary's comment and claimed for Japan the special interests that Kellogg denied. The *NichiNichi* was the most suspicious claiming that the United States was trying to "oust Japan and take her place there." However, the press also took the Tanaka government to task for its handling of Manchuria. Coming after Shidehara who had courted the Western powers, the Tanaka government's openly aggressive approach had alienated the United States and Great Britain, according to the *Asahi* and the *Yamato*.[24]

Reaction to the new American tariff agreement with China was similar to the response to Kellogg's comments. The *Asahi* claimed that China was simply pursuing her age-old practice of "setting barbarians against barbarians" by moving closer to the United States and creating tensions between Japan and America. In addition, the *Asahi* pointed out

> China is our neighbor and we are prone to see her weak points only, but America is separated from China by the Pacific and is apt to be captivated by China. America is too easily charmed by ideal China, whereas it is the habit of Japan to take the outward charms of China at a discount.

The reason for Japanese resentment in this case is because the U.S. government was giving signs through the tariff treaty and in other ways that it wanted to move toward recognizing Chiang Kaishek's Guomindong as the legitimate government of China. While some Japanese expressed support for Chinese reunification, the Japanese government was very concerned that the unification of China under Chiang's nationalist government would damage Japan's interests in Manchuria.[25]

The Japanese government had another concern in Manchuria. Japan controlled the southern railways but the Soviet Union controlled the northern railways many of which had been built before the Russo-Japanese War (1904–1905). Of foremost concern in 1929 was the Chinese threat to take over Russian lines in Manchuria. If the Chinese succeeded, they might attempt to do the same to Japan.[26]

American conservatives on the U.S.-Japan relationship, already suspicious before the Chang assassination, were confirmed in their suspicions. Thomas Millard wrote a series of articles in *The Nation* indicting the Japanese for the assassination of Chang Tsolin, predicting that the Japanese would soon be overlords of China in both Manchuria and the Shantung peninsula, and predicting further that a great Pacific war would eventually engulf the region.[27]

Japanese literature scholar Obata Shigeyoshi wrote a direct Japanese rebuttal to Millard's articles in January 1929. Obata first mentioned incidents against Japanese in China to provoke sympathy for the Japanese there. Then he put forward a series of questions contradicting Millard's assertions about the assassination. Why would the Japanese support Chang against the nationalists and then turn around and kill him? Why did they slow down the Chinese Nationalist Army at Shantung if they wanted Chang out of Peking? Of course Obata was missing some facts that would be revealed in time. The Japanese government had given Chang an ultimatum to withdraw from Peking or suffer the consequences. Japan did not want the instability that would result in Manchuria in case Chang lost a war against the nationalists or turned against the Japanese. The junior officers in the Kwantung Army in Manchuria believed Chang had become too independent to be trusted. Neither did they trust the nationalists. With the rise of the Guomindong in China, the Japanese were running out of options in Manchuria. The assassination was spurred by the realization that events were spinning out of Japanese control in China.

The swift Japanese response to Millard's accusations suggests the Japanese Foreign Ministry was monitoring American media for negative news that required answering. In addition, Obata had access to very detailed statistics about the Japanese in China and Manchuria, statistics that one could only get from the SMR Company and the Foreign Ministry. This tends to support the idea that the rebuttal was initiated by the Japanese government.

IPR CONFERENCE IN KYOTO

The crisis in Manchuria also impacted unofficial relations. The IPR held its third biennial conference in Kyoto in fall 1929. By this time the details of the Chang assassination had leaked out and it was becoming clear that the Japanese were responsible for it.

In this atmosphere, the conference took on increased importance because it became a forum for discussions about the Japanese role in Manchuria. Though it was sponsored by the Japan Council of the Institute for Pacific Relations (JCIPR), the conference was also carefully monitored from the shadows by the Japanese government. The Foreign Ministry had a strong hand in organizing the conference and covered one-third of the conference budget, with money also coming from the South Manchurian Railway (SMR) Company, a quasi-governmental body.[28] The Foreign Ministry had quietly sponsored the Japanese Council of the IPR from its inception, giving travel funds and underwriting the expenses of the Council.[29] In addition, Nitobe Inazô who was the current chair of the JCIPR received a written note from Foreign Minister Shidehara Kijuro concerning how to handle the conference and a briefing from Vice-Minister Yoshida Shigeru on how the Chinese delegates would respond to the Chang Incident (both of these officials became prime ministers in postwar Japan).[30]

The Japanese were very concerned in the months preceding the Kyoto Conference that the situation in Manchuria would blow up in their faces. So the government carefully controlled the media attention surrounding the conference. Japanese embassies and consulates in China sent many detailed reports on developments within Manchuria and other areas. The government also collected newspaper reports on the upcoming Kyoto Conference in the United States and China. Authorities reported on the comings and goings of the foreign participants at the Kyoto Conference. Even the mayor of Kyoto handed in a report on the conference. The Home Ministry in charge of internal security within Japan and the Foreign Ministry received these reports. However, the government allowed the conference to go forward even after it was known that Manchuria would be on the Kyoto agenda.[31]

Japanese who spearheaded the issue of Manchuria at the conference included Matsuoka Yôsuke, Saito Soichi and Inoue Junnosuke. Matsuoka had been a diplomat in the Foreign Ministry until 1921 and then became vice president of the SMR. He later became famous (or infamous) for his blunt style and pro-war approach as foreign minister in 1940–1941. In 1929, he was known simply as "the American" by other Japanese because of his education in the United States and his excellent command of English. It was assumed that Matsuoka was a liberal in 1929, and his involvement in the JCIPR seemed to confirm that position. Few would have guessed that over the next dozen years Matsuoka would move steadily in the militarist direction in his politics, but this became a well-trod path for many Japanese liberals. Saito was the head of the Japanese YMCA which was a powerful and well-respected organization in Japan. The YMCA served the government by confronting the social problems of youth through intellectual and moral training and the government understood its value even though the Christianity inherent within the YMCA's message brought few converts.[32] Inoue, who had been chair of the JCIPR, stepped down to become Finance Minister in 1929. Inoue inaugurated a series of fiscal tightening measures in 1930 that worsened the Depression in Japan and turned the Japanese population against him. He was assassinated in 1932 by a right-wing militant. Of the three only Saito did not have extended government experience but he had connections with the government.

The JCIPR planned to highlight research projects that would demonstrate the benefit of Manchuria to the Japanese economy and the development of the Manchurian economy. While the Japanese government did not intervene in these research projects, by mid 1929 the government expressed concern because Japan nationals were collaborating with Chinese in them.

The government watched the situation closely and received reports from Takagi Yasaka who was a professor of American studies at Tokyo Imperial University and head of research at the JCIPR. The research on Manchuria was presented at the Kyoto Conference and showed evidence that Japan had made huge investments to modernize Manchuria and Manchuria was the economic lifeline of Japan. All sides looked to the conference to defuse the explosive atmosphere surrounding Manchuria. The New York Times headline in July 1929 announced "Pacific Institute Seen as Peace Aid" and gave the conference heavy coverage with twelve articles before, during, and after it. The conference received press publicity from around the world. With Manchuria on the agenda, the world watched to see how the East Asian delegates would respond to one another.

Amidst the elegance and autumnal beauty of Kyoto, 220 delegates attended the conference. Greetings from U.S. president Herbert Hoover and from prime ministers from Australia and Canada were read. Japan's own Prime Minister Hamaguchi Osachi opened the conference with a speech. Hamaguchi characterized Japan as a combination of the best of Eastern and Western civilization and pointed out that the IPR had the strong support of the Japanese government.[33]

Shortly after the conference, Hamaguchi gave approval to a second naval limitation treaty resulting from the London Naval Conference. Even though the Japanese navy wanted a 70 percent tonnage ratio to the British and Americans, ultimately, the Western powers prevailed upon Japan to keep the same ratio (3:5:5, 60%) as the Washington Treaty. Hamaguchi's accomodationist approach and pro-Western stance outraged conservatives in Japan and he was shot by a right-wing radical at a Tokyo Central Railroad station platform. His death in early 1931 caused a crisis among Japanese liberals.

Nitobe Inazô gave a keynote speech emphasizing the importance of the nongovernmental role of the IPR and its focus on the Pacific region. But he also pointed out that the internationalist thrust of the IPR did not preclude or negate appropriate patriotism. "The international mind is not the antonym of the national mind. Nor is it a synonym for the cosmopolitan mind, which lacks a national basis. The international mind is the expansion of the national . . ." Unfortunately, Nitobe's definition of internationalism, which fit within his and other Japanese internationalists' framework very well, did little to dampen the nationalist and partisan atmosphere that permeated the conference. To be fair, Nitobe did encourage the delegates to rise above "national egotism." However, if the interests of the nation dominated the international world, then there was no push to transcend the clash of interests between China and Japan. Indeed, national interests were a strong focus at the conference.[34]

When the Chinese raised the accusation that Japan was responsible for the assassination of Chang Tsolin, newspaper editor Zumoto Motosada stood immediately to object to the accusation. Since it was only the first day and the round table discussions had not yet begun, Nitobe who was presiding stated that the objection could be made later during the roundtable on Manchuria. When the issue came up during the roundtable discussions, Matsuoka Yôsuke responded with an eloquent defense of the Japanese position in Manchuria in English while denying that Japan was responsible for the assassination of Chang.[35] Matsuoka argued Japan had created the conditions for Manchuria to thrive: political stability and economic progress. Japan benefited from this situation but so did China and the West, according to Matsuoka. He made progress and modernity the central argument for the Japanese presence in Manchuria. This fit the Japanese claim that they were modernizing northeast Asia outside of Western imperialism, just as Japan had freed itself from the Western threat through modernization. Matsuoka's argument impressed the foreign correspondents present and they reported his comments positively.[36]

As a result of Matsuoka's presentation, the conference achieved one of its goals, to defuse tensions over the Chang assassination. However, no lasting agreements were reached concerning Manchuria: neither Chinese acquiescence in Japan's presence in Manchuria nor Japanese willingness to leave Manchuria at some future date. The delegates did agree in principal that extraterritoriality practiced in China by all the powers there should be ended and China should regain its full sovereignty over property and legal issues concerning foreigners in China.

The problem with the Kyoto Conference as a model for improving China-Japan and Japan-American relations was twofold. First the unofficial status of the Japanese delegates could be fairly questioned. Distinguishing official from unofficial diplomacy was becoming very difficult in Japan. Second, the delegates from both Japan and China spoke mostly as the voices of their respective nations and so nationalism inhabited not just official diplomacy but also unofficial ties. This situation intensified in the 1930s. Finally, while frank discussion of controversial issues marked the Kyoto Conference, by the mid-1930s, the IPR had stopped taking on controversial issues in open discussion and instead moved into research projects.

The Kyoto Conference might have represented the high point of unofficial diplomacy between the United States and Japan. As tensions increased in the wake of the Manchurian Incident, informal ties became more strained and it became increasingly difficult to find forums where the parties could speak frankly to one another.

CHAPTER 8

"ORIENTAL" DUPLICITY OR PROGRESS AND ORDER: THE MANCHURIAN INCIDENT

IN THE EARLY MORNING OF SEPTEMBER 18, 1931, JAPANESE SOLDIERS FROM THE Kwantung Army planted a small bomb along side the South Manchurian Railway (SMR) near Mukden, where the bulk of the Japanese Army was stationed. As the bomb exploded, the railway, which was built and owned by the Japanese, suffered miniscule damage. Within hours the railroad was repaired and working, transporting Japanese troops to invade Manchuria under the pretext of putting down the Chinese bandits who had supposedly blown up the railroad. Later the next day, reporters were allowed to photograph the blown railroad tie and piece of rail. The damage to the rail was no more than eighteen inches long. This small explosion started a huge conflagration, the event some scholars in Japan such as Saburo Iyenaga have defined as the beginning of the Pacific War.

The Japanese deception was totally transparent. It seemed Japanese officials in Manchuria did not care whether the rest of the world came to the correct conclusion that the Japanese themselves blew up the rail. They set up a small museum exhibit at the point where the tracks had blown showing the broken rail. But no one believed their story of Chinese bandits.

AMERICAN RESPONSE

The deception that mattered most to many Americans was not the blown railroad tracks near Mukden but Japan's larger deception concerning its Westernization and modernization. In the Manchurian crisis, Japan showed that it was an Oriental nation that could not be trusted.

Rodney Gilbert, a former U.S. consul to China and a journalist who wrote for *The North China Daily News* and the *North China Herald*, a Japanese publication in Manchuria and a British newspaper, respectively, argued that in the Manchurian Incident Japan had proved that it was no longer Western at all.

> In maintaining these pretenses, which they know are wholly unsatisfactory to the Occident, they are shedding the frock coat, in which they have been proud to conduct meticulously correct relations with the West and resuming the kimono and with it the Asiatic preference for face above good faith.

Gilbert saw Japan turning from an open Western approach back toward Oriental deceitfulness. While many Americans judged Japanese modernization a success before the Manchurian crisis, the Incident became a turning point, giving new urgency to the question of Japan's modernity. If the Japanese had for a time become metaphorically Occidental, a different metaphor of dressing in a kimono or in this journalist's words "resuming the kimono" described Japan's supposed return to its Oriental nature after the Manchurian Incident.[1]

An earlier analysis by naval intelligence in 1927 of Japan's diplomatic intrigue anticipated the Manchurian Incident. The Japanese had the perfect background to be distrustful in their diplomacy, according to the report.

> Secretive by nature and by training from early childhood—and as naturally inquisitive as children, they are well-fitted to secure and to withhold information . . . The natural skill of her people in intrigue—developed under a feudal system so rigorous that the Samurai instantly punished a fancied breach of manners with his sword—together with a reticence and lack of candor wholly incomprehensible to an American—makes it very difficult for us to negotiate successfully with them.[2]

The author could have noted that the Japanese considered themselves to be poor diplomats because of their shyness. So the same characteristic, a quiet nature, could be either a reason for Japanese success at duplicitous diplomacy or a reason for their failure.

The correspondence of Henry Stimson, who was secretary of state during the Incident, indicates similar sentiments. An employee of the Smithsonian Institution wrote to Stimson,

> We are dealing with wily, egotistic, fanatical and but superficially truly civilized people, who moreover, under the guise of smiles and gifts and condescensions, are filled with envy of us and are our inveterate enemies, for we stand in their way and we have hurt their great conceit and vanity.

The letter ranted against the Japanese, "what trust could ever be had in any new promises and treaties of such a people." Another letter to Senator Borah that was passed onto Stimson condemned the entire Japanese race as liars.[3]

Other journalists argued variously that Japan had revealed in Manchuria that it was not an Occidental civilization at all but a feudal Oriental nation. In an article entitled "The Japanese Smoke Screen" in *The Saturday Evening Post*, Isaac Marcosson concluded Japanese economic exploitation of Manchuria "has shown that her Occidentalization is simply a covering to hide the feudal fist." Marcosson argued that Japan's monopolistic economic tendencies in Manchuria were the result of its still powerful feudalism.[4] Another writer connected Japanese aggression more to the pre–World War I system of the great powers of Europe than to feudal Japan. But he put the word "modernized" within quotation marks to express his skepticism about Japanese modernization.[5]

Upton Close, an American journalist who had spent much time in East Asia, put Japanese modernization within quotes as well. Close, considered an expert on the region, became well known as a radio personality in the late 1930s and 1940s. Upton Close was actually a pseudonym for Josef Wellington Hall. During World War I, Hall served the American government as an intelligence officer in Shantung, where the Japanese had invaded and taken over German possessions. To hide his real identity, Hall signed his dispatches from the field "Up Close" and eventually took the pseudonym Upton Close. Because his reports revealed Japanese plans, the Japanese Army wanted to capture Upton Close, but they did not know his true identity. In a bizarre twist, they offered Josef Hall 3,000 yen to reveal Upton Close's real identity.

Close had a knack for adventure. He and his wife happened to be in China and traveled to Harbin in September 1931 when the crisis began. Travel was dangerous and Close had to bribe conductors and soldiers to arrive safely.[6]

China had been the "Middle Kingdom" for centuries but then in the modern period, Japan had "grown up," according to Close. But Close questioned Japan's modernity, claiming that in Japan "vestiges of an inferiority complex great enough to be significant still remain," citing the still practiced samurai tradition of seppuku (ritual suicide) as evidence.[7]

Another commentator suggested that the samurai were the cause of Japan's superficial modernization.

Outwardly modernized, her leaders talking in the language of the Twentieth Century, Japan is medieval below the surface. Her people are under the domination of an aristocratic military caste actuated by two motives. The first is genuinely patriotic. The Samurai, the hereditary fighting clans, believe that the destiny of the Japanese people is to attain control of all Asia and the Pacific. This control will enable them to dominate the world.

The claim of world domination was a bit outlandish and probably did not represent a significant portion of American public opinion in 1932.[8]

The tradition of the samurai was often blamed for the Manchurian Incident. It seems reasonable on the surface but upon closer examination is questionable. The leaders of the Manchurian Incident, Colonel Doihara Kenji, Colonel Itagaki Seishiro, and Lieutenant-Colonel Ishiwara Kanji, did not hark back to samurai traditions, but looked at Japan with a very modern sensibility. Ishiwara was a devotee of intellectual Kita Ikki, who had fused Marxist and proto-fascist frameworks into a critique of Westernization and capitalism. In addition, the act of fomenting the Manchurian Incident expressed outright contempt for the government of Japan. If a true samurai had done the same thing, he would have been obligated to commit seppuku. In this case, the conspirators were eventually promoted.

Reading like an excerpt from a Fu Manchu novel, an article in *The Living Age*, translated from the Paris weekly, *Marianne*, told the story of the "ruthless" and "diabolical" Doihara, who was promoted to general after the Manchurian Incident. The article on Doihara was reminiscent of the Fu Manchu character. The fictional Dr. Fu Manchu, an evil genius of Chinese origin, was first featured in a series of novels by British author Sax Rohmer (Arthur Sarsfield Ward) during the early years of the twentieth century. Rohmer described Fu Manchu in *The Insidious Dr. Fu Manchu* (1913):

> Imagine a person, tall, lean and feline, high-shouldered, with a brow like Shakespeare and a face like Satan, a close-shaven skull, and long, magnetic eyes of the true cat-green. Invest him with all the cruel cunning of the entire Eastern race . . .

Like Fu Manchu, the Doihara character that emerged from the page fit the Orientalist imagination perfectly. The commentator gave Doihara credit for "masterminding" the Japanese approach to North China from 1931 forward. An exaggeration fitted to suit a Japan that could not be trusted, the article left out the rest of the Japanese military and government. Even though written by a Frenchman, the Doihara article was published in the United States and reached the American reading audience.[9]

American radicals also weighed in on the Manchurian crisis. Wilbur Burton was a homegrown American radical from Indiana in the same vein as Charles Beard, a Jeffersonian suspicious of centralized power wherever it existed. He became a journalist and was stationed in Shanghai during the Manchurian Incident. Burton did not ascribe Japan's fragility to its lack of modernity or inherent militarism. Instead, he noted the sobering realities facing Japan. Japan had industrialized but had few resources to sustain industrialization. It was burdened by a growing population that outstripped the ability of the home islands to support it. It also had a large trade deficit. Burton's views accurately described the Japanese dilemma: Japan faced multiple crises at home and threats from abroad. However, Burton was not necessarily sympathetic to the Japanese cause. He was very critical of emperor system, believing that it contradicted newly inaugurated universal manhood suffrage in Japan.[10]

Mauritz Hallgren, another radical, entered the debate over Japan's actions with an article about the Manchurian Incident in *The Nation* in November 1931. Hallgren, who had little interest in or contact with Japan, later wrote the definitive isolationist work of the interwar period on Wilson and Roosevelt's foreign policies called *The Tragic Fallacy: A Study of America's War Policies* (1937). Hallgren, like Burton, distrusted the Japanese Imperial system, but attacked Western imperialism as creating the justification and necessity for the Japanese to act in similar manner in China. The Japanese were simply doing on a larger scale what the Europeans had been doing in China for decades. Both the Japanese and the American foreign policies were inherently imperialist. However, the influence of these radicals over American public opinion was quite limited because of their strong critique of the American government.[11]

Accusing the Japanese variously of using secretive diplomacy and therefore returning to deceitful Oriental ways, of having a facade of modernity but a feudal military state underneath, and of betraying its promise of Westernization, American commentators shaped public responses to the Manchurian Incident by questioning Japan's modernity. Even Sherwood Eddy, who was in the liberal missionary camp, wrote in *The Challenge of the East*, "The magnificent feudal castle and moat of the ancient Shogun, now the residence of the Emperor stands as a constant reminder that the heart of this great city and all of Japan is still largely feudal and oriental, despite Occidental surface innovations and institutions."[12] If Japan was in fact not becoming modern and democratic, then it was not the nation it seemed and it had betrayed its promise to Americans. This possibility produced intense feelings of distrust among Americans.

SECRETARY OF STATE STIMSON AND NONRECOGNITION

Although American public opinion became more distrustful of the Japanese in the wake of the Manchurian Incident, there was no support for the use of force against Japan. The peace movement in the United States, represented by organizations such as the NCPW, WIL, FPA, and the LNA, was a powerful voice in American public opinion during the Manchurian Incident. These groups were very concerned the Manchurian crisis would destroy the peace mechanisms put into place in the 1920s such as the Kellogg Pact—which outlawed war and was signed by many nations including the United States and Japan but which had no enforcement mechanism—and might lead to a general war. Therefore, they wanted swift action by the U.S. government and the League of Nations to force Japan to pull back its troops. They moved to a strongly anti-Japanese stance and were very pleased when Secretary of State Henry Stimson indicated that the United States would work with the League of Nations to resolve the situation.[13]

Later, Stimson struck out on an independent path away from the League, issuing a statement of American nonrecognition of the Japanese puppet government, Manchukuo, set up in early 1932. This policy received strong support from the peace and religious groups in the United States. Stimson's position moved in concert with their own. After the Japanese bombed Shanghai in spring 1932 with high civilian casualties, anti-Japanese feelings spiked and Stimson, once again showing his sensitivity to American public opinion, toughened the American response. In addition, isolationists, who had disliked Stimson's initial overture to the League, supported Stimson's new independent approach.[14]

An independent American policy suited American tastes well even though it meant a division between the United States and Great Britain and weakened the West's response to the crisis overall. Japanese militarists noted this division among the Western powers and it might have encouraged further aggression later. Nonrecognition appealed to isolationists and peace groups because it was a peaceful response that did not commit the United States to foreign intervention. The policy also expressed support for the Chinese against Japan by stating that the United States would not support any action that abridged the rights of Chinese citizens or its government to make treaties that treated China fairly. Peace groups, anxious for more pressure on the Japanese, also pushed for an embargo against Japanese trade and an unofficial boycott of Japanese goods. While John Dewey and prominent peace activists such as Tyler Dennett and Jane Addams supported the boycott, neither idea had widespread support or was implemented.[15]

Anti-Japanese sentiments produced their own opposition. Roy Mathew Frisen wrote a book called *Japanophobia* in 1933 about the rise of strong anti-Japanese feelings during the Manchurian Incident. Frisen argued that warmongers on both sides had gotten a hold of the Japan debate. This was perhaps an exaggeration given the active role of peace groups in the debate about the U.S. response. But Frisen did point out that anti-Japanese propaganda in the United States, closely watched by the Japanese, confirmed the militarist accusation of an American menace pointed at Japan. Thus, Frisen asserted war talk was dangerous and should be replaced by communication of peaceful intentions.[16]

A smaller segment of the American public maintained sympathy toward Japan. Some support came from business organizations and other hard-headed realists who saw the chaos in China and thought that Japan could exert a stabilizing influence there. Others maintained the Japanese were a bulwark against the penetration of communist influences in North China. In the early stages of the crisis, the *Christian Science Monitor*, the *New York Daily News*, and the *Atlanta Constitution* all defended Japan's actions.[17] The American Asiatic Association, founded in 1898 by cotton exporters, railroad promoters, and mining officials to further American business interests in East Asia, took a pro-Japanese stance. Henry Kittredge Norton, who had become the editor of the association's monthly bulletin, argued that since the Chinese had no effective control over North China, with the exception of the warlords who wrecked havoc on the local population, the Japanese had no choice but to more aggressively protect their own extensive interests and population in Manchuria. Lincoln Colcord, whose family had been involved in the China trade for generations, took a "survival of the fittest" approach in a *Harper's Magazine* article entitled "The Realism of Japanese Diplomacy." Although he did not fully endorse Japan's actions, he condemned the Kellogg Pact and the League of Nations as weak and without enforcement powers. In his view it was idealistic Westerners who were irrational, not the Japanese who were acting out of their rational interests for national survival.[18] William Castle, from a wealthy plantation family in Hawai'i, was concerned that chaos and instability in North China would further the interests of Soviet Russia. Castle had served as ambassador to Japan for a time in the 1920s and was firmly in the pro-Japan camp.[19]

Arthur Schlesinger Sr., historian and father of well-known historian Arthur Schlesinger Jr., wrote an article for *The American Mercury* in 1934 after a trip to East Asia, in which he suggested,

> If we assume however, the sincerity of the rest of the world in wishing the East to be Occidentalized, it may well be the historic function of the Japanese, as the only oriental people who have modernized themselves through an act of self-will, to teach their fellow Asiatics what Europe has failed to do.

Schlesinger's argument was familiar to the Japanese, many of whom believed that their mission was to bring Japanese-style civilization to continental East Asia. Of course they denied that what was being brought was Western civilization. Rather, it was a unique blend of East and West Japan had engineered within its own society and now sought to propagate in the rest of East Asia.[20]

Perhaps the most fervently pro-Japanese were the Christian missionary organizations serving Japan. Far from believing that the Japanese facade of modernity had been pulled off, these groups clung to the belief that Japan was in the throes of modernization and democratization. The missionaries wrote to denounce the embargo and boycott ideas being debated in the United States in early 1932. Their support went not to the Chinese but to Japanese liberals whom they believed had been overlooked in the American rush to condemn the Manchurian Incident. It was their opinion that an embargo and/or boycott would simply turn public opinion against the United States and weaken the hand of liberals associated with the United States in the minds of the Japanese public.

Sidney Gulick, a former missionary to Japan who was well known for his books on Japan and his leadership of groups in the United States sympathetic to Japan, wrote an article for the *New York Herald Tribune* that outlined the recent history of China-Japan relations surrounding Manchuria and the role of the Soviet Union as well. Gulick reported that policy in Japan was no longer in the hands of liberals but was now controlled by the militarists, a frightening turn of events for the Japanese. A series of articles by Willis Abbot in the *Christian Science Monitor* warranted mention in a circular letter from American missionary in Japan, Katherine F. Fanning. She ranked his argument highly because he saw parallels between American control over Cuba and Japanese control over Manchuria.[21]

William Axling defended Japanese actions as necessary for Japan's economic survival in a *Christian Century* article entitled "Be Just to Japan!" Axling, a retired Baptist missionary to Japan, wrote a laudatory biography of Kagawa Toyohiko, a Japanese Christian famous for his work with the poor and his writings in English on the social gospel in Japan. He noted the plight of liberals in Japan, where prominent liberals Premier Hamaguchi, Finance Minister Inoue, and Barons Dan and Wakatsuki were recently assassinated. Axling hoped for the revival of Japanese liberalism in part because he thought liberals were best positioned to resolve the Manchurian situation. While some Americans supposed that liberalism was now dead in Japan, the missionary community believed that the revival of liberalism was key to restoring peace in East Asia and putting Japan back on the track of Westernization. According to Axling, there was a groundswell of antiwar sentiment in Japan. He gave as an example schoolchildren visiting temples and praying for peace. A letter from a Japanese friend articulated the antiwar case.

> The entire Japanese people hate this war and are fearfully troubled over it . . . The Chinese and Japanese are brothers. I can't bear to think of either of them suffering defeat or being slain. I only pray for their reconciliation.

Axling hopefully concluded, "The jingoists are having their fling. But they are a noisy minority."

The United States made a mistake in taking a hard-line with Japan because this only strengthened the militarists and weakened the liberals. Instead Axling suggested an "understanding heart," to see Japan's economic problems and security issues in northeast Asia as Japan saw them. This insightful suggestion was listened to by the missionary community but by few others. The contradictions in Axling's approach also detracted from his plea. Defending Japan's action, Axling then tried to cover himself by suggesting that a peaceful approach would have averted a crisis. Axling, like the missionary community in general, was caught between his attraction to the peace movement and his loyalty to Japan.[22]

Axling's article produced a quick response from one D.W. Learned (probably a pseudonym) in the letters to the editor section of *The Christian Century*. Refuting Axling's assertion that Japan would starve if it didn't take over Manchuria, Learned pointed out that no nation had actually threatened its access to important resources there. In response to Axling's praise of Japan's liberals, the letter ended with "It is no answer to those who criticize Japan's action in China to say that there are many excellent people in Japan; no one attacks them."[23]

A group of 135 missionaries in Japan wrote a letter to a smaller circulation Christian journal arguing that Japan had a "fair claim for peace and order" in Manchuria even though they did not like its methods of obtaining it. In a reference to Japanese liberals recently removed from power, they claimed that "The country is being denied the leadership of some of her most enlightened minds at this time when it is sorely needed."[24]

The Chinese actively wooed American public opinion during the crisis. Stimson received letters from Chinese officials and others encouraging a tough stand against the Japanese. T.V. Soong, wealthy financier and finance minister of China, had many friends in the United States. He did an interview with *Hearst* newspaper reporter Karl Von Wiegand in which he stated that the Chinese would rather have Communist control in the country than Japanese domination. This statement was of course pure propaganda. Soong despised communism but he understood that Americans who were anticommunist would raise their opposition to Japanese domination because it might drive Chinese nationalists into the arms of the communists. Eugene Chen, outspoken former foreign minister of China, asserted in a *New York Times* article that Japan intended to make war on the United States. Publications from the American Committee for Justice to China and The Northeastern Affairs Research Institute circulated through the American media.[25]

Soviet Russia moved more troops to the border with Manchuria in response to Japan's aggression but made no threatening moves with those troops. Inner Mongolia, dominated for centuries by the Chinese Empire, was the one entity in northeast Asia that welcomed the Japanese presence in

Manchuria. Their antagonism toward China led them to embrace Japanese influence there.

American public opinion was divided over the Manchurian Incident in a manner which matched overall American views on Japan. The missionaries and other supporters held fast to the belief that Manchuria was a temporary diversion in Japan's march into progress and modernity, although they were on the defensive and dwindling in number, especially after Japan attacked Shanghai in 1932. Many others believed that Japan was no longer moving in the direction of the West, instead retreating into its past. As a whole, the American public became much more anti-Japanese. They endorsed the official policy of Secretary of State Henry Stimson's nonrecognition doctrine. Newspaper support favoring Stimson's policy ran as high as 80 percent at some points in the timeline of the crisis.[26]

Stimson himself understood the situation in Japan fairly well. He knew that there were serious clashes between liberals and conservatives.[27] He considered Foreign Minister Shidehara a friend and expressed the view that acting too strongly against Japan would simply hurt the liberal cause there. In *The Far Eastern Crisis* (1936), a book he wrote later about the diplomacy of the Manchurian Incident, Stimson stated that because of Japan's traditions (feudal militarism) and recent experiences, the Japanese did not put great trust in the Western European peace-making system built at Versailles and the Washington Conference. He also denied the assertion of many that Japan was locked into its militarist past. "The problem in Japan was not that of a voluntary reversion on the part of her entire people to militarism and the methods of past ages. It was far more complex than that." Stimson, however, did not totally discount the militarism argument. But he saw the complexity of Japan more clearly than many Americans. He had strengthened his knowledge of Japan through time spent in Japan when he was governor-general of the Philippines.[28]

If anything, Stimson was closer to the optimistic missionary argument. He saw popular opinion in Japan turning against the militarists in 1935, promising a more conciliatory policy toward China. Stimson pointed to an upsurge of liberal activity and a recent Japanese election in which support for the militarists had declined. But Stimson was too optimistic and by fall 1937 when the Sino-Japanese War commenced became strongly anti-Japanese.[29]

In 1932, however, Stimson believed that a nonpunitive policy of nonrecognition was the best that could be done under the circumstances. Stimson knew that the United States risked pushing Japanese public opinion squarely into the conservative camp if it punished Japan with official trade sanctions or even an unofficial boycott of Japanese goods. After he was elected president, Franklin Roosevelt endorsed Stimson's policy and confirmed Stimson's belief that Japan would turn back from militarism eventually.[30]

American and Japanese public opinion limited Stimson's options in the Manchurian crisis. He could not act boldly against the Japanese for fear of Japanese public opinion. He could not act boldly to address Japan's economic concerns underpinning the Manchurian Incident because anti-Japanese feeling in the United States did not support it. More seeds of war were planted in the limits placed upon official diplomacy by public opinion in the Manchurian crisis.

NEW TENSIONS IN PRIVATE DIPLOMACY

Sherwood Eddy was in Mukden, Manchuria in September 1931 during the Manchurian Incident. An advocate of the international peace movement, he reacted dramatically to events there. Appalled at the Japanese deception, Eddy sent a cable in the immediate aftermath of the Incident to American and British political leadership and to major American and British newspapers. Included were Ramsay McDonald, prime minister of Great Britain, American secretary of state Henry Stimson, and Senator William Borah, chair of the Senate Foreign Relations Committee. Eddy thought the Japanese deception warranted the immediate attention of American policy makers. He also believed that his rapid active private diplomacy could help save the situation.

> I was present at the capture of Moukden. The evidence of many witnesses interviewed at the time and on the spot points to a premeditated and carefully prepared offensive plan of the Japanese Army without the provocation of any Chinese attack producing bitter resentment when China is suffering with flood disaster and the world is preoccupied ... I testify to evidence of efforts to establish puppet independence governments in Manchuria under Japan military control ... The universal indignation in China taking the form of an economic boycott which the government cannot control. The situation is critical and grave developments are imminent. All the Orient is looking to the League of Nations and the Kellogg Pact signatories for action.[31]

Eddy's sense of outrage and urgency comes through clearly. With this cable, Eddy turned away from Japan and by the mid 1930s he became a strong critic. He denounced the Manchurian invasion as a reckless military adventure in an article in spring 1932 called "Japan Threatens the World." A book entitled *The World's Danger Zone* followed soon after emphasizing the same themes.[32]

Nitobe Inazô and Saito Soichi, head of the Japanese YMCA, signed a cable sent to American YMCA headquarters in New York in response to Eddy's cable. "In view previous close connection YMCA Sherwood Eddy's Mukden affidavit damaging effect stop please exercise influence more careful his expression." They recognized how damaging Eddy's cable was to Japan's reputation in the United States and wanted him to stop. It is possible that the Japanese Foreign Ministry was involved (at the least consulted) in the response. In November, a Japanese consulate official visited YMCA headquarters in New York to encourage the YMCA to try to silence Eddy.[33] Eddy did not stop; in addition to his writing, upon his return to the United States, he did a tour that took him to several cities where he lectured on the Manchurian situation.[34]

Eddy was traveling in China on an evangelical tour at the invitation of the Chinese YMCA when the Manchurian Incident took place. The Japanese invasion boosted attendance for his lectures, which attracted over 200,000 people and at which over 100,000 pieces of literature were distributed. "The ruthless military offensive of Japanese in Manchuria and down the east coast had pierced China's heart awakening her people to the realization of their desperate need." Eddy met with Christian leaders throughout China, sympathizing with their plight.[35]

The Japanese understood that Eddy was doing great damage to their reputation and so he was invited to visit Japan and give testimony (and perhaps be persuaded that Japan's actions in Manchuria were not so bad after all). Eddy stayed in Japan for three days of meetings with various organizations. He met with friendly groups so we can assume that he met with Japanese Christians and liberal internationalist organizations such as the YMCA, the Japan-America Relations Committee, the JCIPR, possibly the Japanese LNA, and even the Foreign Ministry. Eddy did not alter his position and warned the Japanese that their military adventure in Manchuria was a menace not just to themselves or the Chinese but to the world peace process. He was also disturbed by the war fever that had swept Japan encouraging government suppression of dissent and even self-censorship.

Facing strong anti-American sentiment in Japan, strengthening anti-Japanese feeling in the United States, and new problems in Manchuria, Americans in Japan were put under new strain. Personal relationships were put under intense strain. Charles Beard's personal correspondence and presumably his friendship with Tsurumi Yusuke ended with the Manchurian crisis. Tensions erupted on several fronts over minor issues that otherwise would have been paid little attention.

At the same time as Eddy's reports from Manchuria were being made public, another article in *The New York Times* written by Robert Lewis—supposedly an official of the YMCA in China—condemned Japan's actions. Apparently the report also had the hand of the Chinese government at Nanjing in its creation (an American YMCA official in Tokyo reported that the Chinese government had generated the article and had no hesitation to use the YMCA there as a conduit for its propaganda). The Japanese Foreign Office and ambassador to the United States were aware of the article within days of its publication and met with American YMCA officials in Japan and in New York. It turned out that Robert Lewis was not employed with the American YMCA, but the incident demonstrated the explosive, complex triangle between Japan, the United States, and China. Apparently the Chinese government was willing to manipulate unofficial channels such as the YMCA in China to its ends like Japan had done with the media in the United States. The incident also showed once again the careful attention paid by the Japanese government to American press reports.[36]

Much informal diplomatic activity took place among American missionaries stationed in Japan and China. American officials from the YMCA and the American Board of Commissioners for Foreign Missions (ABCFM) in Japan made separate trips to Manchuria to assess the situation. The YMCAs in Manchuria reflected the very diverse population of Manchuria, with 29 million Chinese, 200,000 Japanese, 60,000 white Russians, and 500,000 Koreans. The Americans ran a large YMCA in Harbin, Manchuria that served the white Russian refugees who had settled in Manchuria after the Bolshevik takeover. The Chinese ran six YMCAs in Manchuria from their headquarters in Shanghai. Five Japanese YMCAs were linked to Japanese YMCA headquarters in Tokyo and several Korean YMCAs in South Manchuria were not yet fully integrated with the Korean headquarters in Seoul but corresponded with it. The Japanese for the moment had decided to allow these various groups to continue to exist in Manchuria under independent control. But there were hints that the Japanese intended to amalgamate the non-Japanese YMCAs. The amalgamation did take place eventually during the Sino-Japanese War in the late 1930s.

The American YMCA sent its representative Sidney Phelps who served as the lead American at the Japanese YMCA and the Japanese YMCA sent Secretary General Soichi Saito to Manchuria in March 1933. Japanese officials were well aware that Phelps sympathized with the Japanese position in Manchuria and so Phelps was given red carpet treatment on his travels. He was delighted by this courteous hospitality. It was arranged for him to travel first class instead of coach on the trains; government officials met him at the train stations with cars; he was able to fly in a small airplane to Harbin to meet with another American YMCA official; and he traveled with a government escort for part of the trip, there not only to facilitate Phelps' trip but also to keep an eye on him. The government also arranged for him to meet with all major government officials in the new state of Manchukuo. The Japanese government believed that Phelps could be a useful voice in support of Japan's policies in Manchuria.

Phelps did in fact gain a positive impression and wrote letters and articles back to the American YMCA defending Japan, citing historical grievances in Northeast China such as the Triple Intervention in 1895 and the unfavorable settlement of the Russo-Japanese War of 1905. He maintained that the League of Nations had acted prematurely in condemning Japan, blaming League action for a mass movement of the Japanese public away from the liberal viewpoint and toward the military.[37] Phelps also resolved a situation where the Japanese government had allowed a private opium import company to occupy one part of the YMCA building in Antung on the Yalu River bordering Korea (the company was removed when he reported it). The Chinese and Koreans had accused Japan of encouraging the opium trade in Manchuria to keep the population addicted and cooperative.[38]

Other American missionaries traveled to Manchuria to offer help in resolving tensions. Howard W. Hackett who was the treasurer of the ABCFM in Japan went on a fact-finding mission to Manchuria. His account was much more balanced and comprehensive than Phelps' reports, although he did show an inclination to defend Japan and blame the League of Nations. Hackett traveled in China proper as well to gain the Chinese perspective on the situation. He met with dozens of people including James Yen the Yale graduate who was committed to a rural development scheme for Chinese development and unity.[39]

TENSIONS IN GENEVA

Geneva was the nerve center of the worldwide peace movement in the interwar period. It was the home of the League of Nations and many other organizations concerned with world labor, world peace, and world religious issues. The circuitry of U.S.-Japanese relations had been wired to run between the United States, Japan, and China. But during the Manchurian Incident it also ran through Geneva, where important decision makers sat in judgment and where the world press sent more than 400 reporters during the Manchurian crisis.

The League of Nations set up an investigative body called the Lytton Commission. The commission was tasked with assessing the situation and reporting back to the League. To that end the commission traveled to Manchuria in spring 1932.

During their visit, the Japanese government, through the quasi-governmental corporation of the SMR hosted the delegates. The SMR put on a good show, both literally and figuratively. They feted the delegates and took them to see the substantial investments and sacrifices Japan had made in Manchuria. The SMR made a silent movie about the visit with captions in English that could be shown in the United States to demonstrate the progress and modernity it had created in Manchuria. A work of sophisticated propaganda, the film portrayed Japanese efforts in Manchuria in the best light. It showed the delegates being taken to the coal mines and the great iron and steel works at Anshan. The delegates saw a key battlefield of the Russo-Japanese War where the Japanese had shed their blood to gain their current position in Manchuria—a clever propaganda move to educate the delegates to their hard-won commitments in Manchuria. They were also shown the beautiful buildings and fountains the Japanese had built in the cities of Manchuria. The site of the explosion on the SMR railroad line that provoked the Japanese invasion was also part of the tour although it did not play a central role. Screenings in the United States would have bolstered the Japanese case but there is no evidence film was ever shown there.

Back in Geneva, the Japanese did far less to blunt the negative perceptions of the Manchurian Incident, and this was a mistake on their part. When they did try to soften their image, it was too late. Geneva had hardened its attitude against Japan.

Ambassador to the League Matsudaira held a reception on behalf of the Japanese delegation to the League for the press during the crisis. Only 27 out of the more than 400 journalists came and only 2 actually ate anything. A few days later, the Chinese did the same thing and 270 journalists attended.[40]

Sidney Phelps, YMCA missionary, commented on strong anti-Japanese feelings in Geneva.

> In all our travels we have found no greater misunderstanding of Japan's position or more openly expressed anti-Japanese sentiments, than we encountered among practically all groups in Geneva, including Christian organization leaders, peace society officials, League secretaries, International Labor Bureau experts and especially the press.

At meetings and dinner parties Phelps encountered strong anti-Japanese feeling and little sympathy for the Japanese position. Interestingly, Phelps met with all the major groups in Geneva and worked hard to show them the Japanese perspective: its distrust of Western nations for consistently mistreating Japan, the outrage against immigration restriction laws and outright racial discrimination against Japanese emigrants.[41]

The World's Committee of YMCAs in Geneva, chaired by W.W. Gethman, took a very strong stance against the Manchurian Incident, in opposition to the stance of American YMCA headquarters in New York which was technically noncommittal and probably leaned slightly toward Japan. John Mott, head of the American YMCA during the crisis, had a long and close relationship with several Japanese elites, such as Nitobe and Shibusawa.

In a long letter, Gethman explained their position. He noted that the committee had been warned that strong action would push the Japanese public away from liberals and into the arms of the military. However, in spite of the risks, the committee decided to condemn Japan's actions in

Manchuria. They came to the conclusion that the Manchurian Incident had severely damaged the credibility of mechanisms for peaceful resolution such as the Kellogg-Briand Pact and the League of Nations. The document referred several times to the importance of rallying public opinion to stand for peace and oppose the unilateral takeover of Manchuria by Japan. The committee wanted the Japanese and Chinese to negotiate a solution to the crisis in a multilateral manner that would include Soviet Russia and in which the League would play a mediating role. The statement was sent out to all national committees of the YMCA.[42]

The Japanese YMCA protested almost immediately. Saito Soichi the secretary general of the Japanese YMCA wrote the reply for the Japanese.

... we are constrained to express our amazement and to register our protest against the violation of what your statement so well expresses as the "restraint of precedent and constitutional practice, of recent Committee judgment and guidance." We submit that your action, no matter how great the emotional or moral constraint on your part, in appealing to leaders or constituent movements of our common brotherhood [other religious groups in Geneva] to take action "with a view to influencing public opinion and making a joint approach to your Government," whatever might be the interpretation of the purpose of such Government instructions to their respective representatives at Geneva, is a dangerous political move on your part and if applied to the equally serious and "moral" international situation could only result in the disintegration of our World Brotherhood whose helpful ministrations we so much value and desire now and for years to come.[43]

This was a powerful comment on the damage the Manchurian Incident inflicted on unofficial diplomacy between Japan and the rest of the world.

At the level of official diplomacy, the Japanese followed through on their threat to leave the League of Nations and departed in spring 1933 shortly after the publication of the Lytton Report, which was, after all the propagandizing, a fairly evenhanded assessment of the situation. Even though the editors of the Japanese LNA thought the report was evenhanded, General Araki Sadao, leader of the Imperial Way (Kodo) faction in the army, and minister of war in Japan called the report a "travelogue," and said it had no value whatsoever. The LNA in Japan changed its name to the International Association of Japan after the Japanese withdrew, to align themselves with the anti-Western tone of public opinion in Japan.[44]

A group of younger Japanese intellectuals, including Royama Masamichi and Matsumoto Shigeharu, proposed an alternate solution to the Manchurian Incident. Their plan, published in a pamphlet at the same time as the Lytton Report, recommended a transitional time of self-rule for Manchuria under the supervision of the great powers with a large role for Japan and administration by a regional office of the League of Nations in Tokyo. Although the plan was innovative in proposing a new more autonomous and regionalist approach within the League of Nations, there is no evidence that the Western powers paid any attention to it. They would have likely rejected it because it had no role for China. The Japanese government also ignored the plan and pursued their more aggressive approach to Manchuria.[45]

While Matsumoto and Royama shifted from internationalist to nationalist in the 1930s (Matsumoto took a job with *Rengo*, the government controlled news service and propaganda arm, as Shanghai's bureau chief in 1932 and both Matsumoto and Royama were a part of Konoe Fumimaro's think tank, the Breakfast Society in the late 1930s), after the war, Matsumoto and Royama and others such as Takagi Yasaka and Maeda Tamon regained their internationalism. Takagi and Matsumoto founded an American Studies Association, all these Japanese worked with internationalist organizations such as the International Labor Organization (ILO) and the United Nations (UN), and Matsumoto founded International House of Japan, a Tokyo center dedicated to foreign scholarship about Japan.[46]

JAPANESE RESPONSE

The Japanese responded in a variety of ways to the Manchurian Incident. Even though there were scattered reports of opposition to the war, the public experienced a wave of patriotism and war fever. Great crowds gathered to give enthusiastic send-offs to troops heading to the front in Manchuria. Pro-military organizations sprang up overnight around the country. The government sent out flyers asking for donations so that a volunteer force of 600,000 men could be set up to protect the homeland in case of foreign invasion.[47] A government commission recommended changing the name "Japan" to "Nippon."[48] Japan had come from Chinese usage adopted by the West and Nippon was the correct Japanese pronunciation of the Chinese characters denoting the country.

The military had become radicalized, especially the Kwantung Army. Ishiwara Kanji, one of the junior officers who planned the Manchurian Incident, critiqued the exploitation and corruption of Japanese capitalists and politicians, endorsed Japanese leadership of a Pan-Asian movement, and revered the Japanese Empire and the Imperial House. Ishiwara and other officers had been influenced heavily by the writings of Kita Ikki, a Nichiren Buddhist who asserted that the central problems for Asia were Western imperialism and capitalism. In a Marxist-Asianist fusion, Kita believed that Asians had to unite against the West. He also noted the capitalist exploitation of working peoples and believed Western influences to be responsible for this exploitation. Kita had spent much time in China and believed that Japan and China must work together to overcome the dangerous influences of the West.[49]

The popular magazine, *Hinode* interviewed twelve journalists and retired military personnel together to get their opinions about U.S.-Japanese relations. The interview was published as *Hijoji Tokuhon* (an Emergency Reader), as a supplement to its November issue. First, they made clear that the Manchurian actions had been in self-defense and therefore had not violated the Kellogg Pact or the Washington Treaties and ended by freeing Manchuria and setting up an independent state that was also no violation of the Kellogg Pact. Two interviewees argued that American intentions in the crisis were questionable and that the main aim of the United States was not enforcing the peace process but attempting to "drive Japan out of Manchuria" and getting "Manchuria under her influence," calling the Kellogg and Washington Treaties "mere diplomatic garbs."[50]

Japanese newspapers including the Tokyo *NichiNichi* and *Osaka Mainichi* vociferously defended Japanese actions in Manchuria.[51] The invasion had support from all sectors of society. Supporters were convinced that Manchuria really was Japan's lifeline as policy makers and intellectuals had been asserting for years. Even those who opposed war on principle or worried that a limited incursion in Manchuria would lead to a wider war with China supported the war effort. Liberals were forced by the pressure of public opinion to support the war. They did not like the method of brute force in Manchuria, but they genuinely believed Japan had a right to protect its interests there.

In Japan a war waged in the name of the emperor meant that opposition to the war opposed the emperor as well. This kind of opposition was very rare. The antiwar argument was not seen publicly in Japan because the government had censored it in the public media. However, one article was smuggled out of Japan and published in *The New York Times*.

The writer, Kurato Hirosa, a Marxist, was the head of the Japanese Anti-War Federation. He saw a momentous struggle for control over Japan between the liberals and militarists. If the militarists won and implemented their vision of Japanese imperialism in Asia, it would surely bring war with the United States, according to him. The liberals had failed to combine with working class parties to resist the military group. He rejected the argument made by many that Japan was simply defending itself in invading Manchuria, arguing that it was an extension of Japanese imperialist policies and gave Japan much needed access to raw materials in case of war with the United States or another Western nation.[52]

The Japanese flooded the United States and European press with other statements, articles, and speeches from unofficial diplomats to justify their case in Manchuria. Apparently, private diplomats could make the case in the media more effectively than government officials, who were implicated more directly in Manchuria. In addition, many of these unofficial diplomats had been in government previously or were well-respected on the world stage. Prominent liberals in Japan played an important role in justifying the Manchurian Incident to the West and especially the United States since they had the most positive relationships with Westerners.

A group of very prominent liberal and moderate leaders—Viscount Ishii, Baron Wakatsuki, Prince Tokugawa, Baron Sakatani, and Baron Dan Takuma of Mitsui—all signed a letter sent to the *London Times* suggesting that it was for the sake of stability in China that Japan had to act.[53] The Japanese ambassador to the United States Saito Hirosi went on a lecture tour intended to soften the American response. Prince Tokugawa toured the United States to persuade the American public of Japan's ultimately peaceful aims. The South Manchurian Railway Company did its part publishing several papers and pamphlets in English on the great progress of Manchuria and Manchukuo. Komatsu Takashi traveled to Jehol during the Japanese campaign there and then traveled to the United States to lecture at the Harvard Club about his visit. Komatsu, the chairman and founder of Komatsu Construction Equipment Manufacturing Company, later turned against Japanese aggression in China and was one of a handful of Japanese leaders who openly opposed World War II. This caused him to fall into disrepute in Japan. At war's end, he was one of the people first contacted by U.S. occupation forces seeking assistance and advice as Japan began its postwar reconstruction. Kaheki Mitsuake, a Japanese YMCA leader, was a veritable writing machine, penning four long papers on Manchuria and related subjects in English in the months after the Incident.

Notable internationalists Nitobe Inazô and Tsurumi Yusuke, and journalist K.K. Kawakami also weighed in on Manchuria. Kawakami returned to Japan in 1932 and gave a speech at the LNA. He reported that anti-Japanese feeling in the United States had increased. Kawakami completed his political evolution from antigovernment socialist to pro-Japanese propagandist by writing several books in defense of the Manchurian Incident and Sino-Japanese War: *Japan Speaks* (1932), introduced by Inukai Tsuyoshi who was the sitting prime minister at the time, *Manchukuo: Child of Conflict* (1933), and *Japan in China: Her Motives and Aims* (1938). Kawakami exemplifies in his changing perspective the path of many Westernizers and liberals within Japan who began their careers encouraging Westernization and ended by defending the actions of the Japan in Asia.[54]

Kawakami argued for moral equivalency in an article in the *Atlantic Monthly* entitled "America Teaches, Japan Learns." In a sarcastic note, Kawakami asked if it was not reasonable to assume that Japanese government officials had taken notice of American interventions in Nicaragua, Haiti, and Santo Domingo or read about the American concept of dollar diplomacy. Kawakami quoted

Theodore Roosevelt "I took the Canal Zone and let Congress debate and while the debate goes on, the Canal does also," and thought the comparison—American forces behind a Panamanian secession from Colombia and Japanese forces behind a Manchurian secession from China—to be an excellent one. Unfortunately, the reproach against American moral self-righteousness, while understandable, simply hardened American attitudes against Japan.[55]

Henry Stimson responded to the accusation by portraying the United States as a conservative force maintaining the status quo in Latin America while Japan was revolutionary in its designs for Manchuria. He relied on the scholarship of Professor George Blakeslee who wrote an article called "The Japanese Monroe Doctrine" in *Foreign Affairs* in 1933. Blakeslee announced innocently that the United States had no wish "to seize territory directly or indirectly or to assume political or economic control." He also thought the United States superior to the nations of Latin America and therefore justified in intervention, while Japan could make no such claim over China, which Blakeslee considered to be superior to Japan in some ways.[56]

In an editorial in the English-language section of the *Osaka Mainichi*, Nitobe Inazô, like Kawakami, pointed to Latin America, equating the Manchurian Invasion with the Americans in Cuba and the British in India. "There is no feeling as comfortable as that of self-righteousness. When this is combined with a sense of superiority, we reach a height from which it is easy to fall." He also defended the Emperor as a way of distinguishing a fundamental difference between Americans and Japanese.

> I am not a republican, either by party affiliation or in principle. We [Japanese] too make changes but not for their own sake—particularly, our Ruler's Family has been on the throne for at least two thousand years. We have no desire whatsoever to change it.

Nitobe, who had spent more time in the West than most Japanese, now sought to distance himself from the West.[57]

Tsurumi Yusuke visited Europe and the United States in 1932. Tsurumi spoke in Paris before the Congress of League of Nations Societies in July 1932. He asserted that before the League of Nations became involved in Manchuria, Japanese public opinion had been split. He used the same argument later in an American magazine article.[58] The problem with Tsurumi's argument is one of timing. The League had been involved since very early in the crisis. And reports from Japanese newspapers suggest that from January 1932, the public was unified on the Manchurian issue, before the Lytton Commission began investigating the incident. The other problem with this argument is that the Japanese public had expressed skepticism and even distrust of the

League of Nations at its formation, asserting that the League was a creature of European imperialist powers and therefore would stand against Japan and with the West. Tsurumi also mentioned the American immigration exclusion clause and Smoot Hawley tariff law as forcing Japan to act in Manchuria.[59]

One could conclude from Tsurumi's comments that U.S. domestic policies had in part caused the Manchurian Incident. Japan's population was hemmed in because of American and other anti-immigration laws. In addition, the Smoot-Hawley law, passed by the U.S. Congress in 1930, raised tariffs on Japan's products entering American markets. The Americans had made mistakes in dealing with Japan. On the other hand, it was not fair to put the whole blame on American policy. Tsurumi oversimplified Japanese population and economic problems. For instance, the American exclusion clause had outraged the Japanese public, but it had not driven Japanese to emigrate in large numbers to Manchuria. Less than 200,000 Japanese lived in Manchuria and settlement schemes for Manchuria regularly failed. The Smoot-Hawley tariff was condemned in Japan but did not destroy Japanese trade with the United States. In the period after it was passed, 1930–1939, Japanese trade with the United States boomed. Military activities in China created demand for American oil and scrap metal.

The most important visitor to the United States during the crisis was Nitobe Inazô. Americans considered Nitobe the foremost voice of Japanese internationalism and liberalism. He was also a Christian and intellectual. *Bushido* and his other books described the history and culture of Japan to English-speaking audiences. He has been described as a bridge between Japan and the United States. But Nitobe's reputation outside Japan told only half the story. Nitobe had long been a supporter of the Japanese Empire. He had worked in the colonial administration of Taiwan for a short time and continued to consult with the Japanese government on colonial policies as a part of his faculty position at Tokyo Imperial University. He was concerned that Western values would leave Japan's youth rudderless. When he was headmaster of the prestigious prep First Higher School, he attempted to inculcate the values of bushido and Christianity to give the young men in his charge moral grounding.[60] However, he was also considered a leader of the liberals. During the Manchurian Incident, the latter became a dangerous association. Hamaguchi, Inoue, and Dan Takuma had all been identified as leaders of the liberal camp and had been assassinated for it. Nitobe had to wonder if he was next.

In February 1932, Nitobe went into St. Luke's hospital in Tokyo for back treatment. During his stay a controversy arose concerning a speech he had given in which he stated that militarism was as great a danger as communism. The Army Reservists' Association, a rightwing group, picked up on the comment and demanded that Nitobe apologize and retract the statement. This storm was exactly the kind of incident that could result in a target being put on Nitobe's head and he knew it. Thus it was that Nitobe had to travel from his hospital sickbed to the Reservist's meeting in Tokyo, accompanied by a guard of five uniformed police officers. Before over 100 delegates, Nitobe explained that the statement had been intended to convey the menace of Chinese warlords, not the Japanese Army. Hugh Byas, who covered news in Japan for *The New York Times*, reported that the delegates then would vote to accept or reject Nitobe's apology. Apparently they accepted his apology because no attempt was made on his life.[61]

Shortly after he was released from the hospital, Nitobe traveled to the United States for nine months to plead for understanding on Manchuria. He had vowed never to visit the United States again after the immigration exclusion controversy but broke his vow now to attempt to patch up U.S.-Japanese relations by explaining Manchuria. Nitobe came as a private citizen sponsored by the IPR. He did meet with War Minister Araki Sadao before he left Japan to get an update on Japan's military policy.

Nitobe gave twenty lectures on both coasts of the United States and did two radio addresses on CBS as well.[62] A hostile audience greeted him. One Christian magazine confronted Nitobe with the headline: "The Bankruptcy of Dr. Nitobe."[63] *The New Republic* highlighted an open letter from Raymond Leslie Buell, a professor of history and author of many books. Buell played a large role in the internationalist and peace movement in the United States as the head of the FPA. Nitobe had betrayed the peace process and American faith in Japanese liberalism, according to Buell. Buell scandalized Nitobe by pointing out that he had served the League of Nations faithfully as associate secretary general for seven years but now seemed "indifferent to violations by Japan of the League Covenant and the anti-war pact." Buell's answer to the standard Japanese argument that Japan was only doing in Manchuria what the United States had done in Latin America for decades was that the United States was now cleaning up its act, moving toward a policy of nonintervention. History would show that this was a temporary change, not a long-term reorientation of American policy. Buell had supported Japanese immigrants in the debate over immigration restriction in California in 1924 and had been threatened with tar and feathers. But his life did not hang in the balance like Nitobe's. Buell had at that time "denied the assumption of the exclusionists that it was impossible to bridge the cultural and racial gulf between Orientals and Occidentals." He had more doubts about this now.[64]

Buell and other liberals were outraged because they had been "friends of Japan, not in the sense that we blindly defended the acts of the government, but that we believed Japanese individuals should be justly treated and that we had faith in the ultimate success of Japanese liberalism." He ended by suggesting that Nitobe could have kept his silence instead of endorsing the invasion of Manchuria. Perhaps this might have been an option for Nitobe under other circumstances. However, Nitobe was an opinion leader back in Japan. He had been intimately connected to the League of Nations. There was an expectation that he would have an opinion on Manchuria and the League response. Therefore, he could not hold his silence indefinitely.

While Nitobe might not have liked the military's invasion of Manchuria, he enthusiastically endorsed the creation of Manchukuo as a genuine attempt to create a more stable independent state in northeast Asia. He saw the Japanese as noble in their birth "mother" role of Manchukuo.[65] Buell ended by stating,

> In any case, I hope that before leaving this country you will give new evidence that the faith to which some of us still cling, in the ultimate triumph of liberalism in Japan (as well as in America) has not been misplaced.

Buell never got the evidence he was looking for from Nitobe.[66]

Buell's comment leaves no doubt that his faith in Japanese liberalism was an extension of his faith in American liberalism. He and many other liberals believed before the Manchurian Incident that Japan was becoming like the United States. This notion derived from a very old but still powerful idea in American life that the United States was a model for other nations. Starting with the Puritan idea of a city on a hill, Americans had assumed that theirs was an exceptional nation and a model for the rest of the world. As in the time of the Puritans, this assumption was a recipe for disappointment, and among American liberals in 1932, not just disappointment but also betrayal and disillusionment.

Nitobe's lectures focused on U.S.-Japan friendship, but his radio addresses focused most clearly on Manchuria. In one, Nitobe suggested there were three different attitudes in Japan toward the League of Nations: idealistic, cynical, and realistic. Idealistic Japanese believed in the purpose of the League to support the peace machinery and resolve conflicts. Cynics derided it as a tool of Western imperialists that should not be trusted. Realist liberals thought that though it was imperfect, the League should be supported and nurtured. Nitobe pointed out that the rejection of the racial equality clause at the Paris Peace Conference in 1919 and the U.S. refusal to join the League in the same year damaged the hopes of the idealists and emboldened the cynics. It converted some of the idealists to a more cynical position. The image of the League went from bad to worse in Japan with the Manchurian crisis. The League did not understand the situation in Manchuria, according to Nitobe. Japan had the right to take action in Manchuria because China had violated its treaties with Japan concerning Manchuria. There was no reason, therefore, for the League to be involved.[67]

The League and its friends believed just the opposite. Japan, not China had violated treaties, specifically the Washington Conference Nine Power Treaty that protected China's sovereignty and the Kellogg-Briand Pact (1928) that outlawed war. Nitobe still supported the peace treaties, but he thought they were of a theoretical or ideal nature and not practical in the world of geopolitics. Nitobe saw Japan's invasion of Manchuria as an act of survival. "For before the urge of self-preservation, all peace functions will stagger." League actions therefore did not take adequate account of Japan's situation.[68]

Nitobe believed Japan would be justified in leaving the League under these circumstances. This had to be a bitter conclusion for Nitobe who had been assistant secretary general of the League from its inception in 1920 for seven years and had helped to build its reputation. Nitobe's position was that of a Japanese subject who had been forced by events to make a choice between his internationalist leanings and his more basic connection to his nation and its empire. He clearly believed the latter to be most important.[69]

Nitobe's admiration for the United States had been tarnished by the exclusion clause. Now he, like many liberals, was embittered and disillusioned at the Americans' lack of understanding of Japan's action in Manchuria. His arguments persuaded very few Americans. Very little of the informal diplomacy that Japan engaged in during the crisis had an impact. A few years earlier informal diplomacy at the Kyoto IPR Conference had helped defuse tensions surrounding Chang Tsolin's assassination. But the arguments made at that time by Matsuoka Yôsuke that Japan was a progressive stabilizing force in Manchuria were either ignored or not emphasized during the Manchurian Incident. Instead, a defensiveness pervaded the writings and statements of Japanese unofficial diplomats. At this stage with the Japanese Army in control of Japanese foreign policy and U.S.-Japanese relations in decline, only some sort of appeal to American liberals might have strengthened support for Japan. Just as American liberals did not reach out to Japanese liberals in Japan, neither did Nitobe or other private diplomats reach out to American liberals. Instead they spoke as the voice of the Japanese nation. As a result, the perception that neither side could trust the other became more powerful.

Nitobe returned North America in fall 1933 to attend the IPR Conference in Banff. He became very ill and died shortly thereafter. In death, Nitobe was spared the continuing downward spiral of U.S.-Japanese relations in the 1930s, the Sino-Japanese War, the militarization of Japan, and the Pacific War.

Japanese informal diplomacy has been criticized for being too much in the hands of individuals such Nitobe and Tsurumi. The organizations of informal diplomacy were too weak, according to this view. Certainly there is truth to this argument.[70] However, these informal diplomats' failures in the 1930s also derived from their defense of Japan, since they were seen more often as apologists for the Japanese government and less often as independent voices.

During the Manchurian crisis, unofficial diplomats on both sides were like firemen called to the scene of a roaring inferno with equipment inadequate or too damaged to fight the blaze. As the 1930s progressed, they became spectators to the collapse of the charred ruins of U.S.-Japanese relations.

CHAPTER 9

"AMERICA IS VERY DIFFICULT TO GET ALONG WITH": ANTI-AMERICANISM, JAPANESE MILITARISM, AND SPYING, 1934–1937

THE MANCHURIAN INCIDENT DAMAGED U.S.-JAPANESE RELATIONS SEVERELY. While trust was not always a crucial issue for official diplomats, trust was a very important issue for the American and Japanese public and for the unofficial diplomats who had invested so much of themselves and their resources in healing the wounds of the 1920s, only to find in Manchuria that they no longer recognized the same ideals.

In addition, Americans and Japanese struggled with a crippling Great Depression in the 1930s. The American solution to the economic crisis had been economic nationalism: raise tariffs and refuse to participate in international monetary policies or forgive the debts owed the United States by Europe from World War I. Other nations responded by doing the same and the 1930s became characterized by declining trade and investment internationally; nations became economic islands. The growing popularity of isolationism in U.S. foreign policy accompanied economic isolation. The Japanese dealt with the Depression through autarkic military expansion in northeast Asia to gain greater control over raw materials, trade, investment, and immigration. The statement of Foreign Ministry spokesperson Amau Eiji in 1934, known thereafter as the Amau Doctrine, outlined a Japanese Monroe Doctrine in China that excluded the Western powers. Although inaccurate, the rising perception that the Americans had now closed the trade door by raising tariffs after having closed the immigration door earlier strained relations further and gave Japan a rationale for expansion.

The Japanese wondered who these Americans really were: with their professed love of liberty, yet intense racial hatred and open discrimination. In foreign affairs, Americans on the one hand seemed to exemplify the notion of fair play in their commitment to Wilsonianism, yet Wilson himself had rejected Japan's racial equality clause. The Japanese looked at America's treatment of their Latin American neighbors and criticized American self-righteousness about Manchuria. American policies seemed disconnected from their professed ideals. The United States wanted multilateral naval disarmament but only if the Japanese limits were always lower than their own. The Japanese could be forgiven their conclusion that Americans were hypocritical and untrustworthy.

In an interview with an American intelligence official in 1936, Japanese consul general of Hawai'i Tamura Teijiro summed up the Japanese perspective. Speaking of the naval tonnage disputes, American naval maneuvers in the Pacific, the continuing threat of economic blockade, and the buildup of Hawai'i as a major military base, Tamura chided, "America is very difficult to get along with."[1]

CRITIQUE OF WESTERNIZATION

The growth of anti-American attitudes was part of a much broader and deeper critique of the West unleashed after the Manchurian Incident. Criticism of Westernization among official and unofficial elites began around the turn of the century. One concern was that traditional values such as loyalty to the emperor would be undermined by Western ideas such as Christianity or individualism. Other "isms" attacked were liberalism, materialism, and socialism. Matsuoka Yôsuke had a conversion in the early 1930s to a strongly anti-Western view. An article entitled "Dissolve the Political Parties," in a new scholarly journal *Contemporary Japan*, focused on international relations. *Contemporary Japan*, published in Tokyo in English, had a small following but was respected as a serious scholarly journal. Sometimes its articles were translated into Japanese and it also ran English translations of important articles from major Japanese magazines such as *Chuo Koron* (The Central Review) and *Kaizo* (Reconstruct). Matsuoka ranted about the deleterious effects of Westernization.

The deadlock, confusion, uneasiness, and commotion that reign in every field of Japanese life are, to a very large extent, if not totally, ascribable to our indiscriminate imitation of Western civilization with its dominant colouring of liberalism, individualism, and class consciousness, all of which Westerners themselves are now deprecating.[2]

Matsuoka was talented but erratic. His talent gained him wide influence in the 1930s. His erratic behavior got him dismissed from the post of foreign minister in the summer of 1941. He was indicted for war crimes after World War II but died during his trial.

Dr. Anesaki Masaharu, Japanese professor of religions, argued that Japan's willingness to borrow from the West in strengthening itself earlier had become problematic by the 1930s. Writing for *Asia* in 1936, Anesaki stated "Japan's loss of respect for the Western nations in general has induced her to question the intrinsic values of modern civilization as a whole."[3]

The military entrenched itself among the Japanese population in the 1930s with an anti-Western propaganda campaign through radio, print media, and film. A film called "Japan in the National Emergency" was created in 1933 by the Japanese Ministry of the Army and narrated by General Araki Sadao. Araki, the army minister, a well-known advocate of Pan-Asianism, and a staunch anti-Westerner, was head of the radical Kodo faction in the army. The film portrayed the dual threats of internal Westernization and the external Western powers, opposed by loyal military service in Manchuria and within Japan by rejection of Westernization. In one dramatic scene in the film, a young Japanese girl stood outside in the cold of a Tokyo winter night selling newspapers to make extra money for her family's survival. While she dreamt of patriotic Japanese soldiers suffering for their country in Manchuria, the scene switched to a Westernized Japanese couple dancing cheek to cheek in the late night hours. Dressed in the latest fashions with jazz music blaring in the background, the couple gathered their coats and drove off into the night. In a surprising and literal collision of rampant Westernism and patriotism, the couple drove through the dark and accidentally ran over the young girl. On her death bed, the dying girl exhorted the guilty couple to greater patriotism and selflessness as they expressed deep shame. Illustrating the danger of the pleasure-filled selfishness of Western life, the film made a powerful impression.[4]

Over the summer and fall of 1933, the film was shown to commoners and elites alike all around the country. Prior to public viewing, the film was shown for the Imperial Family on May 29 and at the military headquarters on June 1. It was shown twice at the Osaka Omisuji Gasu (Gas Building Auditorium), where over 1,000 people from the city, executives, youth groups, and Aikoku Fujinkai (patriotic women's group) viewed it. The film warranted a write-up in the journal *Katsuei*, published by the *Osaka Mainichi*. Notably, the film did not contrast ancient Japanese traditions and modernity in the way that Americans thought of Japan, but different versions of modernity: a corrupted selfish modernity of the West versus a patriotic nationalist modernity that bound the nation more strongly together. Stereotypes about patriotic Japan became fodder for political propaganda in both the United States and Japan in the 1930s, the Americans emphasizing the rising dangers of Japanese nationalism and the Japanese pointing to the virtue of it.[5]

Worse yet, the Japanese began to lose faith in the power of public opinion and unofficial diplomacy. According to Consul General Tamura,

> There was a time when Japan and her people cared what America thought . . . now the temper of the Japanese is so that they don't care what anyone thinks and are through explaining. If the time comes to fight, then Japan will fight, the odds be what they may. (Sat straight in chair and slapped desk.) We are going to pursue our course as we see it. Several years ago when I was on duty in Chicago, an American advertising agency with headquarters in New York and offices in Chicago and in San Francisco approached me on an advertising campaign idea to build good will. I thought it was a good idea and got the Japanese Tea Association to sponsor it. It may have done some good but now it wouldn't.[6]

In a lecture before the Toyo Kyokai (Oriental Association), a conservative think tank that lobbied for colonial expansion, Honda Kumataro, former ambassador to Germany, criticized unofficial diplomacy saying that the Japanese should not send unofficial diplomats to the United States as in previous years. Instead, the Japanese should send official diplomats to negotiate directly with the U.S. government. If that did not work, then Japan's military power would speak for the nation. Honda also criticized the American naval buildup and encouraged the Japanese to build a navy that could protect it in the western Pacific.[7]

The Japan Times reported that unofficial good will missions between the two countries were no longer effective concerning a visit of a Japanese naval training squadron to the United States. It praised the official visit of the squadron as a better way to improve relations than the unofficial diplomacy of previous years.[8]

Even Takagi Yasaka, a young professor of American studies at Tokyo Imperial University who was active in the JCIPR, became skeptical about the efficacy of private diplomacy. In a speech to an American Phi Beta Kappa Honor Society in 1935, Takagi described the current period as one of "rampant nationalism," in contrast to the years immediately after World War I that were more internationalist. While Takagi still had faith that "personal friendship" could resolve the problems of the Pacific, he believed that peace without justice was dangerous and took the view that the Japanese needed guarantees of security and justice before they would consider negotiating a settlement in the Pacific. Clearly, Takagi, a former Westernizer, had been affected by the threat consciousness created by the military in the 1930s.[9]

By mid-decade, anti-Western sentiment created a revolution in Japan. The military used anti-Western rhetoric to dominate politics. Japanese liberals like Takagi agreed with militarists that the empire had to be secured. They came under intense pressure to conform to popular opinion in the 1930s. In line with the rest of Japan, they began to see a more threatening West. The army steadily expanded its influence in China. In 1935 Japan withdrew from the London Naval Conference and abandoned the naval tonnage limits of the Washington and London Conferences. Japan embarked on a shipbuilding program thereafter, marking further alienation from the West.

In 1934 prominent Japanese leaders such as Prince Konoe Fumimaro, Prince Tokugawa Iyesato, Viscount Ishii Kikujiro, and Marquis Tokugawa Yorisada founded Kokusai Bunka Shinkokai (The Society for International Cultural Relations) to reorient Japan's approach to internationalism. In tandem with its expanding cultural influence in on the Asian mainland, the Society sought to promote Japanese culture internationally, not Westernization at home. Most of its efforts were focused on educating foreigners about traditional Japanese culture and providing resources and a forum for the study of Japanese culture. Its founding document stated that the Society was organized for the purpose of "dissemination of correct knowledge about the culture of Japan . . ." This implied that foreigners were getting the wrong impression, a negative image based upon Japan's military intrusion into northeast Asia. On a track parallel to Japan's military expansion, the Society had the goal of expanding Japan's culture. The Society linked up with other organizations elsewhere such as the America-Japan Society, the Japan British Society, and the Deutche-Japanische Kultur-Gesellschaft. It sponsored a journal in English that was a clearinghouse of activities related to scholarly research and cultural exchange. It also established culture centers devoted to spreading knowledge about Japanese culture in several major cities including Berlin and New York City.[10]

MILITARY OVERREACH AND THE RESURGENCE OF LIBERALISM

Two events in Japan marked the changing political landscape for Japanese liberalism in the mid 1930s. The trial of Minobe Tatsukichi on charges of lese-majeste and Minobe's expression of remorse and subsequent resignation from the House of Peers put more pressure on liberals in Japan to turn toward the military. On the other hand, the February 26, 1936 attempted coup d'état by right-wing military officers put the military on the defensive and therefore seemed to provide an opening for liberals to retake power in Japan.

Minobe Tatsukichi, a professor at Tokyo Imperial University, was a respected constitutional scholar in Japan. His emperor organ theory of the Japanese constitution grew in popularity in the Taisho and early Showa periods (1912–1930). Arguing that the emperor was one organ of Japan's body politic, Minobe aligned Japanese political theory with Western political scientists who saw the political state as a juridical person who embodied sovereignty. However, Minobe's theories put him at odds with the kokutai (emperor system) interpretation of the emperor's role. Conservative theorists argued the emperor was more than just one organ of the political body. The emperor, according to them, embodied the entire body politic through his unbroken lineage and his divinity. Therefore sovereignty lay with the emperor alone, not with the state or the Japanese people. Even though Minobe's theories were by no means radical and had been widely accepted only a few years earlier, by 1935 the political climate of Japan had become intolerant, and Minobe's theories looked like a threat to the emperor system. One of the most powerful military groups in the country, the Military Reserve Association initiated the attack. Minobe was also attacked in the House of Peers, of which he was a member, and House of Representatives. Both adopted resolutions instructing the government to censor the organ theory. He was forced to resign from the House of Peers and in return, the lawsuit by a MP against him for lese-majeste (treason) was dropped.

The Minobe case forced many liberals into political hiding. Although they had been in retreat ever since the Manchurian Incident, the Minobe case showed that even out of power, liberals were threatened at the level of ideology with political persecution and possible legal prosecution by military and right-wing organizations.

Not all suffered from their association with Minobe's organ theory. An elder statesman, Baron Ikki Kitokuro, who was very powerful politically, had put forward the emperor organ theory in response to conservative arguments in the late Meiji period (1900–1912) even before Minobe's interpretation. Ikki had just been appointed president of the Japanese Privy Council, a powerful council of elder statesmen that advised the emperor on policy matters. He suffered no damaging political repercussions even though the military insisted that all government officials who endorsed the organ theory must be dismissed.[11] This indicated that Japan was not completely under the yoke of the military. One could also point to Ozaki Yukio, the longest serving MP, a staunch believer in constitutional government, and great critic of expenditures for the military. He boldly criticized government spending on the military and the suppression of free speech. Of course Ozaki was uniquely fearless. He knew that his inflammatory words put his life in constant danger. He traveled with an armed bodyguard.[12]

February 26, 1936 dawned cold and snowy in Tokyo. In the first hours of the day, 1,400 Japanese troops loyal to the Imperial Way (Kodo) faction left their barracks with the intention of assassinating leaders and taking over the political institutions of central Tokyo. A coup had begun. Several top politicians were on their assassination list: The Prime Minister Okada Keisuke, Finance Minister Takahashi Korekiyo, Genro Saionji Kinmochi (later taken off the list), Lord Keeper of the Privy Seal Viscount Saito Makoto, Chief Chamberlain Admiral Suzuki Kantaro, and Count Makino Nobuaki, former keeper of the Privy Seal.[13]

The strategic goal was to kill enough of those in power around the emperor to gain control over the Imperial family and therefore the political system. The plotters were also motivated by the court martial trial of Colonel Aizawa, a right-wing army officer who had assassinated an army general in 1935. The trial generated popular support for the Kodo faction and encouraged the coup plotters to act. Ideologically, they were restorationists, believing that those who surrounded the emperor usurped his power and therefore were traitors to the country. The Manifesto of the Uprising mentioned the Minobe incident obliquely, referring to "traitorous scholars . . ." and noted that foreign relations with the United States and other nations were so strained that at any moment war could break out. Declaring that the nation was in "a crucial moment of dangers from within and from without," the rebels acted to save the nation by restoring the emperor.[14]

The coup killed only Takahashi, Saito, and Watanabe. The other three escaped mostly because of the ineptness of the rebels. In a case of mistaken identity, the troops thought they assassinated the prime minister when they had killed his brother-in-law. He later escaped disguised hidden in a group of mourners for his brother-in-law. In the early stages of the coup, the emperor and his representatives led the plotters to believe they had succeeded. However, by the third day, they took a hard-line and the rest of the army backed the emperor's position. The regular army moved in, the rebellious regiments returned to their barracks, some of leaders committed suicide, and the failed coup ended with relatively little bloodshed.[15]

The February 26 Incident, as it became known, rocked the Japanese political system. The army purged itself of the Imperial Way (Kodo) faction including prominent leaders such as General Araki Sadao. Prime Minister Okada escaped death but he and his cabinet eventually resigned.

In the aftermath, there was some evidence to support the hope that liberalism was making a comeback in Japan. A scant week before the February 26 Incident, the general election revealed new strength for moderates and liberals.

Tsurumi Yusuke interpreted the election and the suppression of the coup as victories for liberals in Japan. In a speech at Chatham House in London on October 1, 1936, Tsurumi suggested liberals now had the opportunity to regain power if they could convince the outside world to grant access to the raw materials Japan needed to support its economy. This would help liberals to address Japan's lack of access to world resources and markets that had fueled its depression and support for the militarists.[16]

Tsurumi was peppered with questions in the discussion after his speech. One member of the audience, Freda Utley, a Marxist who wrote on Japan, took Tsurumi to task on his definition of liberalism. Tsurumi equated liberals with those who supported constitutional government in Japan and opposed the militarists. Utley claimed that under Tsurumi's definition of liberalism, "there was not much difference between national and liberal opinion in Japan." Both supported Japanese imperialism abroad and emperor at home. Utley also suggested that the Minobe case had shown liberalism to be a hollow shell in Japan, because no one had dared to come forward to speak in defense of Minobe. Tsurumi defended Japanese liberals, saying that they did in fact support the right of the individual's liberty of thought. But Utley's critique had laid bare unpleasant truths.[17]

After the coup attempt, older leaders in parliament spoke out with new boldness against the military dominance of government. Saito Takao, Hamada Kunimatsu, and Ozaki Yukio all denounced the military's power and insatiable need for more money (military expenditures took half of the Japanese national budget in the 1930s). Of these leaders, only Ozaki was associated with liberals. Even though they had different views on politics, they could agree that military control over the government was making the political parties and the Japanese Diet (parliament) irrelevant.

During parliamentary debates, Hamada accused the military of exaggerating the threats faced by Japan in the international world to bolster evidence for huge budget increases. Speaking from the podium in the presence of War Minister Terauchi, he accused the military of promoting a fascist state. Terauchi responded by accusing Hamada of insulting the army. Hamada rose to cheers and stated "What part of my speech is insulting? I shall examine the record and if I find . . . anything offensive I will apologize by committing hara-kiri. If you don't find those insulting words, you commit suicide yourself." Terauchi backed down from his accusation and the confrontation caused the Hirota cabinet to fall.[18]

Ozaki Yukio also spoke out against the militarism of Japan in parliament, at one point lampooning the army by saying that in neighborhoods and households across Tokyo, dominating and unpleasant personalities were referred to as "army" while people who did their duties properly and pleasantly were called "navy."[19]

Japanese Christian socialist and labor leader Kagawa Toyohiko became a supporter of the international peace movement and an opponent of militarism in Japan in the 1930s. Kagawa traveled to the United States several times in the 1930s. In some ways Kagawa took the esteemed place Nitobe Inazô had occupied among American Christians and peace activists. During a 1935–1936 speaking tour in the United States, Kagawa reportedly reached 750,000 Americans in 150 cities. Kagawa had led a life of service to the poor in the slums of Kobe and choose to live his own life in poverty. He was said to sleep only two or three hours a night, was ill with cancer, and almost worked himself to death several times. This sacrificial image had great power with American Christians sympathetic to Japan. Some called him a Japanese "Gandhi." He also was a prolific writer producing many novels and other works, some of which were bestsellers, translated into English, and read by Americans. Thus, his appeal in the United States was very great.[20]

In a speech Kagawa made in Washington, DC on January 18, 1936, he responded to the basic questions of the U.S.-Japan relationship by denouncing war in general, dismissing the militarists as comparable to mosquitoes, pointing out that the Japanese had been well-tutored in imperialism by Western nations' actions, suggesting that real friendship still existed between the United States and Japan, and arguing that the real problems of the world were economic: the unchristian and unjust exploitation of workers by capitalists. Neither capitalist nor communist, Kagawa was a proponent of buying and selling cooperatives. He started a cooperative movement in Japan and was famous worldwide for his support for cooperatives.[21]

Kagawa's influence on U.S.-Japanese relations, however, was hampered by the exulted position he occupied in the United States. Having been placed upon a pedestal for his commitment to the poor, Kagawa became known as an eastern mystic in the 1930s, according to historian Robert Shildgen. He played this role well. Because his trips were "goodwill" tours, Kagawa ignored the issues that had led to rising tensions between the United States and Japan such as the exclusion clause and the Manchurian Incident. Neither was Kagawa's denial of Japanese militarism very helpful at home or abroad.[22]

American liberals were buoyed by the Japanese electoral victories and saw the February 26 Incident as a turning point that would discredit the military and bring liberals back into power. An article in *The Christian Century* written immediately after the Incident stated,

> However, that the pretensions of the military extremists have received a damaging blow seems beyond question . . . the revelation of the split within the army will encourage all the non-militaristic elements inside Japan to renew the campaign for genuine constitutional government.[23]

Not only would liberals soon be back in power but there was also some confidence that the Japanese government would soon resolve its tensions with China and put the relationship on a stable diplomatic footing. In May 1937, *The Christian Century* reported in its editorial pages that Japanese policy toward China was undergoing a major shift. Noting that Russia looked more powerful in East Asia and China had become unified under Chiang Kaishek, the writer was convinced that the Japanese were moving to form a constructive working relationship with China. A backlash against the military had set in and Manchuria was not helping the economy like the public had been led to believe it would, according to editorials in the *Osaka Mainichi* and the Tokyo *NichiNichi* cited by *The Christian Century*. The editorial concluded,

> but the most important development in the Far East is the fact that Japan itself has changed its mind. The imperialistic thought characteristic of the entire period between the war with Russia and the invasion of Inner Mongolia has begun to pass into eclipse.

It is not surprising that much of the evidence for a renewal of liberalism came from The *Christian Century* and other Christian sources. The foundation for the liberal view of Japan lay with missionaries and other Christians. The view that Japan was back on the path of progress and modernity gained ground among this group in 1936–1937.[24]

In July 1937, the very month when Japan proved its militarism by invading China, Galen Fisher, former head of missionaries to the Japanese YMCA, wrote that the militarists were on the defensive and liberals were recovering. Fisher traveled to Japan in spring 1937 and reported his assessment of the situation in a new small circulation journal called *Amerasia*. Fisher found a very negative attitude among the population toward military governance. The military assessment of the need for Manchuria had been overblown and aggression in China had sown distrust rather than progress.[25]

Fisher concluded the liberals had turned the tide against the militarists. He could not have been more wrong. Three months after his visit, Japan had entered war with China and was moving toward martial law and industrial mobilization at home to fight the war.[26]

Hope for the resurgence of liberalism rested not only with informal diplomats. Joseph Grew, American ambassador to Japan from 1932 to 1942, remained convinced until the actual outbreak of the Sino-Japanese War in 1937 that Japanese liberals and moderates would carry the day. Grew never learned the Japanese language and spent much of his time with a small group of highly influential moderate politicians such as Count Makino Nobuaki and others. Makino believed Japan experienced a pendulum history swinging from left to right and then back again. Accordingly, by the mid 1930s the pendulum was close to swinging back toward the liberals. In late 1935, shortly before the February 26 Incident, another court official Kabayama Aisuke assured Grew that the moderates had taken control under the Okada Keisuke cabinet. Grew wired back to the State Department that "the moderates have gained the upper hand."[27]

Earlier in 1935, John Mott, the former head of the American YMCA, traveled to Japan. Mott's first trip to Japan was in 1896 and he returned for a final visit in 1949, when he visited with Emperor Hirohito for an hour. As the foremost American informal diplomat of the prewar period, Mott had traveled the world many times over. Though his was missionary work, he was a very worldly missionary leader. When Mott stated his confidence after the visit that U.S.-Japanese relations were on solid footing, it was an expression of his faith in informal diplomacy. He stated "personal contacts between our peoples continue greatly to multiply and the network of personal friendship is strengthening from year to year." Mott's optimistic comments appeared despite evidence the Manchurian Incident had damaged personal friendships and the network of informal contacts between Japan and the United States. He expressed hope in the work of Christians on both sides and in the international machinery of peace. "The real America and the real Japan are peace-making, and their influence is destined to become greater."[28]

Not all Americans saw the collapse of the February 26 coup as the beginning of the revival of Japanese liberalism. Many remained suspicious of Japan.

Edgar Snow, an intrepid American journalist stationed in China who was allowed to meet with Mao Zedong at his camp in Ya'nan in western China, wrote of the February 26 Incident in the popular *Saturday Evening Post*. "With this murderous event collapsed the last comfort of Western sentimentalists who had fondly imagined that an awakening would occur in which liberals and Christians would seize power . . ." Snow believed that the period before the Manchurian Incident had not been a genuine exploration of liberalism and democracy but merely a "breathing spell" before the tumult.[29]

Harold Quigley, a political scientist at the University of Minnesota, published an article on the February 26 Incident entitled "Feudalism Reappears in Japan," in the *Christian Science Monitor Magazine* shortly after the event. Quigley published widely on East Asian politics and his recent book, *Japanese Government and Politics* (1932) asserted that the Japanese were moving toward a British model of parliamentary democracy. Much had changed since Quigley researched his book in the late 1920s. Instead of seeing progress for Japan, Quigley now connected the Japanese political system to Japanese feudalism. Arguing that the actions of coup plotters "must be judged in relation to the circumstances in which they occur," Quigley then stretched the circumstances considerably, suggesting the events of February 26 were the result of a 1,000 year old feudal spirit that was still strong in Japan. In reality, the February 26 Incident is better understood in the context of the impoverished economic circumstances of Japan in the 1930s, the cultural crisis of Westernization, the rise of militarism, and conservative renovationist response.[30]

Quigley understood the structure of the Japanese political system but suffered from the same Orientalist views as we have seen from many American commentators. After admitting "The constitution of Japan is like all constitutions . . . largely unwritten," Quigley singled out the Japanese constitution for abuse.

> The decade of party Cabinets from the rise of Hara to the death of Inukai did not, it is clear, establish a purer politics. It is a striking fact that 50 years of pseudo-constitutionalism have left Japanese liberals utterly destitute of leadership.[31]

Another book published immediately before the February 26 Incident, *The Problem of the Far East* (1935), agreed with Quigley. Suggesting that Japan had not yet gone fascist, the authors nonetheless concluded:

> The feudal traditions of loyalty and acceptance of authority have acted as reinforcement of the newly imported capitalist system originally based on entirely different traditions, and the critic of the social foundation in Japan is commonly regarded as a traitor or a rebel. The introduction of the superficial mechanism of democracy has not changed this. The dialectics of democracy can be handled by Japanese politicians with some skill and much enthusiasm. But the authoritarian tradition has always been so strong that the very releases which democratic systems gave have never really been regarded as anything more than an opportunity to extract something from authority. Much has been heard of the corruption of Japanese parliamentary politics. Whether that corruption has been any greater than elsewhere is open to question. But in any case, it can be traced to the fact that the idea of political responsibility has never really caught on in Japan.[32]

Ozaki Yukio and other courageous elder statesmen who risked their lives to denounce the army after the February 26 Incident would surely have stood to object to this and Quigley's distortion.

Winston Churchill, famous British patrician, parliamentarian, and soon to be prime minister, wrote of the rise of the Japanese Empire for the popular American magazine *Collier's* in early 1937. Suggesting that the Japanese were committed to world domination, Churchill emphasized the divergence of Japan and the Western democracies.

> We are therefore confronted with the spectacle of a great nation, equipped with all the apparatus of modern industrialism and the complete armory of

mechanized war, which is in spirit as far removed from the West, whose technical achievements it has copied, as are the Middle Ages from our own.

Like so many other commentators, he linked Japan's actions to its cultural values. "They worship at other shrines; profess another creed; observe a different code. They can no more be moved by Christian pacifism than wolves by the bleating of sheep. We have to deal with a people whose values are in many respects altogether different from our own."[33]

Upton Close's book *Challenge: Behind the Face of Japan*, (1934) published by a major press Farrar & Rhinehart also argued the Japanese were committed to world domination. Both Churchill and Close gave statements of Japanese militarists as evidence. Their mistake was in taking that rhetoric at face value. With a social and political system in the throes of crisis and conflict, and an army ambitious but strained by the task of its activities in China, it was a mistake to take the Japanese seriously on the charge of world domination. Close mentioned the supposedly all-powerful Black Dragon Society (Kokuryukai), sometimes known as the Amur River Society, in connection with a possible Japanese attack on the Panama Canal, which though not true, added an element of danger and excitement. Close's book was later serialized in the *Reader's Digest* and reached a large audience.[34]

The *Reader's Digest* published another article on Japan in its November 1936 issue. Starting with the Japanese past, the writer collapsed all of Japanese history into an Orientalist prelude to industrialization.

> A short 40 years ago the synonym for Japanese was Quaint. They were odd little yellow people who lived in odd little paper houses and bowed odd little grinning bows in odd little silk kimonos, full of such notions as that blowing the nose was a breach of manners, but the reverberation of a belch an exquisite compliment to the richness of the repast. Their country was a kind of Rip van Winkle–Sleeping Princess awakened from centuries of enchanted make-believe, and their efforts to get the cherry blossoms out of their eyes were deliciously funny—so funny that they made you think of Gilbert and Sullivan.[35]

The rest of the article was mostly taken up with discussion of the phenomenal achievement of Japanese industrialism, especially the new competitive edge Japan had gained in textiles. Contrary to the overarching Orientalism that informed its introduction, the article's description of the details of Japanese industrial life were interesting, at least somewhat accurate, and at times downright sympathetic. However, its summarizing comments were the most problematic.

> How long can one century be kept alive within another in the same country, so that a man looking sidewise from his car into the farmhouse where a woman

sits at work looks not only into that house but backward hundreds of years into history as well? . . . For centuries loyalty, not thought, has been the crown of the peasant's life. Freedom to think for himself had no place in such a world. The few who today do think have no chance.[36]

At this point the article turned ominous, mentioning propaganda, censorship, and police terror as effective in keeping the population under control. However, a simple question comes to mind. If the Japanese specialized in "loyalty, not thought," then why did the government need to censor and propagandize its population? Loyal docility surely was its own reward.

The February 26 Incident did not result in Japanese liberals retaking power. Both American and Japanese liberals overestimated the impact of it. Instead of catalyzing liberals, the Incident gave legitimacy to moderates in the military. They did a thoroughgoing purge of radicals and thereby made their case for continuing power. The political narrative remained unchanged. The politicians, through corruption and weakness, had damaged Japan at home and abroad. The rebels were misguided but genuine patriots. The *Osaka Mainichi* and the *Tokyo NichiNichi* asked a question that hinted the problems of the political parties were far from over. "Wherein were the causes and reasons for the sincere young officers being driven to action by their sense of patriotism?"[37]

SPYING

By the time of the Pearl Harbor attack, Americans and Japanese had been spying on each other for several years. This is the impression gained from constant reports in the late 1930s of suspicions or actual incidents of spying. In truth, there are relatively few actual documented cases of private citizens spying in the 1930s. The most famous is that of Moe Berg, a professional baseball catcher. He was sent along with Babe Ruth, Lou Gehrig, and other major league all-stars to play goodwill games in Japan. Berg was a mediocre catcher but very intelligent. He knew Japanese along with several other languages. One day Berg visited St. Luke's hospital, one of Tokyo's tallest buildings, ostensibly there to see the daughter of Ambassador Joseph Grew who had just given birth. Berg never saw Grew's daughter. Instead he went to the roof, pulled a movie camera from under his kimono and proceeded to film the surrounding neighborhoods. The film he took was subsequently used during World War II to map Tokyo for the bombing campaigns against it in April 1945.

Both sides had military attachés located in embassies and consulates who were responsible for gaining intelligence and reporting their findings. While Americans suspected the local Japanese population of spying in Hawai'i, it was not Japanese residents of Oahu but Yoshikawa Takeo, a trained intelligence officer with the Japanese consulate in Honolulu, who gave the Japanese Navy the exact location of the ships to bomb Pearl Harbor.

Charlie Chaplin, the famous comic actor, became very popular in Japan in the interwar period. Japanese identified strongly with Chaplin's melancholy, according to Hiroyuki Ono, an authority on Chaplin. Chaplin hired Japanese immigrant Kono Toraichi to be his driver in 1916. Kono became a close confident of Chaplin and helped to cultivate Chaplin's interest in Japan, arranging for Chaplin's first visit there in 1932. Shortly afterward, Chaplin fired Kono and in 1934 the FBI arrested him on suspicion of espionage. He was released at the time but was quickly interned after Pearl Harbor, spending the war years running the film projector at an internment camp as he had done for Chaplin. Kono had signed a confession of guilt while in custody but there is no other evidence to prove he was actually a spy.[38]

In another incident, an American company National City Bank in Tokyo was accused of spying for the American government when it ordered its branch offices in Japan to take pictures of their buildings for use in promotional advertising. A military policeman observed the picture-taking in Tokyo and reported it to the Japanese press. Soon after articles appeared in all the major newspapers suggesting the photos could be used in an air raid on Tokyo. The press reported that Americans had also taken pictures at a military arsenal, third division headquarters, and the telegraph and telephone offices in Nagoya. The Bank denied this and wanted an official apology. Ambassador Grew was called in but declined to get involved for fear that the incident might get blown out of proportion, instead asking a military attaché to intervene. The attaché met with several Japanese government press officials but they refused to issue an apology.[39]

Bracketed by these erroneous reports from both sides were several other incidents that brought suspicions of spying. There were numerous reports of suspicious looking Japanese fishing vessels in Hawai'i, in the Aleutians, and closer to mainland United States, one reportedly off the coast of Los Angeles.[40]

In the same year two innocent-looking Japanese-American Eagle Scouts, who grew up in Los Angeles, left the United States and traveled to Japan as a part of a special program sponsored by the Japanese government. After three years of education in Japan to foster better U.S.-Japan relations, they would return to the United States. The American naval intelligence officer who filed the report noted that the way the boys were chosen, by a Japanese naval officer instead of by a consulate official, seemed suspicious. Nothing came of these reports.[41]

An even more extraordinary tale was told by the American consulate general in Vancouver, British Columbia, John K. Davis, in 1934. A phone caller instructed him to take down several names and told of a plot to embroil the Americans in a conflict between the Japanese and the Russians. The caller claimed that Soviet Russia was on the verge of attacking the Japanese in Manchuria and had sent several agent provocateurs to blow up Japanese ships in Vancouver and have it blamed on the Americans. Andre Kavolsky was the supposed leader of this mysterious spy ring. No ships were blown up and the caller was never heard from again.[42]

Two reports of American misdeeds came from Tsingtao China. One American, Mr. A.L. Carson was arrested by the Japanese Army and accused of spying for the United States. In another case an American woman, Mrs. Massie, was detained by Japanese sentries but later released. The incident was an apparent misunderstanding brought on by inability to communicate in a common language.[43] Reporting and in some cases publicizing these suspicions, Americans and Japanese showed their deepening paranoia and distrust for each other.

MINER SEARLE BATES IN CHINA

Amidst all these reports in the public eye, one instance of intelligence gathering by a private citizen in this period was never made public. Miner Searle Bates, who is best remembered as a witness at the Tokyo War Crimes Tribunal in 1946 for his first hand experiences of the Nanjing Massacre in November 1937, received his Ph.D. in Chinese history at Yale University and was an American missionary and history professor at Nanjing University between 1920 and 1950.[44]

Having traveled to Japan often and studied its history, Bates was an expert on Japan as well. Bates offered courses on Japanese and Chinese history at Nanjing University. His first Japanese history course, offered in 1923, did not enroll a single student. Thereafter he was able to get enough enrollments to offer the Japan course but it was never his most popular course.[45] He convinced a bright Chinese student from his Japanese history class to write a text about the story of Japan's modernization in the Chinese language. It was the first book of its kind in China and Bates used it in his Japan course for many years. This experience and other observations demonstrated how disinterested and uninformed the Chinese were about Japan. Bates' later work researching Japan owed its motivation to his conclusion that the Chinese lacked basic knowledge about Japan.

Gathering data for reports as he traveled, Bates made three trips to Japan between 1935 and 1936 and four more later on. Although he was never in the employ of the Chinese or American government and therefore not a formal spy, his reports were used by both governments and represented some of the most comprehensive and astute intelligence available on Japan in the mid 1930s. He also prepared recommendations for action directed at

Chinese government leaders on two separate occasions. Bates worked for the Presbyterian missionary organization and so he occupied an important position in China in the prewar period. American missionaries exerted a powerful influence in China and on American attitudes toward China back in the United States. As a history professor at Nanjing University, he also had access to Chinese academics and the wider political world in Nanjing, which was the political capital of China in the 1930s.

Bates' research began when a group of American missionaries and Chinese Christians in Nanjing and Shanghai (Nanjing group) met in 1935 and decided that they should attempt to influence Chinese policy toward Japan. The missionaries believed sound information and informal diplomacy could improve formal diplomatic relations and prevent conflict. Before Bates' first trip, the group set forth a memorandum directed at the Chinese government's policy towards Japan. Written from the Chinese perspective, the memorandum used the terms "our Government" and "our own officials" to set the interests and identification of the writers (as the leading expert on Japan in the group Bates was the lead writer of the memorandum) with the Chinese people.[46]

The Nanjing group argued that the Chinese government should stop appeasing Japan with concessions and begin to take the initiative by negotiating in a vigorous manner to gain better trade terms, arrange for joint economic ventures in North China and exchange experts on economic and technical matters. Recognizing that Japanese control of Northeast China was unavoidable, the memorandum also recommended recognition of Manchukuo. The authors asserted that Chinese leadership should hold the line against Japanese interference in internal administration, control over natural resources, restrictions on normal economic ties and other relations with other countries. China should agree to joint military operations with the Japanese against the communists. Although the Chinese government did not implement the main recommendation of initiating negotiations with Japan, there is little doubt that this report was reviewed by Chinese government officials.[47]

A second memorandum from the Nanjing group, written later and intended only for private citizens, emphasized the importance of informal diplomacy between Chinese and Japanese. The document identified four areas that could be used to bring about improvement in Sino-Japanese cultural diplomacy. First, Chinese visiting Japan should be given contacts of Japanese and missionaries in Japan who could set up meetings and exchanges for them during their stay. Second, Chinese in Japan—the largest contingent Chinese students attending Japanese universities (8,000 students in Tokyo alone)— should be introduced to people and organizations through which acquaintances and friendships could be developed. Third, individuals with contacts in Japan should write to them about conditions and events in China to educate the Japanese about China. The writers realized that the documents would be subject to censorship but some material might get through. Finally, correspondence between organizations in China and Japan might help the flow of communication and information as well.[48] This effort at informal diplomacy was largely ineffective however. Informal contacts between Japan and China declined in the late 1930s.

Bates' first trip to Japan in 1936 was sponsored by the Nanjing group and funded partially by the Fellowship of Reconciliation (founded in 1919 in Europe and committed to world peace). The trip lasted for approximately one month. Meeting with people from the moment he reached Japan, Bates talked with thirty-four Japanese, forty-six missionaries, and nine other foreigners at Kobe College, Kwansei University, and Doshisha University among other venues. He met with Arita Hachiro, ambassador to China who later became minister of foreign affairs, radical leaders, Diet members, the International Relations Association, editors from *NichiNichi* and *Asahi*, student workers, professors of ethics, philosophy, law and constitutional history, the Kagawa Toyohiko organization, an American diplomat, and foreign correspondent Hugh Byas. Not only was Bates gathering data but he also tried to represent the Chinese perspective whenever he could.[49]

Bates' report on Japan was dark. He saw great conformity in Japanese attitudes toward China. Propagandistic education and censorship maintained this conformity and encouraged "extreme nationalism." The Japanese were not getting accurate information about China either. A newspaper editor from *NichiNichi* admitted that his newspaper rarely took government press releases at face value and always tried to confirm the veracity of them through sources in China. The telegrams of correspondents were censored as well so getting accurate information about China was difficult.[50]

Bates also wrote a separate policy report for the Chinese government. Analyzing the temper of the Japanese public, Bates believed that in spite of propaganda and censorship, public opinion was less than totally hard-line on China. A firmer approach mixed with compromise with the Japanese could yield some Japanese compromises.

Another document written by Bates was entitled "PLEASE DESTROY THIS SHEET AFTER MAKING ANY CAUTIOUS NOTES YOU MAY DESIRE TO KEEP," which indicated the delicate nature of Bates' trip to Japan. Bates understood he could be accused of spying. The document contained a list of contacts in Japan and the names of those missionaries in China who had copies of the list. Not only were these individuals in China who held the list potentially in danger but the Japanese contacts, if revealed, might also be in trouble.[51]

Bates included in his intelligence report the state of public opinion and media, attitudes toward China, the economy, the parliament, the Foreign Office, the influence of the army, the liberals, the radicals, Christians in Japan, women, international societies, education, and predictions on the future policy of Japan in China.[52] Some of his reports were translated into Chinese by a colleague at Nanjing University, Dr. Ma Po-an, for distribution among Chinese leaders. Dr. Ma also accompanied him on a visit to Japan in early 1937.

Encouraged to publish an article on his findings in the United States by Harold Timperley, a British newspaper correspondent in Shanghai, Bates sent an article summarizing his findings on Sino-Japanese tensions to The *New York Times Magazine* in early 1937. Given the high stakes of Bates' activities, it is not surprising that he decided not to use his own name. He chose a pseudonym that combined the first names of his sons, Robert and Morton into Robert Searle Morton. The article, at first rejected by the *Times*, made its way to government circles and was picked up and read by State Department officials. A different version was later published in the journal, *Pacific Affairs*, in September 1937 and a year after that an abridged version appeared in *Reader's Digest*. In addition to a summary of his research, Bates noted the great chasm between Chinese and Japanese opinion on almost all aspects of Japan's activities in China.

Bates sounded a mild hope for the future, arguing that in spite of the gulf of opinion, there were "still some men in Japan and China who have enough intelligence and faith to desire a genuine peace and honest neighborliness between the two nations."[53] He also ventured a prescient opinion that Japan's expansionism would eventually fail because the peoples it conquered were unwilling and its own people did not understand them very well.[54]

"A CERTAIN PRESENTIMENT OF FATAL DANGER": THE SINO-JAPANESE WAR AND U.S.-JAPANESE RELATIONS, 1937–1939

BETWEEN 1935 AND 1937, THE KWANTUNG ARMY PUSHED SOUTH OF THE GREAT Wall of China into the area just north of Beijing. In the midst of training exercises on a July night in 1937, the Chinese Eighth Army ran into the Kwantung Army at Marco Polo Bridge at the northern edge of the city. The skirmish that ensued marked the beginning of World War II in Asia.

The Japanese government attempted to negotiate a local settlement of the dispute as they had in so many other instances. This time, however, the Chinese decided to treat the incident more aggressively and brought in reinforcements. The Japanese Army responded by ordering their own reinforcements. A full-scale war broke out around Beijing and spread to Shanghai. Japanese militarists had been waiting for an excuse to plunge farther into China. By the middle of July, the *NichiNichi* and other major dailies now got behind the call for war and the public was mobilized.[1]

However, not all Japanese thought escalation was a good idea. The Japanese general Ishiwara Kanji who was one of instigators of the Manchurian Incident six years earlier warned against military involvement on the mainland of China. He saw the war as a potential quagmire, comparing it to Napoleon's campaign that had become bogged down in Spain. Instead he believed the next war would come against the Soviet Union. But the army leadership did not listen to him and he was reassigned repeatedly until he was forced into retirement. The Foreign Ministry was also against military expansion in China, but had little impact on decision making in Tokyo. The Ministry played catch-up, as in the Manchurian Incident, and its power to influence affairs in China was considerably weakened. The U.S. and British governments both came out strongly against the war but with no plans to intervene.[2]

Why did the Chinese make their stand? Certainly the Chinese polity was more unified behind the nationalist party (Guomindong) leader Chiang Kaishek than ever before. Chiang had effective political and military control over almost all of China. China was more prepared than ever before to engage in a conflict with Japan. Chinese anti-Japanese sentiment had increased. War bounties were reportedly placed upon Japanese combatants. A Japanese general or spy was worth $14.50, a private $5.80, a Japanese tank if captured would net $145, and a destroyer $2,900, according to *The New York Times*.[3] China also moved closer to the Soviet Union. Shortly after the outbreak of hostilities, the Russians and Chinese signed a nonaggression pact. Although this treaty did not amount to an alliance, it was a first step in that direction. In addition, a small group within the Chinese leadership led by Madame Sun Yatsen, wife of the late Chinese revolutionary Sun Yatsen, lobbied Chiang to adopt a strategy of resisting the Japanese Army by drawing it deeply into China.

ANTI-JAPANESE OPINION

American support for Japan disappeared completely with the beginning of the Sino-Japanese War. In a Gallup public opinion poll published on October 24, 1937, only 1 percent favored Japan while 59 percent favored China; 40 percent had no opinion.[4] The poll illustrates how badly U.S.-Japanese relations had deteriorated. Rallies were held on both coasts denouncing the Japanese and in support of China. The New York rally, sponsored by the American League Against War and Fascism and the American Friends of the Chinese People attracted 10,000 people to Madison Square Garden. *The New York Times* reported that bootblacks from San Francisco raised money for the Chinese Army.[5]

But many Americans took little note according to the poll. The large number of Americans not taking sides in the conflict was a reflection of isolationist attitudes in the United States. Americans became concerned about getting entangled in either the European or East Asian conflicts. In 1937 the Ludlow Amendment was considered by Congress. Though never approved, this constitutional amendment, which would have prohibited the U.S. government from declaring offensive war upon another nation without the approval of a voter referendum, had the support of 70 percent of the American population.[6]

American concerns were elsewhere in the late 1930s. The bulk of U.S. magazine articles publishing from 1937 to 1939 focused not on East Asia but on Europe with 902 articles on Germany and 606 on Great Britain. Americans were focused on the threat of Nazi Germany in Europe. The emergence of the Nazis in the American consciousness also hurt U.S.-Japanese relations. Many Americans began to equate Japanese expansionism with German hegemony in Europe and the signing of the Anti-Comintern Pact in 1936 by the Japanese and Germans fueled the comparison.

Frank Slack, an official with the YMCA in New York told of how a Japanese xylophonist performing at Radio City Music Hall was kept in the shadows instead of being shown directly in the spotlight for fear of a negative reaction in the audience. Longtime Japan watcher and former YMCA missionary to Japan Galen Fisher stated: "Public opinion is as strongly against Japan now as it was for Japan in the Russo-Japanese War."[7]

There was little if any room now for the argument made earlier that Japan could become a responsible leader in North China and bring order and progress out of the chaotic situation there. Distrust had risen to the point where Americans believed little of the rhetoric emanating from Japan. Instead, the Sino-Japanese War generated outrage and more and more Americans turned away from the Japanese.

Henry Stimson, though retired from government, became involved in U.S.-Japanese tensions as a private citizen. Stimson wrote *The Far Eastern Crisis*, an influential account of the diplomacy of the Manchurian Incident, in 1935. Though it was in many ways sympathetic to the Japanese situation, Stimson's book maintained that the priority in East Asia was peace and preservation of the Open Door policy in China, including protection of China's sovereignty. A review of the book by Frederick Field, an East Asian expert, pointed out that the United States had few commercial investments in China and little trade: "The strength of his [Stimson's] argument, then, must rest entirely on the special feelings toward China on the part of Americans and special traditions of policy towards the Far East [Open Door] . . ."[8]

Stimson's sympathy for China grew in the early stages of the Sino-Japanese conflict. He corresponded with Chinese academics and students and received a letter from William S. Dodd Jr. who was the head of the China Aid Council, a part of the American League Against War and Fascism. The council had sponsored a well-attended pro-Chinese rally in Madison Square Garden on October 1.[9]

Stimson had been sympathetic to the Japanese situation in 1931 during the Manchurian Incident, although not to the Kwantung Army or its junior officers. In 1935 he wrote that there were early signs of a reaction against the militarists and an upsurge of moderate forces in Japan.[10] By 1937, things had not worked out the way he expected and at the beginning of the Sino-Japanese War, he concluded the Japanese could no longer be trusted.[11]

On October 5, 1937, President Roosevelt gave a speech in Chicago calling for a quarantine of the world's aggressors. The speech condemned aggressor states and urged peace-loving nations to build a quarantine around them, although Roosevelt proposed no specific actions. The solution was left intentionally vague. It pleased interventionists while not alienating isolationists.[12] Stimson wrote a letter to *The New York Times* in support of the speech on October 7, 1937.

> Our American people are aroused and angry at the callous brutality of the Japanese. There is apparently no difference of opinion in their minds as to the merits of the controversy. Their abhorrence of injustice and oppression causes them immediately and universally to sympathize with China, but they do not see how anything can be done about it.

As usual Stimson had accurately gauged American public opinion. Gone was any sympathy toward the Japanese or any hope that Japanese liberals could at some point retake power.[13]

The letter focused instead on how to help the Chinese in their fight against Japan. He rejected the neutrality act that was designed to keep the United States out of the war by embargoing war materiel on both warring parties. He wanted to preserve U.S. support for China's military. Noting that the Japanese had become dependent upon American steel, scrap metal, and oil to fuel its war machine in China in the 1930s, Stimson argued that the Japanese were vulnerable to an embargo on strategic resources. He also wrote a personal letter to Secretary of State Cordell Hull earlier in August expressing the same sentiment.[14]

Many Americans responded with great enthusiasm to Stimson's proposal. Letters poured in praising Stimson for his "courageous and historical letter," expressing "profound respect and admiration." The faculty and dean of the Fletcher School of Law and Diplomacy sent a cable with their "hearty congratulations" to Stimson for his suggestion for an embargo of war materiel against Japan. *The New York Times* published an article on Stimson's letter the next day on its front page, announcing that Stimson favored an embargo on Japanese war materiel. The embargo seemed like a viable alternative for those who rejected active involvement in the war but who wanted to do something to support China. On the other hand, many isolationists believed that an embargo would simply draw the United States into a war in East Asia. The embargo idea died for the moment for lack of public support. However, Stimson laid the groundwork for the embargo that came later.[15]

To see how far Stimson had moved in his support of the Chinese and opposition to Japan, Stimson's letter to President Roosevelt of November 15, 1937 is revealing. During the Manchurian Incident, Stimson had expressed little confidence in the Chinese to run their own affairs. In his letter to Roosevelt, he described China as fighting for "freedom and peace in the Orient today. Her people, representing a peaceful culture almost immemorial, are headed by a government largely influenced by American education and traditions."[16]

Stimson's time in the Philippines as governor-general had imbued him with the sense that all Oriental peoples lacked the virtues of the white race.[17] Now, however, Stimson extolled the merits of the Chinese and his support took on ideological themes, some fairly questionable. First, a quick glance at recent Chinese history of the Boxer Rebellion and warlord control in the 1910s–1920s shows that they were as capable of war and violence as any nation. As to whether the Chinese government modeled itself on our government and traditions, Stimson made the same mistake here that he and others made concerning Japan earlier in the interwar period. China was no more like the United States in its political system than Japan.

Stimson received several letters from Chinese praising *The New York Times* letter. Stimson also entertained well-known Chinese intellectual and soon to be ambassador to the United States Hu Shih in his home in New York City on November 6, 1937. Stimson and Hu Shih debated the proper response to Japan's invasion. Hu Shih apologetically rejected Stimson's nonrecognition doctrine from the Manchurian Incident. Hu, a former student of John Dewey at Columbia University, was a pacifist and believed in evolutionary change up until the outbreak of the Sino-Japanese War. Now he believed only an all-out war against Japan would change the situation. He even rejected Stimson's suggestion of embargo as too timid. Regardless of the debate, the tables had turned and now it was Chinese unofficial diplomats, not Japanese, who were creating connections with the United States.[18]

At the same time, Stimson embraced an argument about Japan he had earlier rejected, that of Japan's feudal militarism.

> Her enemy [Japan], of a feudal military inheritance and today wholly guided by military purposes, is avowedly seeking to overthrow that Chinese government and replace it by one more amenable to Japan's own purposes and interests. These purposes today and for as long as Japan's present leadership continues will be inherently hostile to our own culture and national purposes.

Stimson's shift is indicative of the larger shift of the American public away from Japan toward China.[19]

The feudal militarism argument was strengthened by the war. Freda Utley, a British Marxist, wrote several books about Japan between 1936 and 1939 in part to please Stalin so that he would release her husband from a Moscow jail. The scheme did not work and her husband died in prison. Utley became a severe critic of the Japanese, referring to their "savage, simian efficiency" in her 1939 book, *China at War*. Utley took a view similar to Stimson that the Japanese had not outgrown their feudalism. Utley urged economic sanctions on Japan in 1936 with her book *Japan's Feet of Clay*. Some Japanese credited her with bringing life into a boycott of Japanese goods in the United States with her anti-Japanese writings. Even though the book was badly flawed, it became a bestseller in England and the United States. Utley continued to write on the Sino-Japanese conflict and spent time in China in 1939 as a newspaper correspondent reporting the war.[20]

Writing in *The Atlantic Monthly*, William Henry Chamberlin, an American newspaper reporter for the *Christian Science Monitor* who had been covering Japan since 1934, asked "How Strong Is Japan?" While much of his answer focused on economics and military power, he included the "unique Japanese spirit" in Japan's assets. Invoking Nitobe's *Bushido*, Chamberlin described a military of fanatical loyalty and self-denial. Small offices, dingy furniture, and unshaven men were evidence of this fanaticism in the military. Chamberlin stated that the lack of ostentation characterized the Japanese Army and also the feudal samurai. Here is a case of matching the realities of the time to the evidence available rather than seeking an alternative explanation. That the Japanese Army lacked fanfare was undeniable but the samurai could be quite ostentatious when required to be. In costume and sword, the appearance of the samurai indicated his class status and power in society.[21]

Invoking Orientalism as well, Chamberlin also mentioned that one of weapons of the Japanese in the area of intelligence was their peculiar "reserved and repressed" nature. Because they hid their true feelings and thoughts, the Japanese kept Americans and other intelligence agents in the dark about their true intentions. In reality, since the Manchurian Incident the Japanese had been quite clear about their intention to be very involved in China. There was no subterfuge on this issue.[22]

In his book on Japan, published as *Japan over Asia* (1938), Chamberlin went further. "They [the Japanese] believe first that they are right and they lack the imagination to see other points of view than their own." Pearl Buck, daughter of missionaries to China who had lived in China most of her life and who was famous for her Pulitzer Prize–winning book *The Good Earth* (1931), had become entranced with the Chinese people but exhibited a virulent hatred of the Japanese. Her review of Chamberlin's book in 1938 included her own comment on the Japanese.

There seems, however, to be something beyond the usual in the case of the Japanese. That they are efficient and practical must be granted. But the lack of imagination which characterizes all of their life and even their art, as colonial rulers makes them unnecessarily harsh, uncomprehending, and unaware of the sufferings of people more cultivated and more sensitive than themselves. They so easily give gratuitous insults . . . For as Mr. Chamberlin describes them, and I think truly, the Japanese are a simple-minded people, not at all astute and they have the rigidity, the lack of tolerance, the absence of humor of the somewhat stupid.[23]

Even those Americans who had more sympathy for the Japanese situation embraced the explanation that Japan had only a facade of modernity. Nathaniel Peffer, a journalist and historian who taught at Columbia University, wrote several books on East Asia before World War II. Peffer took a realist approach to the problems of East Asia. He had a generally sound understanding of Japanese economic interests in China. Even with this approach Peffer felt the need to address questions about Japan's modernization in an article in *Harper's Magazine*.

The much acclaimed miracle of transformation into a modern state in fifty years was, like all miracles, subject to cold internal criticism. It has always been fair to question whether there was a transformation, or just a superimposed exterior. Railways, telegraphs, an effective navy and some textile mills do not constitute a modern society. In reality Japanese institutions had changed but little. They remained the institutions of a peasant-handicraft society with the peculiar inflections lent by Japanese feudalism, to which were attached the accouterments of the West. These were adjuncts to Japan however, not an integral part of Japan. Or it might be said that Japan had donned an extra outer garment, but the body and spirit were the body and spirit of medieval Japan.[24]

After openly questioning Japan's modernity, Peffer then contradicted himself by stating that Japan had without a doubt successfully Westernized and modernized and that Japan's struggles were not unique but the very same struggle as all the modern industrial economies. "Fundamentally, Japan's problems are those of the West, the problems of a country industrializing by power-machine production and organized without restraints on private interests or regard for social consequences." If they had the same problems as the modern industrialized West, then how could they be anything but modern people?[25]

A year later Peffer published a second article in *Harpers* about the Sino-Japanese War. In it, he noted that the Japanese had become stalemated in China and in the case of a long war would lose eventually because their resources would be exhausted. He also suggested that Japan had underestimated China's resolve at the outset.

If Japan had not underestimated the enemy but instead had thrust into China with the full force of its trained manpower and modern armament, China might have been crushed before it could gather its scattered powers. But if Japan had not underestimated the enemy it would not have been Japan and there would have been no war. It would not have been a country dragged at the heels of a military clique, insular, semifeudal in its ignorance of the world, overweening in pride and intoxicated by fantasies of world conquest that the country is not strong enough to sustain.[26]

PANAY INCIDENT AND NANJING MASSACRE

The Panay Incident further inflamed American opinion against Japan. The Panay, an American gunboat moored near Nanjing, was used as a refuge by American embassy personnel during the Japanese invasion of Nanjing. On December 12, 1937, Japan airplanes dive-bombed the Panay and sunk it. Two Americans were killed and 48 injured. The American public was outraged but concerned that the incident could lead to war between the United States and Japan. Thus, it also fueled more support for the antiwar Ludlow Amendment. The incident split the American Congress between strict isolationists who wanted no further engagement and those who wanted economic sanctions against Japan. The Japanese Foreign Office, well aware of strong anti-Japanese feelings in the United States, apologized immediately and paid an indemnity to the Americans. The Tokyo newspaper *NichiNichi* set up a relief fund for Panay victims that raised 7,012 yen given to Ambassador Grew in a ceremony in January 1938.[27]

In the immediate aftermath of the Panay Incident, the Japanese Army entered Nanjing, the capital of China. The fierce resistance of China at Shanghai, the evacuation of Nanjing by the Chinese government, and the generally strong feeling in the Japanese Army against the Chinese people led to widespread rape, murder, and pillage in Nanjing. The atrocities to this day are known as the Rape of Nanjing.

The Rape of Nanjing has become a symbol for either the deep brutality of the Japanese Army or a mean-spirited propaganda campaign waged against Japan by Chinese and others, depending upon who is telling the story. While American writers have studied the atrocities and reported them to a shocked audience ever since they began, conservative nationalists in Japan deny that Nanjing atrocities ever took place. Iris Chang's book, *The Rape of Nanjing*, though seriously flawed, raised the profile of the event in the United States. Japanese primary and secondary school textbooks generally whitewash the Rape by calling it an "Incident." This denial of its own history along with visits to Yasukuni Shrine by the Japanese prime minister where fourteen Japanese war criminals are enshrined has led to severe diplomatic tensions between China and Japan in recent years.

Americans began receiving information about the atrocities at Nanjing shortly after they happened. The Japanese entered Nanjing on December 13.

There were several American reporters in Nanjing at time, including Hallett Abend working for *The New York Times*. By December 19, the *Times* reported that the Japanese high command was working to end the atrocities against Chinese civilians. However, the atrocities continued at a high level well into 1938, according to the eyewitness account of Miner Searle Bates.

Bates, a missionary who taught history at Nanjing University, was on the scene when the Japanese entered Nanjing and he became the chair of the Emergency Committee of the University of Nanjing. Some 17,000 Chinese fled to the university, which was part of the Safety Zone set up by a volunteer International Committee of Twenty Europeans and American doctors, missionaries, and businessmen for the protection of civilians from the Japanese Army.[28]

Bates, as the head of the Safety Zone at Nanjing University, wrote several letters of complaint to the Japanese Embassy in Nanjing, which was located near the university. His first letter of December 16 described the rape of several female students and the disappearance of others. The rest of the letters detail similar outrages.

> In our Agricultural Economics Compound (Hsiao T'ao Yuan) more than thirty women were raped last night by soldiers who came repeatedly and in large numbers. I have investigated this matter thoroughly, and am certain of the correctness of the statement.

Bates also pointed out that the Japanese Army had lost an opportunity to show that it was a better organized and more disciplined organization than the retreating disorderly Chinese Army. Bates later gave eyewitness testimony to the Nanjing atrocities at the Tokyo War Crimes Tribunal in 1946.[29]

There have been differing assumptions about the effect of Japanese traditions on the fighting soldiers of Japan. Some historians today argue that Japanese soldiers were locked into the martial traditions of Japan's past and this explains why the Sino-Japanese War and later the Pacific War were fought with such violence and ruthlessness. On the other hand, there were others, Japanese and Americans, who believed that the arbitrary violence and ruthlessness of the Japanese Army was attributable to just the opposite: the lack of training in the bushido code of the samurai.

Charlotte Deforest, president of Kobe Women's College, reported to her sisters in the United States that four Japanese Army officers who refused to obey the order to destroy and plunder Nanjing a year earlier decided instead to commit ritual suicide and were buried by missionaries. She and her Japanese friend found out about the atrocities through magazine articles sent by an American friend that slipped through the censors. They agreed that if more Japanese soldiers followed the bushido ethical code, the atrocities of Nanjing would not have happened. Deforest argued that the lower-class origins of many of the soldiers in the Japanese Army meant that they had no chance to be educated in bushido.[30]

Thus, the Japanese soldier was seen either as a prisoner to a militarist past, or as too modern, having thrown out the old ways precipitously. Neither version was accurate. Although samurai certainly had rules to live and die by, the code of bushido was a modern invention of Nitobe Inazô, a Japanese Christian who gave a Christian slant to it in his book *Bushido*. Japanese Christians and Charlotte DeForest idealized samurai behavior. The samurai could be quite brutal. On the other hand, neither did the samurai commit atrocities on scale that would have instructed the Japanese soldiers at Nanjing.

It is not clear that Japanese soldiers acted as samurai, either the good version or the bad version. More likely, their atavism replicated the cruel experiences they suffered as army recruits. There is also evidence Japanese soldiers saw their Asian counterparts as inferior. In addition, the army was driven by dreams of hegemony that derived from modern nationalism, not from the samurai. Any education about samurai ideals was a part of the nationalism with which they were imbued. However, when the Nanjing atrocities were made public in the United States, they turned even more people against Japan.[31]

IMPACT ON OFFICIAL DIPLOMACY

Strong anti-Japanese sentiment in the United States had a concrete impact on official diplomacy. Those who were against Japan rejected any mediating role for Americans.

Ambassador Grew, on the other hand, favored American mediation. In August and again in October, he met with Foreign Minister Hirota and suggested that the United States act as a "go-between" to negotiate a settlement of the war. Grew believed the Japanese had gotten themselves into China too far and too fast and were seeking a negotiated settlement on favorable terms rather than a prolonged war. In late August, Grew cabled the American State Department with a request for approval to mediate. Secretary of State Hull made it clear in a return cable that American public opinion was outraged at the actions of the Japanese military and this made it impossible to act as an intermediary.[32]

The Japanese reached out again to the British, Americans, and the Germans in October and early November to solicit an impartial broker. The British had to bow out because anti-British feelings were too high in Japan. The Germans did step in and attempt unsuccessfully to broker a peace settlement. The Americans represented another choice to resolve conflict. Grew received a briefing by Hugh Byas, the newspaper correspondent of *The New York Times*, indicating the Japanese were hoping for a quick victory at Shanghai and then a favorable peace settlement. In October, for the second time, Grew requested State approval to mediate. After some hesitation, State refused on two grounds: first on the principle that a negotiated settlement might violate the Washington Nine Power Treaty by damaging further China's already weak sovereignty, and second on the grounds that the Americans had a "strong distaste" for any negotiation that would support a Japanese victory. Just as Secretary of State Henry Stimson's options were limited by a negative response to the Manchurian Incident in 1931, strong negative American perceptions of Japan limited Grew.[33]

The principle of public support for diplomacy was well understood. Galen Fisher suggested to his friend and former colleague Saito Soichi, head of the Japanese YMCA,

> The President and State Dept. will not go far ahead of public opinion, as represented by the leaders of various powerful associations and interests. These leaders are exceptionally well informed about the Sino-Japanese conflict, due to the full news dispatches and many special publications by such agencies as the F.P.A., IPR, national peace Conference, Mission boards, and to the daily radio news broadcasts which always feature it. In driving across the continent three weeks ago I was amazed to see how small town papers were carrying the Associated Press and United Press dispatches much like the city dailies.[34]

Fisher, who argued just before the conflict broke out that liberals in Japan were on the verge of a comeback, now urged Japanese liberals to lay low and not push for an end to the war. Fisher became convinced that the only way to push the militarists in Japan out of power was for them to suffer a catastrophic defeat in China. Responding to Saito's impending visit to the United States as well, Fisher suggested that Saito not defend the actions of Japan in China to American audiences but emphasize possible mediation to end the conflict, and the continuing cooperation of American and Japanese Christians.[35]

MISSIONARIES IN THE MIDDLE

The Sino-Japanese War put American missionaries in Japan in a very uncomfortable position. Torn between their love of Japan and their loyalty to the United States, some missionaries would have preferred that the Americans declare a policy of neutrality so that they could negotiate a settlement. If Roosevelt invoked the Neutrality Act by declaring both sides belligerents, the United States could not aid China, since the act banned trade in military goods to belligerents in a war. Others hoped for a negotiated settlement. They also criticized American imperialism as stimulating Japanese hegemony in Asia.[36]

Controversy erupted among missionaries over whether to condemn or sympathize with Japan. A. Livingston Warnshuis, who had served as a Reformed Church missionary to China from 1900 to 1920, was the head of the International Missionary Council, located in New York City. In December 1937, Warnshuis issued a confidential statement called "Prospects for Peace in the Far East," apparently not that confidential because it ended up in the hands of several members of the missionary community. It was exceedingly critical of the Japanese, rejected the possibility that Japan had economic motives in China, and attributed the Sino-Japanese War to the Japanese belief that they should lead East Asia and eventually the world in what he called Japanese "messianism." In a direct reference to Japanese feudal militarism, Warnshuis stated, "The struggle between feudalism and modernism still continues." Turning to American policy toward Japan, Warnshuis asserted it "would be treasonable to the established American policies to recognize now Japan's conquest of China," for the following reasons: the peace movement would be devastated by any concessions to Japan, trade with China damaged, and the abandonment of American support for China would be a cynical about-face and damage American prestige in the entire region.[37]

Warnshuis's arguments aroused the ire of Arthur Jorgensen, head of the American YMCA mission in Japan. Attacking his arguments in a letter he sent Warnshuis, Jorgensen asserted that economics was at the center of why the Japanese were in China and called Japan's messianic language "window-dressing." Jorgensen also compared Japanese imperialism in East Asia with American imperialism in the Philippines at the turn of the century. He even suggested at one point that General Araki Sadao was actually imitating the American rhetoric of salvation in the Philippines, and applying this language to China. While Jorgensen's statement was short and general, it points to a shared framework of hegemony of both Americans and Japanese in East Asia. Warnshuis responded to Jorgensen's letter with a vigorous defense of his arguments, at one point suggesting in a conspiratorial tone that Japan had been working on a China invasion from before the time of the Twenty-One Demands in 1915.[38]

Jorgensen and other American missionaries in Japan also responded as a group and sent an open letter to fellow Christians in the United States. The letter expressed dismay over the war while withholding blame from any side, calling it a "Greek tragedy." The letter implicated American policy decisions such as the immigration exclusion clause, tariffs, and the naval buildup as adding to the atmosphere of fear in Japan thereby contributing to the causes of the Sino-Japanese War.[39]

JAPANESE DEFENSE

In response to the open letters from American Christians, Japanese Christians sent their own open letters to the Christians of the world (but focused on an American and Western audience). They dismissed China's status as an independent nation, accused China of practicing duplicitous diplomacy (Americans had often accused the Japanese of the same thing), blamed Chinese ill-treatment of Japanese living in China and the boycott against Japanese goods, and credited the Chinese with winning the propaganda war in the United States and turning the American population against Japan. One of the letters was signed by forty-five of the most important Christian leaders in the country, although Kagawa Toyohiko, the popular Christian preacher and Saito Soichi, YMCA leader, did not sign it.[40]

A letter from Doshisha University, the most important Christian university in Japan located in the ancient capital of Kyoto, signed by the Japanese faculty claimed that the Japanese had no territorial ambitions in China and desired only the "mutual benefit" and unrestricted trade in North China. Doshisha had become very nationalistic and followed the antiforeigner line of the government. Doshisha's board of trustees removed President Dr. Yuasa Hachiro in December 1937 because he was pacifist and too connected to the American missionary movement. The letters followed arguments set forward by the government about its purposes in China, which belied their unofficial origins.[41]

These Japanese Christians revitalized a nationalist movement begun in the late Meiji Period (1890–1912) to make Christianity Japanese by fusing it with Japanese ideas such as bushido and purging the foreign element from it. Given the climate of fear and suspicion of the West, the Japanization of Christianity seemed an even more urgent task in the late 1930s and it also offered Japanese Christians cover against a government very suspicious of Christian organizations with connections in the West.[42]

But there were also calls to improve U.S.-Japanese relations. Kikuchi Kan, in a speech at the U.S.-Japan Friendship meeting in Hibiya Park in Tokyo told his audience of the two nations' historic friendship going back to the Perry Expedition opening Japan to the West. "I believe that we should never fight America," Kikuchi asserted to great applause. It is likely, however, that beyond his sympathetic audience, this attitude of friendship was far less prevalent.[43] Some Japanese Christians responded to the war with Christian pacifism. Yanaihara Tadao, well-known professor of colonial economics at Tokyo Imperial University and a Christian, was forced to resign his position because he refused to endorse the war and renounce his pacifism.[44]

Arthur Jorgensen believed there was considerable opposition to war, although on the surface, the Japanese seemed unified in support of the war. Jorgensen claimed there was intense pressure by the government upon groups and organizations to demonstrate their "loyalty and readiness to back official policies." In this atmosphere, Japanese Christians were singled out and watched very carefully.[45]

Charlotte DeForest, president of Kobe College, reported in spring 1938 that a questionnaire from the Japanese Military Police was sent out to Japanese church leaders and faculty at Christian universities. The questionnaire was seen as a trap to trick Japanese Christians into revealing their true feelings. The subjects intimated divided loyalties: "The relation of our Emperor and the Christian God," "The relation of the Imperial Rescript and the Bible," "Conception of religious liberty," and "Relation of Christianity and the Japanese Spirit."[46]

There was long-standing precedent in Japan to see Christians with some suspicion. The seventeenth century policy of isolation, execution of Christian missionaries, and a ban upon Christianity marked the beginning of this trend. Japanese Christians were accused of divided loyalties when the Imperial Rescript on Education was issued in 1890. The Rescript confirmed the divinity of the emperor and the duty of loyalty of Japanese subjects. In a famous case at the time, Japanese Christian Uchimura Kanzo hesitated to bow before the Rescript and later admitted that he hesitated because of his commitment to Christianity. Uchimura was fired from his position at prestigious First Higher School and castigated in the press, but went onto become a famous Christian leader of the Mukyokai or Non-Church movement in Japan. Japanese Christians responded in the 1890s with a vigorous defense of their loyalty to Japan and their interest in seeing Christianity Japanized and placed at the center of Japan's moral universe. They partially succeeded in the years during and after the Russo-Japanese War.[47]

By 1937, however, a vigorous defense of Christianity was ill-advised. Japanese Christians kept quiet. However, this did not help their cause abroad. Many Americans saw the lack of open resistance as more evidence of oriental submissiveness. However, the central issue was government pressure to endorse official policy, not prescriptive cultural traditions.

Japanese Christians stated that their friendship with Chinese Christians was undeterred. In a speech to American missionaries in Japan, Reverend Tagawa stated that "Japan under whatever circumstances must make friends with China and collaborate with her." By spring 1938, there were very few friendly feelings left on the Chinese side. A goodwill mission of Japanese Christians was sent to Beijing in May 1938 under the leadership of Saito Soichi. There they were to hold a conference with Chinese Christians. But the conference never happened. To a man, Chinese Christian leaders in Beijing refused to meet with the Japanese delegation.[48]

THE RUIN OF THE IPR

East Asia seemed to be falling apart in 1937. In a similar way, private diplomacy between the United States and Japan fell apart as well. It did not start in 1937 however. Earlier in the decade the effects of the Manchurian Incident and Japanese anti-Americanism could be seen in tensions surrounding unofficial diplomacy. Unofficial diplomacy was increasingly viewed with distrust.

Not surprisingly, the IPR suffered. Certainly the most important mechanism for improving U.S.-Japanese relations at the unofficial level in the interwar period, the IPR had been founded on the "collective principle of international relations," wrote Glen Fisher, in a history of the IPR on its tenth birthday in 1935. The IPR's paradigm was consistent with the time in the 1920s when it seemed that nations were beginning to accept collective security through the League of Nations and collective disarmament through the Washington Conference, according to Fisher. The atmosphere in 1935 was very different. Japan had left the League of Nations and abandoned the Washington Agreements. Germany was soon to leave the League and abandon the Versailles Treaty. An arms race was building and violent conflicts between nations in Europe and East Asia were brewing. While in 1925 internationalism was thriving, by 1935, internationalism was dying.[49]

While the IPR struggled with the decline of internationalism, internal problems also beset the organization. After the Manchurian Incident, the JCIPR was watched carefully by the Japanese government. Because the Foreign Ministry had been intimately involved in financial support of the JCIPR, the Japanese government could now dictate its future.

In 1935, the JCIPR merged with the Japannese LNA, which was renamed the JIA after Japan left the League of Nations in 1933. The JIA was the private citizen arm of the Foreign Ministry. Given the deterioration in Japan's relations with the West, the JCIPR and the Foreign Ministry found the merger a practical step. Also the JCIPR had been struggling financially. JCIPR leaders believed the merger would consolidate dwindling liberal support in Japan. They also believed linking with an arm of the Japanese government would give them more power and legitimacy within Japan. Tomoko Akami suggests that for IPR leaders the Japanese state was "the regime of truth . . . The state was morally right." In addition, the IPR was under increasing scrutiny by the government because of their foreign connections and the merger offered cover since the Japan International Association was closely linked to the Foreign Ministry.[50]

Although the merger was a solution to the problem of the Western nature of the IPR and the weakening of Japanese liberals, unofficial diplomacy was undermined because the JCIPR was increasingly closely connected to the Foreign Ministry. The JCIPR lacked separation from government and could not speak with an independent voice. The whole idea behind the IPR was to use unofficial channels and private diplomacy to improve U.S.-Japanese relations without the confining restrictions of official government policy.

The feeling of the IPR headquarters in New York was that the JCIPR risked becoming a propaganda arm of the Japanese government with the merger. Later, during the Sino-Japanese War, the JCIPR did just that, sending out pamphlets created by the Foreign Ministry to other national councils of the IPR justifying the Japanese invasion of China. William L. Holland, a New Zealander in charge of the IPR's research agenda, had considerable experience dealing with the Japanese. He was sent to Japan after the start of the Sino-Japanese War to gain approval for a new research initiative. He confronted JCIPR leaders about the flyers, suggesting that they were nothing more than government propaganda. During his trip, Holland attended an expensive dinner sponsored by JCIPR. The conversation was forced. Tsurumi Yusuke, who had the strongest ties with IPR leadership, took the role of distracting Holland from the recent Japanese invasion of China and Western condemnation of it through meaningless banter. Undeterred, Holland openly condemned the Japanese invasion to his Japanese IPR colleagues in an emotional outburst. Several of his Japanese counterparts "seemed ill at ease and they left early."[51]

The Sino-Japanese War created additional problems for the IPR, throwing the New York headquarters into confusion. The war put its cherished goals of creating peace and understanding in the Pacific in danger. The organization began a soul-searching examination of what it could do to revive its agenda.

Edward Carter, head of the IPR headquarters in New York, traveled to Europe to consult. The leadership of the English branch of the IPR, a section of the Royal Institute of International Affairs at Chatham House, though far removed from the Pacific, insinuated themselves into a leadership position within the IPR in the mid 1930s. At their meeting with Carter, they threw a series of hard questions at him. Even now, verbatim, these questions sear into the very heart of the internationalist agenda.

> What was the Institute going to do to stop the war? Does not the outbreak of war mean the end of the IPR? Does not the war prove the utter futility of the kind of work which the Institute has done in the past ten years? Have the leaders of the Institute courage enough to announce that the Institute has failed and proceed to liquidate it? Does not prudence demand that the Institute cease its activity during the war in order to preserve itself intact for service in the interest of peace when the war is over?[52]

As a consequence of his trip and internal discussions with other IPR leaders—J.W. Dafoe who was the chair of the Pacific Council and William Holland, the research secretary along with Carter initiated a new study of the Sino-Japanese War. Richard Tawney, the well-known English economic historian, helped to formulate research questions for the so-called Inquiry Project: How will China recover from the ravage of war? What are the roots of Japanese aggression in China? What steps has China taken leading to a policy of united national resistance against Japan? There were also questions concerning the future of Mongolia, the applicability of the Washington Treaty principles, the major issues that might require international negotiation in the aftermath of the war, and the impact of the conflict on the European powers in China. Tawney's questions were reworded later as more neutral statements to make them more palatable.[53]

The questions implicitly took China's side against Japan. Because the questions were China-focused and sympathetic to China, the leadership recognized that tension might flare up between the headquarters and the Japanese Council. Meeting summaries reveal that while there was concern about the Japanese reaction, the leadership never intended to allow Japanese disapproval to stop the project. "Every effort should be made to refrain from taking any steps that would make either the Japanese or Chinese councils feel that they would be criticized by the other councils if they did not find it possible to co-operate." This approach was a crude face-saving gesture that would allow the project to go forward despite the disapproval of the Japanese.[54]

Holland was sent to Japan to gain approval with instructions to describe the project in general terms. The Japanese gave a general approval that was later rescinded. However, the study was approved by the other national councils so it went forward. While the Americans were victorious, the Japanese became further alienated, and the stake was driven in deeper. The U.S.-Japanese relationship in the IPR was now in mortal danger.[55]

In July 1938, the JCIPR responded formally in a letter written by Yamakawa Tadao, Vice-Chairman of the JCIPR, a former high-ranking diplomat, and member of the House of Peers. Yamakawa stated that the IPR should do "purely academic and strictly objective research . . . And now I look at the program of the project again. Honestly I cannot help finding it as something other than purely academic and strictly objective."[56]

The Japanese were telling a fundamental truth about the research program, but they did so only because it fit their immediate need to discredit the IPR. The IPR research program had never actually been objective, but had become more academic with the move to long-term issues in the mid 1930s. But the letter does not end here. Instead, it became a platform for the JCIPR to openly break with the Americans, rather than pursue a more diplomatic approach as in previous times:

> Now let us come back to the IPR. As you will see clearly, we are at the moment at war—de facto—with China. And, should there be, among the groups in the States, some who thinking that, Japan being disunited between the militarist group and those who advocate a more liberal policy, the time will come sooner or later when the present Government is replaced by more liberal Government with which the third Powers may be able to confer more comfortably, endeavor to bring about a situation which is likely to accelerate the fall of the present

regime in Japan it is a grave mistake. If the IPR itself were to base its activities on such a theory, not only would it be a grave mistake but would also it would signify a fundamental and lamentable metamorphosis of the IPR. It will be suicidal for the IPR to plunge headlong into actual political controversies. Some of the members of the IPR have, I understand, been advocating boycott against Japan; some others are urging the authority to adopt interventionist policies; they are doing this through public speeches or publication of articles in their "private capacity." If such be the predominant atmosphere among those who are, it is proposed, to be entrusted with the project of inquiry, which should purely academic, strictly objective, and certainly not political, would it be prudent action on the part of the Pacific Council or the International Research Committee or the Secretariat to encourage the prosecution of such a project, or would it be more prudent to reconsider the matter altogether . . . I do feel a certain presentiment of fatal danger in the air.[57]

The letter was very open and blunt about tensions in U.S.-Japanese relations (very un-Oriental!). Yamakawa expressed a suspicion of partiality that was accurate, for some American IPR leaders had already engaged in anti-Japanese rhetoric outside of the IPR. The letter contained a menacing and somewhat paranoid warning about American attempts to influence internal Japanese politics. The IPR was not engaged in any attempt to overthrow the Japanese government.

This was a crucial moment for the IPR. While previously, the organization had at least striven to be fair, the Inquiry Project was clearly not impartial.

The Foreign Ministry and the leadership of the JCIPR leveled even stronger criticism against the American Council of the IPR and the international headquarters in New York behind closed doors. A confidential report written by the Japanese Ministry of Foreign Affairs in 1939 claimed that the American Council had become infiltrated by Soviet Communists who had turned the American IPR into a "propaganda agency" to disseminate pro-Chinese, pro-Soviet, and therefore anti-Japanese views. The report also pointed out that American Council members participated in several pro-Chinese groups such as the China Relief Committee, Friends of the Chinese People, The American Committee for Non-Participation in Japanese Aggression, and even mentioned the new magazine *Amerasia* as presenting dangerous pro-Chinese views.[58]

The writer of the report blamed the Japanese themselves in part because they had been too passive during IPR international meetings and had allowed proposals to be passed without open critical inspection. Claiming that German Jews dominated the American Council, the report also demonstrated anti-Semitic prejudice that had become more common in Japan in the 1930s.

Frederick Field, who headed up the American Council, was identified in the report as the most important person in this supposed conspiracy against

Japan. Field was heir to the Vanderbilt family fortune. He worked for the American IPR fulltime for free and according to the report also donated $5,000–20,000 a year to the organization. Dedicated to several organizations sympathetic to China's plight, Field was unquestionably quite pro-Chinese. The report identified several others including Owen Lattimore, Phillip Jaffe, who edited *Amerasia*, Bruno Lasker, and S. Kurt Bloch as forming a "pro-communistic camarilla" along with Field. Although several of these associates were students of Communism and were later harassed by Joseph McCarthy during the 1950s for their links to Communism, the writer exaggerated the influence of Stalinism within the IPR in the late 1930s. In the late 1930s, American leftists were rapidly shedding their Stalinism and beginning to question the Soviet regime. Rather, it was their pro-Chinese sentiments that most threatened Japan. As in other cases, the Japanese substituted pro-Communist for pro-Chinese accusations because threats of communist conspiracies rallied anticommunist elements at home and abroad.[59]

The other influential person who threatened the Japanese was Edward Carter, the head of the IPR international headquarters in New York. Stating that one of Carter's best friends was the Soviet premier Molotov, the writer painted Carter as anti-Japanese and pro-Soviet and therefore pro-Chinese. Not certain exactly where Carter stood, the document portrayed him as either a "competent stooge" for the pro-Communist cabal or a "ruthless Machiavellian" out to enhance his own power. There is no doubt Carter had tilted toward the Chinese. However there is no evidence to support the communist accusations.[60]

The document had a conspiratorial tone; it read more like an excerpt from a spy novel than a dispassionate assessment of IPR leadership. The tone of the report indicated the rift between Americans and Japanese within the IPR had become a gaping chasm. The thinly veiled hostility of Japanese toward the American IPR and the clearly pro-Chinese, anti-Japanese stance of American IPR leadership demonstrated that the IPR no longer operated as an effective unofficial channel for improving U.S.-Japanese relations. The Japanese continued to protest against the inquiry, stopped attending IPR meetings, and with the outbreak of war in 1941, the JCIPR was eventually disbanded.[61]

PROPAGANDA AND CENSORSHIP

As it had during the Manchurian Incident the Japanese used propaganda to persuade Americans that its cause was righteous. However, the Japanese made less of an effort to openly polish Japan's image in the United States than during the Manchurian Incident. No major unofficial diplomat traveled to the United States to justify the Sino-Japanese War as with Tsurumi Yusuke in the immigration dispute or Nitobe Inazô in the Manchurian crisis.

Americans and Japanese were more distrustful of the other and more skeptical of unofficial diplomacy and open professions of friendship by 1937.

Instead, the Japanese government took its project to influence American public opinion underground, hiring Americans to write positive articles about Japan. One such person, Frederick Vincent Williams, an American journalist, was paid large sums of money by a secret Japanese agency, The Committee for the Current State of Affairs (Jikyoku Iinkai), to plant positive stories in the American press in the 1930s. Williams worked diligently for the Japanese writing a book in 1938 called *Behind the News in China* intended to counter stories of Japanese atrocities emerging from China. He stated that the behavior of the Japanese military in China was exemplary, implying that the stories were Chinese propaganda. The book was serialized in the *Osaka Mainichi* as well. Eventually, Williams' association with the Japanese government was uncovered and he was tried and convicted in an American court on counts of conspiracy and violations of the Foreign Agents Act.[62]

The Japanese sponsored many other Americans to propagandize for the Japanese in the United States, including Mr. Fisher, a writer for *The New York Times*, Henry Cotkins and a Mr. Thompson from the *San Francisco News*, orator Newton Bull, Dr. Brooks Emeney who worked at the Japanese embassy in Washington, DC, and David Wilson who worked at the Japanese consulate in Portland. Altogether, at least nine American agents worked for the Japanese government writing propaganda in the 1930s.[63]

Japanese propaganda aimed at an American audience was many times either badly done or simply missing. A short English-language flyer created by Yenji Takeda at the Imperial Hotel in Tokyo was intended to inform American hotel guests of the root causes of the situation in China. The flyer described the Chinese as the aggressors and blamed Chiang Kaishek for anti-Japanese propaganda. In the midst of the Japanese invasion of China, it was difficult to sustain the notion that the Chinese were actually the aggressors or as Williams had claimed, that the Japanese military was blameless.[64]

A more effective piece of propaganda was a film produced by the International Cinema Association of Japan in 1937. Entitled "Why Defend China?" the film focused on the positive benefits of the Japanese occupation of China. It showed neat-looking Japanese educational institutions in China, Japanese soldiers feeding Chinese children and elderly and protecting a religious shrine, and happy-looking lazy Chinese rickshaw drivers. Contrasting the happy conditions of Japan-occupied China with Soviet occupied Outer Mongolia, the film showed a house burning down and soldiers putting out the flames. The narrator spoke flawless English with a southern accent. Intended to show American audiences the positive nature of Japan's role in China, the film could have been an effective tool of propaganda but there is no evidence it was actually shown in the United States. Presumably, the Cinema

Association decided not to distribute it because they believed that anti-Japanese sentiment had risen to the point where any attempt to defend Japan's actions would inflame opinion against them further.[65]

The Japanese reserved their best propaganda efforts for their own population in the Sino-Japanese War, however. Barak Kushner in *The Thought War* notes that the goal of Japanese propaganda and censorship, or what the Japanese themselves referred to as the "thought war," was to link the warfront in China with the population at home.[66]

The Japanese engaged in extensive censorship starting long before the Sino-Japanese War but with much more emphasis during the war. Newspapers, magazines, and books had for decades been subjected to censorship. Now the censorship was stricter and personal letters became censored as well. Arthur Jorgensen, YMCA missionary to Japan, evaluated Japanese propaganda and censorship as very effective. He pointed out that the one source of news about the war in China was the official Japanese news agency the *Domei Tsushin* (United News Agency). The *Domei* was a mouthpiece for government policies. It was known to publish articles in China that did not appear in Japan and vise versa. "Censorship is tight as a drum so far as magazines, newspapers, books, etc., are concerned . . ." To illustrate his point, Jorgensen asked if the reports about large scale evacuation out of China by Americans was true or just Japanese propaganda. It turns out to have been propaganda because most Americans stayed in China until 1941 and some were interned in China by the Japanese for the duration of the war.[67]

One of these Americans, Miner Searle Bates, a missionary and history teacher at Nanjing University, confirmed that the Japanese public was being kept in the dark about the war in China. Bates traveled frequently to Japan and he found the net of censorship ever tighter. The press had strict instructions on issues and subjects they could not report on, at one point a list of over 200 items. Bates claimed that one had to be careful even in oral discussions at small group meetings because there could be military police infiltrators present.[68]

Other American missionaries living in Japan wrote about censorship in their letters home, either warning that they could not explain the whole truth for fear that the letter would not be sent, or in rare cases being able to avoid the censors by putting a letter or manuscript in the hands of an American returning to the United States. Some missionaries even warned those who wrote from the United States to be guarded in their comments because Japanese military police were reading incoming letters and might punish the recipient.[69]

The Japanese military issued censorship and propaganda guidelines specially designed for North China in September 1937. In a list of items that could not be published, the word "puppet" could not be used in association with Manchukuo, it could not be published that Chinese soldiers bombed a plane or were victorious, Japanese defeats and/or the suffering of soldiers were off-limits, general opposition to Japan or to the Japanese Emperor was not permitted, and most ironically in the midst of a vicious war, the phrase that most mildly described the situation "peace does not reign" was not permitted. Any foreign news that did not give credit to Japan could not be published.[70]

Among the items that were permitted (in fact required) to be published were heavy losses by the Nanjing Chinese Army, dissension among its ranks, its connections with communist elements, its disorderly behavior, and its imminent annihilation. The Nanjing government was targeted for propaganda as well. Reports of failing finances, corruption, and exploitation of the peasants were to be published.[71]

The Japanese required a positive portrayal of their own soldiers. Their fighting men should be portrayed as having high ideals. They were good friends of the Chinese and sacrificed themselves for this friendship. Japan, Manchukuo, and China represented the yellow races and were all becoming friendly according to the censorship regulations.[72]

Propaganda and censorship effectively kept the Japanese public in the dark about the Sino-Japanese War. Japanese audiences were shocked to hear of the intense anti-Japanese sentiment in the United States reported by Saito Soichi, the head of the Japanese YMCA, upon his return from a visit to the United States in spring 1938. Not only did they lack access to reports of anti-Japanese feeling, they also did not know that the reason why the Americans had come to hate Japan was damning news of Japanese actions in China. Saito spoke to a group of Tokyo businessmen and later to government officials who knew nothing about what was going on in China.[73]

In 1939, an American Luther Tucker, the head of World's Student Christian Federation for East Asia, ran afoul of the censorship laws. Based in Shanghai, Tucker traveled to Japan to keep Japanese Christians fully informed about the war there. To do so, he distributed a pamphlet concerning federation activities that apparently had damaging statements concerning Japanese troop behavior in China. In Kobe on October 12, as he and his family were boarding their ship to depart Japan, Japanese military police (thought police) took the family off the boat and Mr. Tucker into custody. He was held in Kyoto for about two months, although he was kept at a hotel, not a jail, and he had access to reading material, foreign food, and other comforts not normally allowed detainees. He was tried under the Japanese sedition law and military penal code. Found guilty, Tucker was sentenced but the sentence was commuted, he was deported, and he arrived in Shanghai on December 21.

The case caused a media sensation. The American press picked up the story and Cordell Hull, the American secretary of state got involved, calling the parents of Tucker in New York and assuring them that he was doing everything he could to free Mr. Tucker. It is likely that Tucker was treated so well and let off so easily because he was an American and because of the media attention surrounding the case.

The Tucker case is instructive in two ways. First, it confirms the tightness of Japanese censorship. Second, it illustrates once again the distrust that lay between the United States and Japan. Americans were scrutinized very carefully by this time in Japan. American missionaries were called in for interviews and underwent surveillance by military police.

Given effective censorship and propaganda, it is not surprising that the Japanese population backed the war with little dissent. Because Japanese had little idea of what was actually happening in China, they were susceptible to propaganda that showed the Japanese Army winning the war and serving the Chinese people there. This is a better explanation for the so-called "blind obedience" of the Japanese population than the argument that the Japanese had a feudalistic culture of submission.[74]

JAPAN AND CHINA: BROTHERS OR ENEMIES

The propaganda also revealed a perverse line of thought about the relationship between Japan and China. While Japan was tearing China into pieces, its troops, commanders, and politicians expressed the salvation of the Chinese. Shiratori Toshio, former ambassador to Sweden, expressed it well. "It [the invasion] represents a brave attempt on the part of Japan to rehabilitate Asia by saving the Chinese people at whatever cost to herself . . ."[75] The rhetoric concerning expansion into China after the outbreak of war in 1937 was filled with perverse and paradoxical themes that fused brotherly love and zeal for conquest.[76] Interestingly, Shiratori was no radical ideologue but a practical diplomat. He published a book called *The International Position of Japan*, a realist assessment of the Sino-Japanese War and foreign nations' responses.[77]

Morbid expressions of love for the Chinese became grafted onto the war effort. One Japanese military commander, Kawanami wrote a short poem in the aftermath of a battle with a Chinese regiment. The poem was an expression of regret and sorrow at the killing of Chinese soldiers whom the commander considered his Asian brothers. It was published in the American journal *Asia*. Its reading must have filled American China sympathizers with outrage, although it was intended to demonstrate the purity of Japanese intentions in China.[78]

Amerasia, a new small market journal started by Phillip Jaffe and Robert K. Reischauer, ran an article giving the Japanese perspective on Japanese affection for China. Reischauer, the elder brother of Edwin O. Reischauer, died in Shanghai during fighting in 1937. In the article, Takeuchi Tatsuji, who received a Ph.D. from the University of Chicago in 1931, tried to convince Americans of Japan's pure intentions in China. "We are fighting in China because we love the Chinese." According to Takeuchi, Americans did not understand this statement because they were too wedded to a fact-based and rational orientation. This paradox only made sense to the oriental mind. Here, Takeuchi invoked the oriental/occidental dichotomy that Americans had come to emphasize in U.S.-Japanese relations, only this time to justify the Japanese invasion.[79]

In a rebuttal in *Amerasia*, Frederick Field, an IPR leader, rejected Takeuchi's argument. "I doubt that the longest and most involved possible dissertation on national psychology could ever convince me that these phrases [Japanese are fighting China because they love the Chinese] really made the slightest sense to the Japanese themselves." Field also rejected the standard argument that Japan was motivated by the need for self-sufficiency in its invasion of China. He fell back on a different cultural argument, the feudal militarism argument, suggesting that underneath its modern industrial facade, Japan was still a feudal agricultural nation.[80]

As often as the Japanese expressed brotherly love for the Chinese, anger and hatred also seeped out of writings about China. Prince Shimadzu Tadashige, a member of the House of Peers and a retired rear admiral, wrote an article for *Asia* in 1938 arguing that basic human concepts of love, peace, and justice along with important religions originated in the Orient. On the other hand, the Occident brought war, hatred, and imperialism in Asia, according to Shimadzu. Japan had worked as a bulwark to stop Westerners from fully invading China and by so doing saved China and itself. And the past and present and futures of China and Japan were fused inextricably. "In the independence of China lies the independence of Japan, and vice versa." He also cited Sun Yatsen's endorsement of Japan as evidence of this close relationship.[81]

Then Shimadzu's message turned darker.

> To accuse Japan of having motives antagonistic to the national integrity of China is to pass the limits of ordinary propaganda: it is one of the greatest and most provocative of fabrications to be traced to those bent upon mischief. The Manchurian Incident of 1931 and the present conflict between China and Japan are a direct outcome of the propaganda of these mischief-makers.[82]

Shimadzu identified Chiang Kaishek, along with the financiers and warlords who supported him, and supporters in the United States as the mischief-makers. In Shimadzu's convoluted thinking, those who denounced Japan's actions were to blame for Japan's actions. It neatly took responsibility for the war out of Japanese hands.

Hasegawa Tetsutaro, who was the director of The International Young Women and Children's Society in Japan, sent a letter addressed to an American friend Alfred Stearns with whom he had attended Andover College, but he also addressed it "To the Intelligentsia of the world." He wrote

> China is not a nation in reality. And what country knows her as well as Japan? Chinese racial trait is something abnormal. Foreigners who have been in China and studied her need no further explanation. It is common in China for a stricken man to be stripped of his clothing and belongings by his own people. Even murder and burglary are not considered as vices.[83]

What are we to make of these simultaneous expressions of good will and brotherhood and visceral hatred? Is one propaganda and the other truth? There is no doubt that anti-Japanese propaganda and the boycott against Japanese goods in China created antipathy among Japanese. The hostility was real.

But one can also find deep roots in Japan for the "saving China" argument. After the Russo-Japanese War, the same argument was used for Korea by Japanese Christians Ebina Danjo and Kozaki Hiromichi. Not adept propagandists, they believed genuinely that just as Japan had modernized and made progress, so the Japanese could bring progress and modernity to the rest of Asia outside of Western imperialism. Add to this the Pan-Asianist ideology, and the basis for arguing that the Japanese were simply saving their Asian brothers in China and moving China into a world of progress is an understandable result. To be sure, the censorship and propaganda of the Japanese government in the late 1930s solidified these ideas. However, these ideas were not themselves crude propaganda as much as the growth and consolidation of a nationalist paradigm of expansion.

CHAPTER 11

THE MARCH TO WAR

THE SINO-JAPANESE WAR PUSHED U.S.-JAPANESE RELATIONS ONTO THE ROCKS. It destroyed what little was left of informal diplomacy and solidified the perception that the Japanese were controlled by the impulses of feudal militarism.

However, the United States had no interest in military involvement in East Asia in 1937. Strong isolationist views prevailed and the public and their president were focused on events in Europe, not East Asia. While the populace was sympathetic to China, the United States had very few concrete interests in China. Its trade with China was 2 percent of its total. There were no deep historic ties. The Open Door policy, which had provoked so much anguished discussion about protecting China's sovereignty, had been originally designed not as a vehicle for sovereignty but to rationalize the economic exploitation of China by the United States and other Western nations. China was the sentimental favorite but this support was based upon a myth that was not worth protecting by force of arms. So the existence of a Japanese Army occupying large stretches of Chinese soil provoked outrage but not military action.

There were even those who argued for rapprochement with Japan. John Hersey, a bold young journalist, wrote an article in *Life*, a popular new magazine, arguing for closer U.S.-Japanese relations. *Life* magazine was founded in 1936 by publisher Henry Luce as a large circulation photo magazine with contemporary news articles. By 1940, it had become one of the most popular magazines in America. Hersey noted that two major newspapers, the *Chicago Tribune* and the New York *Daily News* both endorsed closer relations with Japan, asserting that the United States had little investment in China, that Japan was an important customer, and that a negotiated settlement with Japan might remove Japan from parts of China.[1] A survey of American business executives done in September 1940 showed that 40 percent of the 15,000 people questioned favored accommodation with Japan in the form of a new trade treaty; 35 percent wanted to do nothing but only 19.1 percent favored an embargo.[2]

Hersey's article also discussed Joseph Grew, the U.S. ambassador to Japan. He believed that Grew was just the ambassador to patch up the U.S.-Japan relationship. Because Grew was tall and athletic, the Japanese would "stand in awe of giants" such as Grew. According to Hersey the Japanese "are stunted physically" and they have "a mass inferiority complex." Orientalist stereotypes aside, Grew had in fact cultivated the Japanese and was popular there. This did not however translate into "awe" as Hersey assumed.[3]

American opinion of Japan was shaped in the last years before Pearl Harbor by a conflicting discussion about American priorities and an intensifying distrust of the Japanese. In the words of journalists covering Japan, the Japanese were described variously as stunted, divine, mysterious, medieval, hypochondriac, blindly devoted, and/or mythological.

In another article in *Life*, Japan's premier Konoe Fumimaro was caricatured. Noting that Konoe exercised more power in Japan than any other individual, the writer then described him in a dichotomous fashion as athletic but of constant ill-health (or at least a prolific hypochondriac according to the article), Western-leaning but "shrewdly oriental," mundane and enigmatic in personality but divine and aristocratic by lineage from the ancient and honored Fujiwara family. The description was emblematic of American thought concerning Japan. No wonder Americans distrusted Japan.

More subtle but still important, the article was structured starting not with the rise of Konoe but with the death of Japan's last Meiji oligarch Prince Saionji Kinmochi. Described as the last great liberal of international status in Japan and the one last representative of Japan's period of modernization, Saionji upon his passing symbolized the death in Japan of liberal westernized modernity. To replace him, Konoe signified a new mysterious oriental approach based upon ancient values and culture. It did not matter that these descriptions of Saionji and Konoe were inventions. The power was in the description not the truth of it. Saionji was as much of a staunch imperial nationalist as Konoe. He simply conceived of cooperation and emulation of the West as a good strategy for Japanese growth and prosperity. Konoe had moved from a more pro-Western stance to a more conservative perspective focusing on Asia in the 1930s. The shift was a typical one for Japanese politicians in the 1930s and as much as Americans did not like the trend, there was little that was enigmatic or bizarrely oriental about it.

Other articles echoed the view that the Japanese had abandoned modernity and were retreating into their past. Entitled "Rise Again Amaterasu," an article on state Shintoism written by Harold Fey, associate editor at the *Christian Century*, suggested that while state Shinto in the Meiji period was accepted as secular, now state Shinto was considered by constitutional scholars to be an official religion of the state. Even Japanese Christians endorsed state Shinto, according to Fey, who cited a statement by a Japanese professor of religion at a Methodist seminary in Tokyo. Fey's assertion that all Japanese including Christians were under the spell of the "cult of the emperor," is problematic given the great pressure on Japanese Christians to conform to official dogma. It was not blind devotion but official pressure that moved Japanese Christians to endorse state Shinto.[4]

What had seemed rational, the progressive secularization and liberalization of the Japanese state, now reversed itself and Japan plunged irrationally into its past by reviving an ancient religion, Shinto. This narrative of reversal made sense to an American public that had been fed a steady diet of skepticism about Japan's modernity. But the story didn't fit with the Japanese situation. The Japanese had steadily cultivated Shinto as a state religion by using its symbols in the educational system beginning in the early Meiji period (1870s). Shinto was used by the Japanese government to buttress its claims to the past and therefore to universalize the modern Japanese state and strengthen its legitimacy. There was no reversal but instead a strong continuous effort to build state ideology and institutions from the late Meiji period onward. To his credit Fey did point out that this approach was by no means unique and could be identified to a certain extent in all modern states seeking to legitimize their power.[5]

In addition to the debate about Japanese identity, both sides discussed the role of misperceptions. Some denied the reality of the role of misperceptions in the decline of the relationship. The new Japanese ambassador to the United States, Admiral Nomura Kichisaburo gave an interview with the London *Daily Sketch* in March 1941 stating, "As far as I understand the situation, the United States understands quite well Japan's fundamental foreign policy and does not accept it. What is responsible for the long list of divergences dating from the Manchurian Incident is not so much 'misunderstanding' as it is fundamental differences in policy." On the face of it, this forthright statement makes a great deal of sense. It cut through the Orientalist and modern liberal/feudal militarism debates about Japan that preoccupied Americans.[6]

However, problems appear when we consider the issue of misunderstandings at a deeper level. While denying that misunderstandings played a role in tensions, Nomura, a big bluff diplomat with a reputation of openness, revealed his own significant misunderstanding of conditions in the United States. Upon his arrival in the United States, he was said to be "shocked" at the almost universal distrust of the Japanese among Americans.[7]

Others used the misperception debate to dismiss real issues. Robert Aura Smith, who was the cable editor at *The New York Times*, noted the contentious debate between Americans and Japanese about whether or not the

Japanese should be allowed a Japanese Monroe Doctrine in East Asia, like the Americans had in Latin America. Japanese commentators brought up the issue of American hegemony in Latin America arising from the Monroe Doctrine repeatedly when challenged on their position in Manchuria and China. Smith dismissed these similarities out of hand, claiming they were based upon misperceptions. The American Monroe Doctrine was about principle, not hegemony, according to Smith. Now the comparison the Japanese made, instead of being applicable and worthy of consideration, became just one more example of the misperceptions that plagued the relationship.[8]

A series of articles attempting to counter misperceptions appeared in the more scholarly *Annals of the American Academy*. This journal did not obtain a wide circulation but the articles do confirm issues that made their way into other larger forums. Galen Fisher, a former Japanese YMCA missionary, wrote an introductory article called "Understanding and Misunderstanding Japan." Fisher had been a proponent of the liberal modernity argument for Japan in the 1920s and even before the outset of the Sino-Japanese War had maintained that liberals in Japan would retake power in parliament and form a government. That was all in the past. Like so many other opinion leaders, he now embraced the feudal militarism argument. Emphasizing the unique and ancient Japanese culture to his audience, Fisher remarked on the "antiquity and unity of [Japan's] social order." More specifically, Fisher pointed out that while Europe and the United States had outgrown feudalism centuries ago, in Japan "feudalism exercises a far stronger influence on the contemporary Japanese chiefly because it flourished in Japan until 1872 . . ."[9]

This statement was not particularly problematic but the conclusions Fisher drew from Japan's apparent closeness to feudalism were more troubling. After claiming that Europe grew to modernity through the "fires" of political revolutions, war, and intellectual and industrial revolution, Fisher described Japan as "rusting at anchor under the sealed seclusion and Great Peace imposed by the Tokugawa regime." Japan stood still while the West progressed according to Fisher's view, which ignored the real intellectual and political tumults Japan experienced in the Tokugawa period. This "arrested development" according to Fisher meant that many of the "lineaments of feudalism appear in modern Japan, much as features like a high nose or heavy eyelids crop out in a family line." State control over the patterns of life, the Japanese "poker face" which allowed for no expression of emotion to be seen their visage, and blind obedience to the emperor were the visible results of apparently still active feudalism.[10]

Going further, Fisher argued that the "suppression of originality and its exclusion of stimulation from abroad is also to be blamed—or credited—for having cramped the Japanese genius . . ." One does not have to look far to refute this argument. The ero-guro-nansensu (erotic, grotesque, nonsensical) movement of the interwar period was a very creative artistic and social movement committed to the funny, weird, and erotic in Japanese culture. And if the supposed lack of originality began in the Tokugawa period, how does one explain the tremendous sense of artistry and humor Hiroshige used in depicting scenes from the Tokaido Road in his famous Tokaido Road paintings in the same period. The Tokaido Road works, rather than a copy, were so original they became models for Western painters in the late nineteenth and early twentieth centuries.[11]

Fisher concluded that his goal was to clear away the puzzle that was Japan. Doubtless he made the Japanese seem less mysterious but as he clarified so he also confirmed the outlines of an argument that locked Japan into an imagined past. Another article in the same issue of *Annals* mentioned cultural issues as the cause of misunderstandings. "Dissimilarity of blood and culture have provided fertile ground in which seeds of distrust and suspicion could grow into open antagonism." These attempts to clear up misunderstandings simply added weight to the misunderstandings that already existed.

Japanese commentator Go Toshi, president and editor of the *Japan Times* who had spent several years in the United States, outlined the Japanese view of "misunderstandings" in the same issue of *Annals*. Go Toshi accused the American State Department of willfully manipulating public opinion by "misrepresenting the situation in China," sensationalizing the news coming from China to portray Japan in a bad light.[12]

The Japanese alliance with Germany also became a ground for misunderstanding. While Americans accused Japan of damaging the U.S.-Japan relationship severely by allying itself with Germany and Italy in the Axis Pact in 1940, Go Toshi accused the American government of leaving Japan to shift in the wind instead of reaching out for a compromise when the European war broke out in spring 1940. According to this perspective, the United States had forced Japan into the Axis alliance by its opposition. Denying that the Axis Pact was an aggressive move, Go Toshi argued the Japanese saw it as a peace pact, designed to show Japanese strength and therefore keep the Americans out of the European war and the Sino-Japanese War. Here Go Toshi misunderstood American public opinion. The American public had been fed a constant stream of negative information about Hitler throughout the 1930s. Americans therefore distrusted any nation that allied itself with Hitler. The Japanese apparently did not understand this fact. The explanation for this misunderstanding and Nomura's surprise about the anti-Japanese mood of American public opinion is that the Japanese government put less emphasis on understanding American public opinion than it had during the Manchurian Incident.[13]

It is likely that the Japanese government came to the conclusion that some tension with the United States was a reasonable price to be paid for its aggressive approach in China. As the temper of American public opinion became less crucial to Japan's foreign policy formulation, the Japanese government paid less attention to understanding American public opinion, though it still tried to manipulate it through propaganda. In addition, the Japanese Foreign Ministry lost power and influence in the 1930s and their knowledge of American opinion therefore did not matter as much to the militarists who controlled and directed Japan's policies. Censorship also contributed to the problem. Important statements of American sentiment were censored out of the Japanese media.

Negative public attitudes resulted from the perception gaps on both sides. A U.S. Gallup poll taken in May 1939 showed that 74 percent favored China and only two percent favored Japan in the Sino-Japanese War. This marked an increase of 15 percent from the beginning of the war. The poll suggested the isolationist impulse to remain neutral was waning. Americans now endorsed a boycott on Japanese goods by a two-thirds majority and 72 percent supported an embargo of arms against Japan. Another poll three months later showed even stronger support. Americans now endorsed the canceling of the U.S.-Japanese Treaty of Commerce and Navigation of 1911 and supported an embargo on war material by a whopping 81 percent.[14]

By this time the Japanese had themselves begun to poll their population about the U.S.-Japan relationship. In 1940, the Japan University Professors League undertook a poll of Tokyo Imperial University student parents and guardians concerning Japanese foreign policy. Out of a survey of 11,789 respondents, 6,428 or 54 percent said they would support a war against the United States if it tried to stop Japan from securing resources in the Dutch East Indies and 40 percent declined to answer the question, which indicated the Japanese were not necessarily as unified or blindly obedient as Americans assumed. On the issue of the ongoing war in Europe, the respondents favored Germany heavily (82%) over Britain (3%) although the results also made clear that the Japanese did not want to get involved in the European war. While there were many who were undecided about the question of war in the U.S.-Japan relationship, Japanese antagonism to the United States was still quite high. On questions short of war, as in American public opinion, there was little support for the other and much support for their enemies, Germany for Japan and Great Britain for the United States.[15]

While American public opinion was firmly against Japan, American policy was characterized by drift, according to Harold Quigley, East Asian expert, who wrote in the *Atlantic Monthly*. Great distrust of the Japanese made movement toward Japan impossible. Strong pro-Chinese sentiment enabled support for the Chinese but not enough support to justify American entrance in the war. Quigley noted the ties of the American public to Christianity in

China, ties kept open by missionaries there, and the American belief that under its influence China was becoming more democratic, although this view was as mythic as it was strong. Caught between support for China and commitment to isolationism, American policy drifted.

The drift, however, was in the particular direction of punishing Japan short of war. An embargo would meet the criteria of doing something while not engaging in war.[16] Calls for an embargo had emerged not among official diplomats but among private citizens such as Henry Stimson. Roosevelt was in tune with public opinion in wanting some form of action against Japan. However, joining the war in East Asia was out of the question because Roosevelt believed that the United States would have to enter the war in Europe eventually and he did not want to fight a two-front war. Public pressure for an embargo mounted as photos of the Japanese loading oil at American ports and accompanying stories of large purchases of oil by Japan filled the front pages of American newspapers, inflaming American public opinion.[17]

Widespread support for an embargo made it the most viable option for the Roosevelt administration to use against Japan. But not all agreed that an embargo would bring the Japanese to their senses. Kenneth Latourette, long-time expert on Japan, claimed the embargo had the dangerous potential to bring about war between the United States and Japan. In an article entitled "A Church-Made War with Japan?" Latourette pointed out that the very people who hated war, Christian activists and missionaries, were through their calls for an embargo against Japan forcing the United States and Japan to the point where war might become impossible to avoid. Other experts noted much the same; missionaries from China and supportive church groups had led the charge against Japan. Noting that moral arguments for an embargo were so strong as to make it seem immoral to argue against it, Latourette then outlined the consequences of an embargo. Japanese determination was so great that Japanese liberals and Christians who had initially opposed the Sino-Japanese War would swing in favor of the war in China, according to Latourette. Precisely gauging the Japanese temperament, he outlined the problems and consequences of an embargo and boycott.[18]

A complete boycott would bring even more serious retaliation. The Japanese are tense with a war psychology. They are a proud people. Relations between the United States and Japan have long been chronically strained. The Japanese have not forgotten our treatment of their fellow countrymen in the United States or our immigration law of 1924. It would not take much to start reprisals . . . The more radical elements in the Japanese army would shake off restraint. Japanese retaliation would provoke American counter-reprisals.[19]

Latourette's solution to the problem was a combination of waiting out the situation, confident in eventual Chinese victory in the war, and endorsement of church-based unofficial diplomacy. In reality, Latourette's solution was not much of a solution at all. Waiting did nothing to help the Chinese and the declining effectiveness of unofficial diplomacy made it a dubious tool for resolution.

How seriously did the Japanese take the embargo threat? Japanese commentators were well aware of the Gallup poll showing great support for an embargo against Japan. However, Kiyo Sue Inui, a Tokyo Imperial University professor of international relations, discounted the poll because he was also well aware that the Americans were isolationist and did not want to go to war. Because Kiyo Sue Inui had lectured at Occidental College and the University of Southern California there, he had an excellent grasp of the situation in the United States.

The Gallup poll indicating something like 82 per cent., later 86 per cent., in favour of embargoing certain materials, reputed to be used for war purposes, to Japan, is often cited as the index figures of American public opinion. On the other hand, according to General Hugh Johnson, "99 per cent. of the American people do not care to have war with Japan, while 80 per cent. Of the people do not know what it is all about." Without questioning the high standard of American intelligence, the writer is inclined to agree with the general and is unwilling to accept the Gallup figures as a well considered American opinion. Rather he prefers to treat them as the hearsay American opinion, that of the floating mind or as an expression of America's sociality.[20]

This Japanese view is significant because it dismissed the embargo potential, instead choosing to emphasize American isolationism and relative indifference. What Kiyo Sue Inui did not understand is that there was no contradiction between antiwar opinion and strong support the embargo. The embargo was the most logical choice, given the American fear of war and yet strong American support for some sort of action.

However little even the best informed Japanese understood of American sentiment, many Americans themselves did not see the full consequences of an embargo of strategic resources. When Kiyo Sue Inui was in the United States in 1940, he recognized that Americans both official and unofficial assumed the negative reinforcement of the abrogation of the trade treaty and the talk of embargo would chasten the Japanese and prevent them from further aggression. The view that the embargo was not in fact provocative is confirmed by Americans in other writings. "The average American might be willing to apply economic pressure from a secure position behind five thousand miles of open Pacific, but he was still unwilling to provoke Japan into retaliation."[21]

The embargo was assumed to not be an aggressive act, according to this view. Just the opposite was true, according to Kiyo Sue Inui, who argued that the ratcheting up of the embargo pushed Japan into the arms of the Axis partners. The implication is clear as well that implementation of a total embargo would further alienate the Japanese and would have serious consequences, maybe this time directed against the United States.

> The American intelligentsia, China missionaries, college professors, journalists and others who are interested in collective security, and sanctions against Japan, were not quite so militant as to advocate a full-dress war with her in the hope of subjugating or defeating her. They are sincere in their belief in sanctions. The saddest part was that they saw nothing beyond its immediate consequences. Never did they dream of the ultimate implications of their type of "power politics."[22]

In 1939, President Roosevelt moved to abandon the U.S.-Japanese Treaty of Commerce and Navigation of 1911 with Japan and implement a licensing system for strategic resources such as oil, scrap iron, and steel and spare parts for airplanes. Roosevelt was also given the power by Congress in the National Defense Action Act of 1940 to place a total embargo on goods going to Japan. The licensing system was like a water spigot. The Roosevelt administration turned the spigot tighter and tighter against Japan between 1939 and 1941. In September 1940 the United States embargoed scrap metal. Then in the spring of 1941, Americans acted without public announcement to cut Japan's oil exports. The United States would decide on an ad hoc basis how much oil Japan was going to get in a particular month. The Japanese could only guess how much oil they would be allowed to buy. In the late summer of 1941, oil exports to Japan were being cut again and again until oil stopped flowing altogether. The Japanese were almost entirely dependent upon the United States for these crucial items. To Roosevelt, the embargo represented action short of war. It was also intended to buy the United States time to build its military.[23]

On the other hand, the Japanese saw the embargo as a provocative half-measure that ensured that war would come sooner rather than later. The assumption that the Japanese somehow wouldn't notice that they were able to buy less and less oil each month was foolish. The embargo pushed Japan into a corner and forced it to find new sources of oil. If the actual oil cutoff was the work of a single man, Assistant Secretary of State Dean Acheson, as historian Walter Lafeber suggests, all the more reason to criticize it.[24]

For all the concern about Japanese diplomatic cunning, the Americans now pursued a sneaky diplomacy of an unannounced oil embargo that grew every month. The Roosevelt Administration would have had better success with direct communication and action that sent a clear signal than with this secretive action. Commentator Robert Aura Smith suggested the same.

It is not jingoistic to suggest that a clearer definition by our own State Department of the limits of American patience will be useful. A forthright declaration of what we propose to defend may assist the Japanese in deciding what they can, and cannot afford to attack.[25]

For the third time in the U.S.-Japan relationship, anti-Japanese public opinion limited the options of official diplomacy. In the Manchurian Incident and in the beginning stages of the Sino-Japanese War, official diplomacy had been restricted by an unfavorable public opinion of Japan. In this case, by pushing the U.S. government toward an oil embargo, distrust of Japan moved the two nations closer to war. No doubt other factors such as the predominance of Europe, the desire to buy more time, and the unwillingness to act too aggressively in international affairs because of isolationism played into the calculation that an embargo was the best choice. But public opinion played a large role in these considerations as well.

By September 1941, the full extent of the American embargo had become clear to the Japanese public. In addition, the Americans froze Japanese assets. The Americans had succeeded in shutting down Japanese economic interchange with the United States completely by this time. An article outlining the embargo and asset freeze was published in the *Kaizo* (Reconstruct) in that month and later translated in *Contemporary Japan*. It ended by suggesting that the Japanese needed to "thoroughly acquaint all our nationals with the true character of the freezing order."[26]

Official diplomats on both sides now recognized that time was running out for the U.S.-Japan relationship. In the spring and summer of 1941, American and Japanese diplomacy intensified to try to find a solution to the crisis in China and Japan's occupation of French Indochina (the Japanese had moved troops into northern Indochina in September 1940 and southern Indochina in July 1941 with the connivance of Germany which persuaded the Vichy government in France to give its stamp of approval). Though Nomura Kichisaburo was a friend of Roosevelt and the kind of diplomat Americans warmed to, he had little diplomatic experience, having served as a naval officer for most of his career. Exceedingly suspicious of Japanese intentions in Southeast Asia and well aware that any negotiated settlement could lead to charges of appeasement, American Secretary of State Cordell Hull was in no mood to compromise. And the Japanese government, led by Konoe and Matsuoka Yôsuke, still maintained that it was trying to keep the peace, but its action in moving into Indochina was expansionist and warlike. This was a recipe for a catastrophe, not a negotiated settlement.[27]

At issue was Japan's control of Indochina and China proper and Japan's alliance with Germany. The Japanese were willing to back off from Indochina and put the Axis alliance on the table. However, the Americans wanted a troop withdrawal from China as well. The Japanese would agree to only a selected withdrawal of some troops. In return the Japanese wanted a partial lift of the embargo on oil and scrap metal and American mediation of the China conflict and settlement on terms favorable to Japan. Even though the diplomacy was frantic and substantial—Saburo Kurusu, a career diplomat was sent to the United States in November 1941 to help Nomura with negotiations—the basic terms were out of reach. Japan wanted the United States to join its side on the China crisis and settle it to the detriment of China which in the parts they controlled would become another puppet state. The United States wanted to get Japan out of both China and Manchuria. Essentially both sides were asking for the thing that the other side could not give up under any circumstances. This made for surreal negotiations that went nowhere. The Japanese took their own rhetoric concerning their regional bloc called the Greater East Asia Co-Prosperity Sphere too seriously to recognize that others might not see it that way, and the Americans could not escape the view that the Japanese had turned their backs on modernity and the liberal West.[28]

Into this cauldron two private citizens, one Japanese and one American, reached out to officials with plans to stop the march to war. Father James Drought was vicar general of the Maryknoll Society, a Catholic organization. Like many before him, Drought believed that channels outside of government offered an opportunity to solve U.S.-Japan tensions. In this case, Drought used unofficial channels to get official diplomacy rolling. He came into contact with several Japanese officials who had connections with Prince Konoe and was able to get an initial proposal for settlement reviewed and approved by the Japanese government. In April 1941, Drought presented a draft of a Japanese proposal to Cordell Hull. In the same month, Nomura accepted the Drought draft as a basis for the start of secret negotiations between Hull and himself that lasted from April until the attack on Pearl Harbor.[29]

While it would be inaccurate to say that Drought had produced a realistic offer from the Japanese to the Americans, his ideas caught the attention of the Japanese who were interested in probing the American side to see how many concessions they could gain. Drought's draft proposed that Japan's troops remain in China after a peace settlement for a "joint defense against communism." And it obligated the Americans to cease aid to China if China refused to negotiate a settlement. In effect it put all of the important cards in Japan's hand. The Americans however had their own reasons for starting talks even if the proposal was one-sided. Hull and Roosevelt needed time more than anything else and the negotiations bought them time. On the other hand, the expanding embargo made time short (shorter than anyone realized). Negotiations were also a way to see how much commitment the Japanese had to the Axis alliance. Serious compromises and a settlement were unlikely given this situation.[30]

Kagawa Toyohiko, the famous social gospel preacher, also engaged in last-ditch diplomacy during his trip to the United States as part of a Christian delegation to salvage U.S.-Japanese relations in 1941. While he was there Kagawa met with an old friend who had attended Princeton Seminary with him, E. Stanley Jones. Suggesting that Jones visit Admiral Nomura, Japanese ambassador in Washington, Kagawa outlined a bizarre proposal to avert war. The Americans would convince the Dutch to give up New Guinea in the South Pacific to Japan. This would provide the Japanese with a realistic place to send their excess population and in turn it would discredit the militarists' argument that forceful expansion was necessary because immigration doors had been shut in the West. The proposal was outdated and unrealistic. While immigration had fueled tensions in the 1920s, U.S.-Japanese problems had gone way beyond immigration by 1941. Jones, however, liked the proposal and believed it would also allow the Japanese to leave their alliance with Germany. He shuttled around Washington with Kagawa's plan over the next several months, meeting with Japanese diplomats Nomura and Kurusu and eventually gaining an audience with President Roosevelt on December 3, 1941.[31]

Jones did not present Kagawa's plan but instead forwarded a Japanese diplomatic proposal that Roosevelt send a cable to Hirohito with a direct plea to stop the impending war. Prominent Japanese such as Yale University professor Asakawa Kan'ichi and businessman Ayukawa Yoshisuke supported the effort. The cable was sent on December 5. Apparently Kagawa also sent cables from Japan to Jones and Roosevelt stating that the Japanese prime minister wanted to meet with the president. Nothing came of Kagawa's intervention and while earlier in the year Drought was able to get negotiations rolling, nothing came of them either. That both private citizens intervened directly speaks to the powerful role they believed private citizens could play in diplomacy. Their failure is a symbol for the failure of private diplomacy in general.[32]

Many of the mechanisms for unofficial diplomacy had been destroyed at the outset of the Sino-Japanese War. The IPR, the foremost organization for mediating the unofficial U.S.-Japan relationship, had suffered from very great tensions and was now helpless to stop the march to war. Instead, the American IPR leader Edward Carter used his connections in the U.S. government to place IPR research initiatives and research personnel into the State and War departments to help with war planning. The JCIPR had long before become connected to the Foreign Ministry.

Tsurumi Yusuke, a veteran unofficial diplomat, started the Institute of the Pacific, a small organization that supported Japan through writing and publicity encouraging tourism in Japan's expanding empire in Asia. His letters and writings reveal complete support for the expansion of the Japanese Empire, calling it a Pax Japonica. His evolution from a liberal internationalist to Japanese nationalist and propagandist was by this time complete and his earlier service as an unofficial diplomat promoting U.S.-Japanese friendship all but forgotten.[33]

Tsurumi gave a speech at the Kokusai Bunka Shinkokai (Society for International Cultural Relations) building in Tokyo to the Japan-American Student Conference (JASC) in 1940. The JASC had been started in 1934 by some Japanese students concerned about the deteriorating U.S.-Japanese relationship. The JASC was held annually and alternated between Japan and the United States. The conferences were suspended during World War II but resumed after the war and are still held today. Tsurumi gave his standard speech defending Japan's actions in China and blaming U.S. tariffs and immigration exclusion. James Halsema, an American student, remembers discussion of Tsurumi's speech dominated the next day's roundtable. The Japanese students defended Tsurumi and their empire. But Halsema thought in general that the conference was far too controlled by authorities whose goal was to convince the American students that Japan's cause in East Asia was righteous. One Japanese student compared Japan to a mother who tells her children what they must do, and according to Halsema, the Japanese students admitted readily that they held no resentment at censorship and thought control because it served the interests of the nation. Halsema was skeptical that the conference would make any difference in U.S.-Japanese relations.[34]

JAPANESE CHRISTIAN DIPLOMACY

Religious groups now stepped to the forefront. The ties between missionaries and Japanese Christians had deteriorated over the years. Many missionaries had been sent back home, in part because the Great Depression had reduced funding levels for missionaries everywhere and in part because the Japanese government continually pressured the missionaries to go home. The government continued to pressure Japanese Christians on the issue of divided loyalties. In addition, the Japanese government now planned to amalgamate all religious organizations into one department of the government.

The government forced Christians into two organizations, one for Catholics and one for Protestants, the Kenehonkadisto and Nepunkadisto. According to historian Mark Mullins, these organizations were

> raising money for warplanes and began every religious service by bowing to the imperial family or the emperor. Sermon topics were sent from the government directly to churches, and for the most part churches conformed to this

directive. Various new religions and Christian denominations became the target of investigation, persecution, and arrest by the special police until the end of World War II.[35]

Although on the surface, it seemed that the Japanese state had simply repressed the Christian movement, the situation was more complex. In a response similar to the one taken by the IPR in Japan (JCIPR) in their union with the Japan International Association (JIA) in 1935, Christians themselves argued that the move was voluntary and expressed enthusiasm for the changes. In fact, the Christian movement in Japan had studied the possibility of church union for several decades and Japanese Christians had a tradition of deemphasizing denominations. The cooperation between the government and nongovernmental organizations in achieving state goals is characteristic of modern Japan, according to historian Sheldon Garon, who calls this phenomenon "state management." Garon notes that even after the Religious Bodies Law was abrogated after the war in 1945 by the SCAP occupation authorities, many Japanese Christians requested that the new law continue to regulate religious expression. This suggests that at least some of the changes were genuinely voluntary and not just at the behest of the state.[36]

The goal of government pressure was to rectify the thought of Christian groups by clarifying their relationship to the emperor and the Japanese state and thereby make patriots out of them. The Japanese Government emphasized that Christians had to choose between their loyalty to their god and their loyalty to the emperor. This was an old trick that had been used in the 1890s to tar Japanese Christians with the charge of disloyalty. Japanese Christians at that time had argued forcefully that Christianity was needed by the Japanese state to bring moral progress. They effectively refuted the accusations. And they were samurai Christians and so they had strong credibility in Japanese society.[37]

However, in the late 1930s, Japanese Christians were in a weaker position and had fewer tools for resistance. Christians felt obligated to invoke emperor system ideology and visit state sponsored Shinto Shrines. One missionary described the situation.

> Regimentation, pressure from above in thinking, and living precariously are the accepted thing today, and yet the government seems to be very clever in keeping the balance. When there is growing resentment against certain restrictions, before the point of danger is reached the pressure is relieved and the situation saved.

In addition, in the late 1930s, new emphasis was placed upon an old dictum that Christianity in Japan ought to be nationalized or "Japanized" and missionaries in some cases were asked to leave because they were seen as an unwelcome foreign intrusion. As Christianity was nationalized in Japan, it became much more difficult for Japanese Christians to act as mediators between Japan and the United States.[38]

In the spring of 1941, however, there was a last-ditch attempt by Japanese and American Christians to save the relationship. Japanese Christians led the effort. The Japanese National Council of Churches decided to send a delegation to the United States with the goal to "preserve the peace between Japan and the United States." The major Japanese Christian leaders of that time came to the United States: Bishop Abe Yoshimune of the Methodist Church, Reverend Kozaki Michio of the Congregational Church, Soichi Saito of the Japanese YMCA, Miss Michio Kawai of the Japanese YWCA, MP Matsuyama Tsunejiro, Dr. Yuasa Hachiro, and Christian activist Kagawa Toyohiko. The delegation arrived in April 1941, stayed for about two months, met with American Christians in Chicago and New York, gave speeches across the country, and held two conferences, one in Riverside, California and another in Atlantic City, New Jersey.[39]

From the beginning, the visit was flawed. If the Japanese delegation was to impact American public opinion, they would have to have full access to the media. However, instructions for the Japanese delegates stated "no publicity–the quieter the better." The instructions also emphasized that no publicity should get back to Japan. The Americans generally agreed. This limit reflected fear about exposing the delegation to the now almost universal distrust for Japan in the United States and likewise exposure to censure and harassment if news of the meetings reached the Japanese media.[40] In addition, a document called "Some Negative Aspects of Christianity in America," most likely written by a Japanese Christian, probably circulated among the delegates. Highly critical of American Christianity, the document claimed American Christians pursued policies that were "partisan, half-baked, unbalanced, unguarded . . ." in support of the embargo and other issues. Although the purpose was unclear, one can clearly see Japanese nationalization of Christianity and the alienation from American Christianity in it. As the Japanese had so many times before, the delegation invoked the Monroe Doctrine to compare Japan's interventions in China and Indochina with American interventions in Latin America. Abe Yoshimune, the leader of the delegation, defended the church union concept and the Religious Bodies Law. Far from overcoming the antagonistic nationalism that existed on both sides, the meetings were drenched with it.[41]

And yet, Abe, who had been a church leader for over thirty years, had been to the United States often, and had made many friends among American Christians, couldn't help but comment upon the rapid transformation of Japan and Christian movement in Japan in the late 1930s. In unforced moments at the beginning of his speeches, Abe gave Americans a glimpse into the mind-set of Christians and possibly many others in Japan by admitting that there was confusion among the Japanese.

> As I have often stated during these days, the situation in Japan is as if our people felt that "the common sense of yesterday is not the common sense of today." That means that we really do not know where to go nor what we are.

Whether Abe stated this to reveal the thoughts of his heart or to placate American Christians is impossible to tell. But the grain of truth is unmistakable and it is a truth that many Americans could identify with in 1941. One's friends were no longer friends but enemies; the successful collaboration of the past had become the intractable problems of the present and future.[42]

Although the effort was genuine, and Christians felt positively about the visit, the delegation had no impact on the march to war. The visit came too late to be effective. And the unofficial diplomacy that it represented suffered from the same problem it had throughout the interwar period: nationalism was so strong that it drowned out calls for a more truly international perspective. This fact was compounded by the deterioration of the web of unofficial connections between Japan and the United States.

Writing before the trip, a commentator in *The Christian Century* put it well.

> Indeed, when it comes to these political issues in the Pacific the conference is likely to provide a striking illustration of the limitation of action by religious forces *after* a political situation has deteriorated to the point of tense crisis [italics in original] . . . To put the problem concretely, if the Japanese delegates should agree that the present policy of their government in China is an unjustified aggression, what chance is there that they could, at this juncture, persuade the Japanese people to demand an abandonment of that policy. Or if the American delegates should agree that the Oriental exclusion policy of the United States constitutes an unjustified insult to Japanese sensibilities, what chance have they at present of persuading the American public to demand the abandonment of that policy? Or what chance have both delegations of inducing their government to abandon their present reliance on military measures?[43]

The attempts to stop the march to war in 1941 were too late to save the peace. War broke out on December 7 with the Japanese bombing of Pearl Harbor and the general invasion of Southeast Asia later that month.

IMPACT ON THE POSTWAR WORLD

THE PACIFIC WAR WAS NOT JUST ABOUT RESOURCES OR THE GEOPOLITICAL rivalry between the United States and Japan but also about links between those issues and the public's view of the country they fought. It was a war made by public perceptions of the other as well as by oil, scrap metal, and military strategy.

Given the central place of public opinion in the making of the Pacific War, the negative images that Americans and Japanese brought into the war can help to explain several important characteristics of the war. First, John Dower's *War Without Mercy* makes more sense given the prevailing negative views and deep distrust on both sides at the outbreak of the war. The sense of betrayal and outrage that shook American opinion is matched by the steadily building sense of betrayal and outrage of the Japanese at the hands of the great powers of the West including the United States. The Japanese betrayed their promise of liberal modernity in the rise of militarism and a violent, seemingly atavistic expansion into Manchuria and China. The Americans betrayed their promise of democratic fairness at the Washington Conference and in anti-Japanese discrimination culminating in immigration exclusion. A war of hatred was the logical result of this atmosphere.

Second, the rising antagonism and pressures to conform on both sides help explain how private citizens committed to internationalism and peace in U.S.-Japanese relations became estranged from one another and became staunch nationalists serving their nations in the Pacific War. Loyalty to nation trumped friendships and trans-pacific cooperation. The struggle to define international cooperation allowed both governments to co-opt internationalist efforts. Trust was broken and spying became a concern on both sides.

Thus, the seeds of the Pacific War were planted long before they germinated. They germinated as the Pacific War began.

The IPR in its role as the organization with the most expertise on Japan sponsored conferences and meetings to discuss the future peace and reconstruction of Japan after Pearl Harbor. The meetings focused much attention on the question of what lay in the Japanese mind. Theories explaining Japanese thought and behavior, especially its wartime atrocities, abounded. Freudian theories posited that the Japanese were repressed. One scholar even blamed the violence of the Japanese Army on Japanese toilet-training habits, the so-called Scot Tissue theory. Though ridiculous, these and other theories dominated discussion about how to reconstruct Japan.[1]

The U.S. Army signal corps made a film about Japan called "Japanese Behavior" in 1944. Though never released, the film confirmed views that prevailed elsewhere, articulating theories of Japanese behavior. Rejecting a blatantly Orientalist approach, the film tried to demonstrate the confusion among the Japanese people about modernization, showing film clips of Japanese dressed in a mix of western and traditional clothing who had to choose between a martini or a glass of sake. It also used theories of sociology to show that the Japanese were so-called ladder people. The Japanese always had someone above and someone below them in their social hierarchy. Intended to explain how Japanese would follow suicidal orders or fight to the death, the film invoked stereotypes about the Japanese.

The accumulation of knowledge about the Japanese was important because this knowledge was used in the planning of the American occupation of Japan after World War II. This is especially true of Ruth Benedict's well-known and influential book written between 1944 and 1946 and published in 1946 as *The Chrysanthemum and the Sword*. Benedict, a cultural anthropologist who studied with Franz Boas, was hired by the U.S. War Department to write an analysis of Japanese culture in an attempt to know the enemy better. One can see Boaz's influence in Benedict's emphasis on culture. "No one is unaware of the deep-rooted cultural differences between the United States and Japan."[2]

This book was considered the authoritative work on Japan in its time, influenced approaches to Japan in the postwar occupation period coming out of Washington, DC, and was used as a model for studying history and anthropology across the country in the 1950s–1960s.

Benedict was a part of a group of intellectuals hired by the U.S. Military to study Japan and make it comprehensible to Americans fighting the war. Geoffrey Gorer, Gregory Bateson, Margeret Mead, and several others all participated in the "national character" studies that dominated wartime anthropological approaches. The goal of Benedict's study was to make a supposedly irrational and closeted Japanese culture clear to Americans. She used the book to study the cultural peculiarities of the Japanese and explain their violent attack on the United States as a product of a neurotic, highly pressurized culture. Chapter by chapter Benedict discussed Japanese commitment to hierarchy, loyalty, proper place, duty, and reciprocal obligations. She concluded that these cultural characteristics created a great deal of tension and repression which in turn fueled irrational and violent behavior. The return to an Orientalist posture is unmistakable in Benedict's obsession with Japanese culture—politics and diplomacy apparently played almost no role in Benedict's explanation of Japan's turn to war—and its strangeness, only to be understood even dimly through anthropology and psychology. Here Japanese inscrutability, a prominent feature of late nineteenth-century Orientalism, returned with force.[3]

Benedict distanced herself from the prewar argument of missionaries and others that Japan was becoming just like the United States, following a universal liberal route to modernity. She called the prewar ideas the "brotherhood of man" argument (an implicit but clear reference to the influence of Christian missionaries in shaping American thinking about Japan in the prewar period). Suggesting that those who saw the Japanese as fundamentally the same as Americans suffered from their own neurosis, she wrote, "But to demand such uniformity as a condition of respecting another nation is as neurotic as to demand it of one's wife or one's children." She also hints at a deeper agenda by suggesting that the attempt to make another culture like our own was "wanton" and implicitly pointing to an imperialist mind-set within American missionaries as the problem. Benedict's criticism can be seen as an indirect attack on the views of people like Sidney Gulick, Sherwood Eddy, and Galen Fisher.[4]

Benedict's own view was that the occupation should be lenient. Her book's conclusions helped shape an American view of Japanese focused on the peculiarities of Japanese culture: hierarchy, obedience, loyalty, and duty. Her book became the authoritative account of Japanese culture and is widely cited even today. The foundation for her view was the prewar argument that the Japanese were not really modern people.

NOTES

INTRODUCTION   THE SEEDS OF WAR

1. John Dewey, *China, Japan and the USA: Present-Day Conditions in the Far East and Their Bearing on the Washington Conference*, New Republic Pamphlet No. 1 (New York: Republic Publishing Company, November 12, 1921), 9.
2. Ibid., 26.
3. Ibid., 63.
4. Richard F. Calichman, ed., *Contemporary Japanese Thought* (New York: Columbia University Press, 2005), 105.
5. George H. Gallup, *The Gallup Poll: Public Opinion, 1935–1948* (New York: Random House, 1972), 39.
6. Richard Smethurst, *A Social Basis of Prewar Japanese Militarism: The Army and the Rural Community* (Berkeley: University of California Press, 1974).
7. Akira Iriye, *Cultural Internationalism and World Order*, 45. John F. Howes, *Nitobe Inazô: Japan's Bridge across the Pacific* no, leave in, first reference.
8. *Current Research Program*, American Council, Institute of Pacific Relations, October 31, 1938, Rare Book and Manuscript Library, Columbia University, New York, 5.

CHAPTER 1   AMERICAN PERCEPTIONS OF JAPAN: LIBERAL MODERNITY OR FEUDAL MILITARISM

1. Analysis of the *Reader's Guide to Periodical Literature* by James Uregen, October 2003.
2. Walter Lafeber, *The Clash: U.S.-Japanese Relations Throughout History* (New York: W.W. Norton, 1998), 84.
3. Hirao Ren, "The Campaign of Education among Americans and Why," *The Japanese Student*, Vol. 1, No. 2 (December 1916), 2.
4. Sheila K. Johnson, *The Japanese through American Eyes* (Stanford University Press, 1988), v.
5. A.B. Simpson, *Larger Outlooks on Missionary Lands* (New York: Christians Alliance Publishing, 1893), 551, 542.
6. Edward Said, *Orientalism* (New York: Random House, 1979).
7. Johnson, *The Japanese*, v.

8. Joe Hennings, *Outposts of Civilization: Race, Religion, and the Formative Years of American-Japanese Relations* (New York: New York University Press, 2000), Chapter 4.

9. Ibid., 109–111.

10. Ibid., 105–106. Mari Yoshihara, *Embracing the East: White Women and American Orientalism* (New York: Oxford University Press, 2000). Stefan Tanaka, "Imaging History: Inscribing Belief in the Nation," *The Journal of Asian Studies*, Vol. 53, No. 1. (February 1994), 24–30.

11. J.O.P. Bland, *China, Japan, and Korea* (New York: Charles Scribner and Sons, 1921), 318.

12. Editorials, Dr. Frank Crane, "What the Orient Thinks of Us," *Current Opinion*, April 1922, 450–453. Bland, *China, Japan and Korea*, 176–177.

13. William Elliot Griffis, "Japan, Child of the World's Old Age: An Empire of Mountainous Islands, Whose Alert People Constantly Conquer Harsh Forces of Land, Sea and Sky," *National Geographic Magazine*, Vol. 63, No. 3 (March 1933). *The Mikado* was on several reading lists including this one: "Books on Japan," *Literary Digest*, Vol. 72 (January 1922), 71.

14. Sidney Gulick, *White Peril in the Far East: An Interpretation of the Significance of the Russo-Japanese War* (New York: Fleming Revell, 1905), 29.

15. Nitobe Inazô, *Bushido*, seventeenth edition (Tokyo: Charles E. Tuttle Company, 1984), 189–192. William Henry Chamberlin, "How Strong Is Japan?" *The Atlantic Monthly*, Vol. 160 (December 1937), 788–789.

16. Thomas Millard, *The New Far East* (New York: Scribner's Sons, 1906), 18.

17. George William Knox, *The Spirit of the Orient* (New York: T. Y. Crowell & Co., 1906), 254–255.

18. Ibid., 62.

19. Ibid., 289–290.

20. Knox, *Spirit of the Orient*, 256–257.

21. Akira Iriye, *Cultural Internationalism and World Order*, 41.

22. Arthur Judson Brown, "Twenty Books on Japan Worth Reading," *Missionary Review of the World* (October 1923), 874.

23. Sidney Gulick, *White Peril in the Far East*, 88.

24. Ibid., 106.

25. Sherwood Eddy, *The Challenge of the East* (New York: Farrar and Rhinehart, 1931), 120–124.

26. Circular Letter, Sherwood Eddy, September 20, 1922, Found in Sherwood Eddy Biographical File, Kautz Family YMCA Archives, St. Paul, MN, hereafter referred to as KFYMCA Archives.

27. Galen M. Fisher, *Creative Forces in Japan* (New York: Missionary Education Movement of the United States and Canada, 1923), 35.

28. Putnam Weale, *An Indiscreet Chronicle from the Pacific* (London: George Allen and Unwin, Ltd., 1923), 2. See also H.M. Hyndman, *The Awakening of Asia* (New York: Boni and Liveright, 1919), 126.

29. Jesse Willis Jefferies, "What Japan Is Thinking," *New York Times Current History* (1921), 927.

30. Bland, *China Japan and Korea*, 176–177.

31. Stephen King Hall, *Western Civilization and the Far East* (London: Methuen and Co., 1925), 30, 118.

32. Ibid., 279.

33. Andrew Gordon, *Labor and Imperial Democracy in Prewar Japan*, (Berkeley: University of California Press, 1991).

34. Marguerite Harrison, *Yellow Dragon and Red Bear* (London: Brentano's Ltd., Published in United States by George H. Doran Company, 1924), 40.

35. Ibid., 53–54.

36. Stanley Hornbeck, *Contemporary Politics in the Far East* (New York: D. Appleton and Company, 1918), 214.

37. Fujitani Takashi, *Splendid Monarchy: Power and Pageantry in Modern Japan* (Berkeley: University of California Press, 1998).

38. Modris Eksteins, *Rites of Spring: The Great War and the Birth of the Modern Age* (New York: Anchor Books, 1989).

39. Russell F. Weigley, "The Role of the War Department and the Army," *Pearl Harbor As History: Japanese-American Relations, 1931–1941*, Dorothy Borg and Shumpei Okamoto, eds. (New York: Columbia University Press, 1973), 186.

CHAPTER 2   JAPANESE RESPONSE
TO ORIENTALISM

1. E.E. Speight, "The English Reading of Young Japan," *The Living Age*, excerpted from *Japan Advertiser*, Vol. 316 (March 17, 1923), 663. Robert Nichols, "Young Japan and Its Reading," *The Literary Review*, Vol. 3 (July 7, 1923), 818.

2. Rev. S.H. Wainright, "What the Japanese are Reading," *The Missionary Review of the World* (December 1923), 991–992.

3. Tsurumi Yusuke, *Contemporary Japan*, (Tokyo: The Japan Times, 1927), 88–92.

4. Quoted in Genzo Yamamoto, "The Pacific War as Civilizational Conflict," *Historically Speaking*, Vol. 4 , No. 1 (September 2002), 26–27.

5. Nitobe Inazô, "The Manchurian Question and Sino-Japanese Relations," and "Japan and the United States," *The Works of Nitobe Inazô*, Vol. IV, Takagi Yasaka, ed. (Tokyo: University of Tokyo Press, 1972), 221–233, 259.

6. Nitobe Inazô, "Character of the Occidentalization of Japan," *The Works of Nitobe Inazô*, Vol. I, 444.

7. Ibid., 441, 442, 451, 461.

8. Ibid., 442–446.

9. Ibid., 455–456.

10. Tsurumi Yusuke, *Contemporary Japan*, 187–196.

11. Ibid., 209–211.

12. Katsuji Kato, "Editorials," *The Japanese Student*, Vol. 3, No. 6 (March 1919), 179.

13. Kawashima Saijiro, "A Word to Japan and America," trans. Katsuji Kato from *Dai Nihon*, August 1921, *The Japan Review*, Vol. 5, No. 12 (October 1921), 214–215.

14. Shibusawa Eiichi, "American-Japanese Relations and World Peace," (translated from *Taiyo*, 1919) *The Japanese Student*, Vol. 3, No. 8 (May 1919), 257.

15. *The Autobiography of Ozaki Yukio: The Struggle for Constitutional Government in Japan*, trans. Fujiko Hara (Princeton: Princeton University Press, 2001), 327–328.

16. Ibid., 328–329.

17. Akira Iriye, *Cultural Internationalism and World Order*, 45–46.

18. Professor Yoshino Sakuzo, "Japan's Rising Tide of Liberalism," *The Living Age*, November 22, 1919, reprinted from *Japan Advertiser*, September 11, 1919, 154.

19. Ibid., 154–155.

20. Baron Yoshiaki Fujimura, "China As Seen by Foreigners," *Japan Review*, Vol. 5, No. 4 (February 1921), 62–63.

21. T. Okamoto, "American-Japanese Issues and the Anglo-Japanese Alliance," *The Contemporary Review* (1920), 355.

22. Yamato Ishibashi, "Industrial Plight of Japan," *Asia*, Vol. 19, No. 9 (September 1919), 906–908. Fujimura, "China as Seen by Foreigners," 62–63. Gordon Chang, *Morning Glory, Evening Shadow: Yamato Ichihashi and His Internment Writings, 1942–1945*, 56.

23. Kenkichi Mori, "Japan's Effort in China," *The Japanese Student*, Vol. 2, No. 3 (February 1918), 92–93.

24. Ryutaro Nagai, "Japan between Scylla and Charybdis," *The Living Age* (November 22, 1919), 445. Sharon Minichiello, *Retreat from Reform: Patterns of Political Behavior in Interwar Japan* (Honolulu: University of Hawai'i Press, 1984), 1–2.

25. Nagai, "Japan between Scylla and Charybdis," 445–446. See also a report of Japanese reaction to the Versailles Treaty in Quarterly Letter, V.S. Peeke, Series IV, No. 4, July 20, 1919, 2. Found in V.S. Peeke Papers, Yale Divinity School Library Special Collections, Hereafter referred to as YDSL, New Haven, CT.

26. Jon Thares Davidann, *A World of Crisis and Progress: The American YMCA in Japan, 1890–1930*, Chapter 2. Setsuo Uenoda, "When East Meets West I. Japan's Right to Empire," *Asia*, Vol. 19, No. 12 (December 1919), 1214–1217.

27. Ozaki, *Autobiography*, 324.

28. Ibid., 326.

29. Ozaki Yukio, "Kokka no sombo to kokusai remmei," ("The League of Nations and the Fate of the Nation") *Kokusai Chishiki* (International Understanding), February 1921, 2–3. National Diet Library, Tokyo.

30. Nitobe Inazô, "Why Is Japan in the League of Nations," *International Gleanings from Japan* (Tokyo: The League of Nations Association of Japan), Vol. 3, Nos. 10, 11 (October–November 1927), 1, 7, 8. National Diet Library, Tokyo. Nitobe Inazô, "Dr. Nitobe Answers Japanese Objections to the League," *International Gleanings from Japan*, (March 1928), articles first published in *Japan Times*, 3, 7, 10. Ebina Danjo, "Urging the Awakening of the Nation to the Spread of the Attitudes Surrounding the League of Nations," *Kaitakusha* (March 1920), 15.

31. Shigetomo Sayegusa, "A Practicable World Order," *Contemporary Japan*, Vol. 2 (June 1933), 62–63.

32. Anesaki Masaharu, "Bunka mondai toshite no kokusai remmei," ("The League of Nations and the Problem of Culture") *Kokusai Chishiki* (International Understanding), November 1920, 20–21.

CHAPTER 3   WAR TALK AND JOHN DEWEY:
TENSIONS CONCERNING CHINA

1. Charles Edward Russell, "The Japanese-American Relations," *The Japan Review*, Vol. 5, No. 11 (September 1921), reprinted from *New World*, 207.

2. Captain Mizuno Hironori, "Can Japan and America Fight?" *The Living Age*, translated from *Chuo Koron*, Vol. 29 (August 11, 1923), 254–260.

3. Kenneth Scott Latourette, "Japan: Suggested Outlines for Discussion of Japan, Her History, Culture, Problems, and Relations with the United States," printed by Townsend Harris Endowment Fund Committee of the Japan Society, New York, seventh edition, 1934–1935, Kenneth Scott Latourette Papers, YDSL, 29–30. Eleanor Tupper and George E. McReynolds, *Japan in American Public Opinion* (New York: MacMillan Company, 1937), 155.

4. James Reed, *The Missionary Mind and American East Asia Policy, 1911–1915* (Cambridge, MA: Harvard University Press, 1983).

5. James Thomson, *Sentimental Imperialists* (New York: Harper Collins, 1981).

6. Margaret MacMillan, *Paris, 1919* (New York: Random House, 2002), 320–322.

7. Rodney Gilbert, "Downfall of Tsao the Mighty: Minister Literally Bites the Dust," *The North China Herald*, May 10, 1919, 348–349.

8. Quoted in Jay Martin, *The Education of John Dewey* (New York: Columbia University Press, 2002), 317.

9. Ibid., 318–319.

10. John Dewey and Alice Chapman Dewey, *Letters from China and Japan*, Evelyn Dewey, ed. (New York: E.P. Dutton and Company, 1920), 308.

11. Martin, *The Education of John Dewey*, 322.

12. Ibid., 323–325.

13. Jessica China-Sze Wang, "John Dewey as a Learner in China," *Education and Culture*, Vol. 21, No. 1 (2005), 69–70. C.F. Remer, "John Dewey's Responsibility for American Opinion," *Millard's Review*, Vol. 13 (July 10, 1920), 321–322.

14. MacMillan, *Paris, 1919*, 326.

15. Ibid., 10.

16. Ibid., 14.

17. K.K. Kawakami, "China and Japan at the Washington Conference," *The Japan Review*, Vol. 6, No. 1–2 (January–February 1922), 17.

18. Editorial, "The Chinese Inconsistencies," *The Japan Review*, Vol. 5, No. 14 (December 1921), 253.

19. John Dewey, *China, Japan and the USA: Present-Day Conditions in the Far East and Their Bearing on the Washington Conference*, New Republic Pamphlet No. 1 (New York: Republic Publishing Company, November 12, 1921), 7.

20. Ibid., 9.
21. Martin, *The Education of John Dewey*, 326.
22. Nathaniel Peffer, "The Playground of the Spoilers: Would War with Japan Solve the Far-Eastern Problem?" *The New Century* (January 1922), 380–384.
23. Ibid., 384.
24. Russell, "The Japanese-American Relations," 207.
25. Count Soyeshima Michimasa, "The Relations between America and Japan," *The Japan Review*, Part 1, Vol. 5, No. 10 (August 1921), 174–175.
26. Sakatani Yoshiro, "Why War between Japan and the United States Is Impossible," *The Japan Review*, Vol. 5, No. 11 (September 1921), 193.
27. T. Okamoto, "American-Japanese Issues and the Anglo-Japanese Alliance," *The Contemporary Review*, Vol. 119, No. 663 (March 1921), 358.
28. Stefan Tanaka, *Japan's Orient: Rendering Pasts into History* (Berkeley: University of California Press, 1993), Chapters 3–4. Soyeshima, "The Relations," 203.
29. Mark Caprio, "Japanese and American Images of Koreans," *Trans-Pacific Relations: America, Europe, and Asia in the Twentieth Century*, Richard Jensen, Jon Thares Davidann, and Yone Sugita, eds. (Westport, CT: Praeger, 2003), 106–112. See also Jon Thares Davidann, *A World of Crisis and Progress: The American YMCA in Japan, 1890–1930*, 131–137.
30. Soyeshima, "The Relations," 203.
31. Davidann, *A World of Crisis and Progress*, 148.
32. Sakatani, "Why War," 193.
33. Soyeshima, "The Relations," Part 2, 201.
34. Ibid., 201–202.
35. Sakatani, "Why War," 194, 195.
36. "Editorial Comment," *Physical Training* (Published by the Physical Director's Society of the YMCA, New York), Vol. 10, No. 6 (April 1913), 172.
37. Letter, Franklin H. Brown, National Committee of the YMCA of Japan, Tokyo to Elwood S. Brown, New York, KFYMCA, 2–3.
38. Ibid., 3.
39. Ibid., 5.
40. Ibid., 7–11.
41. Russell, "The Japanese-American Relations," 208. Soyeshima, "The Relations," Part 2, 202.

CHAPTER 4   THE WASHINGTON CONFERENCE, THE KANTO EARTHQUAKE AND JAPANESE PUBLIC OPINION: VICTORIES FOR LIBERALS?

1. Akira Iriye, *Cultural Internationalism and World Order* (Baltimore, MD: Johns Hopkins University Press), 18–19, 51.
2. Arthur Link, *Woodrow Wilson: Revolution, War, and Peace* (Arlington Heights, IL: Harlan Davidson, 1979).
3. Sherwood Eddy, "Everybody's World," *World Outlook*, Vol. 6 (August 1920), 40–43.

4. Walter Lafeber, *The Clash: U.S.-Japanese Relations Throughout History* (New York: W.W. Norton, 1998), 143. See also Roger Dingman, *Power in the Pacific: The Origins of Naval Arms Limitation, 1914–1922* (Chicago: University of Chicago Press, 1976), 11, and Neil Earle, "Public Opinion for Peace: The Tactics of Peace Activists at the Washington Conference on Naval Armament," *Journal of Church and State*, Vol. 40, No. 1 (Winter 1998), 1–2.

5. Shigetomo Sayegusa, "A Practicable World Order," *Contemporary Japan*, Vol. 2 (June 1933), 62–63.

6. Count Uchida, "Foreign Relations of Japan," *The Japan Review*, Vol. 5, No. 4 (February 1921), 56–57.

7. Ibid., 58.

8. Dingman, *Power in the Pacific*, 184–195, 218.

9. Uchida, "Foreign Relations," 58–59.

10. Ibid., 59–60.

11. Kawashima Saijiro, "A Word to Japan and America," trans. Katsuji Kato from *Dai Nihon* (August 1921), *The Japan Review* Vol. 5, No. 12 (October 1921), 212.

12. Ibid., 213.

13. Kawakami Isamu, "Disarmament: The Voice of the Japanese People," *The Japan Review*, Vol. 5, No. 10 (August 1921), 177–178. Dingman, *Power in the Pacific*, 182–184.

14. Editorial, "Japan and the Washington Conference," trans. by Kato Katsuji, from *North China Standard*, *The Japan Review*, Vol. 5, No. 13 (November 1921), 246.

15. Baron Kanda Naibu, "Japan at the Conference," *The Japan Review* Vol. 6, No. 1–2 (January–February, 1922), 14.

16. Ibid., 15. Editorial, Bruce Bliven, *New Republic*, November 16, 1921, 24–26.

17. Lafeber, *The Clash*, 131–132.

18. Extraterritoriality provided that citizens of the countries occupying China would have all the rights and privileges of their home countries while in China, including trial by their own countries, not Chinese courts.

19. Kato Katsuji, "Japan and China at Washington," *The Japan Review*, Vol. 5, No. 11 (December 1921), 258, 259. Editorial, Kato Katsuji, "Chinese Inconsistencies," *The Japan Review*, Vol. 5, No. 11 (December 1921), 253.

20. Noel Pugach, "American Friendship for China and the Shantung Question at the Washington Conference," *Journal of American History*, Vol. 64, No. 1 (June 1977), 67–86.

21. Kawakami, K.K., "China and Japan at the Washington Conference," *The Japan Review*, Vol. 6, No. 1–2 (January–February 1922), 16–17.

22. Dr. S. Washio, "Japan's Salutary Defeat," *The Living Age*, reprinted from the *Japan Advertiser*, February 11, 1922, 322–324.

23. "Japanese Press Opinions on Washington Conference," *The Japan Review* Vol. 6, No. 2 (March–April 1922), 42, 43.

24. Pugach, "American Friendship," 75–85.

25. Foreign Comment, "Oh Hateful and Haughty America," *Literary Digest* (January 28, 1922), 17–18.

26. Editorial, "A Japanese Project Against Anglo-Saxon Domination," *Literary Digest*, Vol. (August 18, 1923), 22–23.

27. Foreign Comment, "Oh Hateful and Haughty America," 17.

28. Dr. Iyenaga, "How Japan Views the Arms Conference," *Current History*, Vol. 16 (April 1922), 22–23.

29. Dr. Wilhelm H.H. Roth, "Japanese Public Opinion," *Los Angeles Times*, April 1932, Office of Naval Intelligence. Lafeber, *The Clash*, 193–143.

30. Lucian Swift Kirtland, *Samurai Trails: A Chronicle of Wanderings on the Japanese High Road* (New York: George H. Doran Company, 1918), 105–110. See also *Finding the Worthwhile in the Orient* (New York: Robert M. McBride and Company, 1926).

31. Lucian Swift Kirtland, "What Japan Thinks of Us," *Travel*, August 1923, 10–11.

32. Ibid., 15.

33. Arthur Jorgensen, "Public Opinion and the Washington Conference," *The Pioneer* (Kaitakusha), January 1922, 10.

34. Administration Report, Russell L. Durgin to Foreign Department, International Committee, February 27, 1922, KFYMCA, 1.

35. John Dewey, "Public Opinion in Japan," *The New Republic*, November 16, 1921, 15–18.

36. Ibid., 17.

37. Quoted in Thomas C. Kennedy, *Charles Beard and American Foreign Policy* (Gainesville, FL: University Presses of Florida, 1975), 48–49.

38. Cited in Robert Dallek, *Franklin D. Roosevelt and American Foreign Policy, 1932–1945* (New York: Oxford University Press, 1979), 16.

39. Otis Manchester Poole, *The Death of Old Yokohama* (London: George Allen and Unwin, Ltd., 1968), 9.

40. "Aged Survivor Jolts Collective Memory of Tokyo's Fatal Day," *Asahi News Service*, Tokyo, September 24, 1999, 13.

41. "Testimony by Survivor of Great Kanto Earthquake," *The People's Korea*, December 1, 1999, 1–2.

42. Naval Attaché's Report, "Intelligence Report on Japanese Earthquake Disaster," October 29, 1923, Office of Naval Intelligence, 1.

43. Naval Attaché's Report, "Weaknesses in Japanese Naval Character," December 8, 1923, Office of Naval Intelligence, 3.

44. Naval Attaché's Report, "Intelligence Report on Japanese Earthquake Disaster," October 29, 1923, Office of Naval Intelligence, 1.

45. Letter, H.S. Sneyd to Frank B. Lenz, May 1, 1926, Report of the Yokohama YMCA, 1–4. Letter, F.H. Brown to George Gleason, July 31, 1925, 1–2, Report of the Yokohama YMCA,.

46. Charles Reifsnider, "Has Japan the Stamina to Recover? A Look," *Asia*, Vol. 23, No. 12 (December 1923), 924–925.

47. Tsurumi Yusuke, "Japan and America," *The Saturday Evening Post*, Vol. 197, No. 6 (February 6, 1925), 140.

48. Tsurumi Yusuke, "What Young Japan is Thinking about: A Liberal Generation Faces Chaos that Comes from Disappointment and Disaster. Which Way Will the Balance Swing?" *The Outlook*, September 24, 1924, 130.

49. Leonard A. Humphreys, "The Japanese Military Tradition," *The Modern Japanese Military System*, James H. Buck, ed. (Beverly Hills: Sage Publications, 1975), 32.

CHAPTER 5 IMMIGRATION EXCLUSION

1. Report, B. Haworth, "Photograph Marriage, Racial Development, Military Service," March 10, 1920, Navy Department, Office of Naval Intelligence, 2.
2. Letter, Richard L. Halsey, Inspector in Charge to Secretary of Labor, October 24, 1921, U.S. Department of Labor, Immigration Service, 2–3.
3. Hirao Ren, "The Campaign of Education among Americans and Why," *The Japanese Student*, Vol. 1, No. 2 (December 1916), 62.
4. Ibid., 194–195.
5. Obata Shigeyoshi, "Another Phase of American-Japanese Problem," *The Japanese Student* (December 1917), 47–48.
6. Ibid., 50.
7. Ibid., 49.
8. Juiji G. Kasai, "The New Japanese-American Relations," *The Japanese Student*, Vol. 2, No. 5 (June 1918), 193. Shidehara Kijuro, "The United States and Japan," *The Japan Review*, Vol. 5, No. 7, 118.
9. Shidehara, "The United States and Japan," 117.
10. Abe Isoo, "The Anti-Japanese Problem," *The Japan Review*, Vol. 5, No. 9 (July 1921), 153.
11. Jon Thares Davidann, ed., "Crossroads Hawai'i," Unpublished Manuscript under review at University of Hawai'i Press.
12. Ibid.
13. Anesaki Masaharu, "The Races and Race Agitation," *The Japan Review*, Vol. 5, No. 6 (April 1921), 92.
14. Ibid., 92–93.
15. H.M. Uchikata, "A Problem for Tomorrow," *The Japanese Student*, Vol. 2, No. 5 (June 1918), 201.
16. Editorials, "Dr. Harada's Report," *The Japan Review*, Vol. 5, No. 7 (May 1921), 114–115.
17. John Higham, *Strangers in the Land*, third edition (New Brunswick, NJ: Rutgers University Press, 2002).
18. Izumi Hirobe, *Japanese Pride, American Prejudice: Modifying the Exclusion Clause of the 1924 Immigration Act* (Stanford, CA: Stanford University Press, 2001), 230.
19. David Roediger, *The Wages of Whiteness: Race and the Making of the American Working Class*, revised edition (London: Verso, 1999).
20. V.S. McClatchy, "Japanese Immigration and Colonization," Brief Prepared for the Consideration of the State Department, October 1, 1921, second edition, 4.
21. Interview, Mayor James Phelan, *Sunday Boston Herald*, June 16, 1907, 1.
22. K. Allerfeldt, "Race and Restriction: Anti-Asian Immigration Pressures in the Pacific North-west of America during the Progressive Era, 1885–1924," *History*, Vol. 88, No. 1 (January 2003), 53–73.

23. Dr. Thomas Green, Immigration and Its Effect upon the Present and Future Condition of the United States, Address to the Maryland Society Sons of the Americans Revolution, April 19, 1922, 2.

24. *Literary Digest* (December 1, 1923), 19.

25. Ibid., 20.

26. Ibid., 19–20.

27. Sandra Taylor, *Advocate of Understanding: Sidney Gulick and the Search for Peace with Japan* (Kent, OH: Kent State Press, 1984), Chapters 7–10.

28. Sidney Gulick, "Problems in American-Japanese Relations," *Asia*, Vol. 17, No. 7 (September 1917), 526–528.

29. Arthur Judson Brown, "The Immigration Bill," *The Japanese American* (1924), 3–4.

30. Taylor, *Advocate of Understanding*, 149.

31. Colonel John P. Irish, "How Shall Japanese-Americans in Idaho Be Treated?" *The Japan Review*, Vol. 5, No. 7 (May 1921), 119–120.

32. Ibid., 120.

33. Ibid., 122–123.

34. Ibid., 119.

35. "California Press on Anti-Alien Land Legislation," February 1915, compiled by Northern California Peace Society, Berkeley, CA, 1.

36. Taylor, *Advocate of Understanding*, 158–161. Eleanor Tupper and George E. McReynolds, *Japan in American Public Opinion* (New York: MacMillan Company, 1937), 183.

37. Quoted in Taylor, *Advocate for Understanding*, 162.

38. "Japanese Wrath at Exclusion," *Literary Digest* (June 14, 1924), 8–10.

39. Ibid., 163.

40. Hirobe, *Japanese Pride, American Prejudice*, Chapter 3.

41. Irish, "How Shall Japanese-Americans in Idaho Be Treated," 123.

42. Letter, Geo. D. Swan, September 11, 1925, Correspondence and Reports, Japan Collection, KFYMCA, 1.

43. Quarterly Letter, V.S. Peeke, Series V, No. 8, July 20, 1924, V.S. Peeke Collection, YDSL, 2. See also "Methodist Missionaries Attack U.S. Immigration Law," *The International Gleanings from Japan*, Vol. 2, Nos. 8 and 9 (August–September 1926), 4.

44. "Japanese Carry Protests to Shrines," *The New York Times*, July 2, 1924, 21.

45. Hirobe, *Japanese Pride, American Prejudice*, 33.

46. "Table of Contents," *Kokusai Chishiki* (International Understanding), July 1924.

47. Telegram, Edward C. Jenkins to C.S. Phelps, April 23, 1924, Correspondence and Reports, Japanese YMCA Archives, Tokyo, Japan, 1. Anna Lousie Strong, "Three Men of Japan," *Asia*, Vol. 26, No. 3 (March 1926), 228.

48. Quoted in Hirobe, *Japanese Pride American Prejudice*, 29–30.

49. Tsurumi Yusuke, "Japan and America," *The Saturday Evening Post*, Vol. 197, No. 6 (February 7, 1925), 143. Frank Luther Mott, *A History of American Magazines, Vol. 5, 1895–1905* (Cambridge, MA: Harvard University Press, 1938). Mott listed the *Saturday Evening Post* as number one in 1905. Circular

Letter, S. Ernest Trueman to Friends, June 30, 1924, Nagoya YMCA, Japanese YMCA Archives, 2.

50. Ibid., 2.
51. "Are Japanese People," *Literary Digest* (April 26, 1924), 22–23.
52. "Foreign Comment: Japanese Rage at Exclusion," *Literary Digest* (May 21, 1924), 18.
53. Ibid.
54. Ibid., 19.
55. Fujisawa Rikitaro, "On Japanese American Relations," *Kokusai Chishiki* (International Understanding), July 1924, 8–13.
56. Editorial, B.W. Fleisher, "Who Owns the Pacific?" *The Japan Advertiser*, December 11, 1924, 1. Wilfred Fleisher, "Farewell Bid to Castle," *The New York Times*, May 23, 1930, 1.
57. K.K. Kawakami, "Japanese Looks across the Pacific," *Contemporary Review*, No. 131 (April 1927), 474–482.
58. Ibid., 481.
59. K.K. Kawakami, "Japan's New Ambassador of Peace: An Interview with Mr. Matsudaira," *The Outlook*, Vol. 139 (April 15, 1925), 575–576.
60. Tagawa Daikichiro, "America, Let's Reason Together," *The Living Age*, No. 327 (October 17, 1925), 145.
61. Ibid., 146.
62. Hirobe, *Japanese Pride, American Prejudice*, 25–26.
63. B.W. Fleisher, "Who Owns The Pacific?" 1–2.
64. Letter, George Swan to E.C. Jenkins, December 18, 1924, 1, KFYMCA.
65. John Dower, *War Without Mercy: Race and Power in the Pacific War*, 124–146.

CHAPTER 6 THE LIBERAL CHALLENGE: RESPONSES TO IMMIGRATION EXCLUSION

1. Bamba Nobuya, *Japanese Diplomacy in a Dilemma: New Light on Japan's China Policy, 1924–1929* (Kyoto: Minerva Press, 1972), 77–80.
2. Harry Emerson Wildes, "Japan Returns to Feudalism," *The Nation*, Vol. 123 (October 27, 1926), 436–438.
3. Louis Fischer in "America, Japan, and Russia," *The Nation* (March 25, 1925), p. 317.
4. K.K. Kawakami, "The Basis of Japanese Diplomacy," *Current History*, Vol. 26 (June 1927), 401.
5. Tsurumi Yusuke, *Contemporary Japan*, 94–97.
6. George D. Swan, 1925 Annual Report, Correspondence and Reports, Japan Files, KFYMCA, 1.
7. J. Merle Davis, General List of Specific Suggestions on Conference Agenda, IPR Collection, Sinclair Library, University of Hawai'i at Manoa, A-2, folder 5, 2.
8. Viscount Kentaro Kaneko, "Roosevelt on Japan," *Asia*, Vol. 32, No. 9 (November 1932), 538–541. J. Merle Davis, General List of Specific

Suggestions on Conference Agenda, IPR Collection, Sinclair Library, University of Hawai'i at Manoa, A-2, folder 5, 2.

9. Yamaoka Michio, "The Role and Activities of the Japanese-American Relations Committee in the Formation of the Japan Pacific Council," trans. George M. Oshiro, *Rediscovering the IPR: Proceedings from the First International Research Conference on the Institute of Pacific Relations*, Paul Hooper, ed., 46–48.

10. Thomas C. Kennedy, *Charles A. Beard and American Foreign Policy*, 50.

11. Letters, Charles Beard to Tsurumi Yusuke, from July 17, 1924, to November 15, 1933, located in Tsurumi Yusuke Papers, National Diet Library, Tokyo, Japan. There were 13 letters in all.

12. Tsurumi Yusuke, *Contemporary Japan* (Tokyo: The Japan Times, 1927), 10.

13. Ibid., 16–19. Tsurumi Yusuke, "Japan and America," *The Saturday Evening Post*, February 7, 1925, 137–140.

14. Editorial, "Japan—Enemy or Friend?" *The Nation*, Vol. 120 (March 25, 1925), 309.

15. Ibid., 309.

16. Miriam Beard, "Our War Advertising Campaign," *The Nation*, Vol. 120 (March 25, 1925), 322.

17. Ibid., 323. Miriam Beard, *Realism in Romantic Japan* (New York: MacMillan Company, 1930).

18. Charles Beard, "War with Japan: What Shall We Get out of It," *The Nation*, Vol. 120 (March 25, 1925), 311.

19. Charles and Mary Beard, "The Issues of Pacific Policy," *Survey*, Vol. 56 (May 1, 1926), 189.

20. Margaret DeForest Hicks, "New Forces in Old Japan: Will the Radical Colt Take the Bit in His Teeth," *Century Magazine*, Vol. 111 (April 1926), 728–729.

21. "Democracy's Dawn Delayed in Japan," *Literary Digest*, Vol. 100 (February 16, 1929), 18.

22. "Rapid Americanization of Japan," *Literary Digest*, Vol. 106 (August 2, 1930), 41.

23. "Japan Goes in for Our Popular Songs," *Literary Digest*, Vol. 110 (August 15, 1931), 15.

24. Jim Marshall, "The White Peril," *Collier's*, October 19, 1935, 9. "Evidences of Americanization of Japan," *Literary Digest* (September 23, 1933), 9.

25. Henry J. Reilly, "The Americanization of Japan: The Younger Generation is Modernizing the Mikado's Realm," *World's Work*, Vol. 52 (October 1926), 649.

26. Sarah M. Lockwood, "Japan—One Face East, One Face West," *World's Work*, Vol. 59 (December 1930), 49–51.

27. Dr. Emil Lederer, "What Is Wrong with Japan?" from *Frankfurter Zeitung*, September 28, 1924, translated and reprinted in *The Living Age*, No. 323 (November, 15, 1924, 363). Harry Emerson Wildes, "Japan Returns to Feudalism," *The Nation* (October 27, 1926), 436–438. Henry Kittredge Norton, What the Japanese Think of America," *Travel*, No. 47 (August 1926), 12–15, 43.

28. Roderick Matheson, "The Myth of Japanese Efficiency," *Current History*, Vol. 26 (May 1927), 190, 192–195.

29. Ibid., 190.
30. John Dower, *War Without Mercy: Race and Power in the Pacific War*, 98–108.
31. "Japan's Advances Fail to Win China," *The New York Times*, June 24, 1938, 1.
32. K.K. Kawakami, "A Reply," *Current History*, Vol. 26 (May 1927), 196.
33. William Elliot Griffis, "Japan's Progress in Rebuilding an Empire," *Current History*, Vol. 27 (February 1928), 681.
34. William Elliot Griffis, "A View of Japan Then and Now," *Missionary Review of the World*, Vol. 51 (January 1928), 28.
35. Quarterly Letter, V.S. Peeke, Series V, No. 7, May 20, 1924, V.S. Peeke Papers, YDSL, 2. Quarterly Letter, V.S. Peeke, Series V, No. 14, January 20, 1926, 2, and Quarterly Letter, V.S. Peeke, Series V, No. 18, January 20, 1927, 1–2.

CHAPTER 7   NEW EMPEROR, NEW TENSIONS IN MANCHURIA

1. Herbert Bix, *Hirohito and the Making of Modern Japan* (New York: Harper Collins Publishers, 2000), 190.
2. Ibid., 192–194.
3. Hugh Byas, "Lavish Kyoto Rites of Accession Start," *The New York Times*, November 10, 1928, 1. Hugh Byas, "Hirohito Ascends His Historic Throne with Ancient Ritual," *The New York Times*, November 11, 1928, 1.
4. Byas, "Hirohito Ascends His Historic Throne," 1.
5. Stanley High, "Is Japan Going Democratic?" *Harper's Magazine*, Vol. 158 (January 1929), 218–220.
6. Elsie Weil, "Heirs of the Japanese Sun Goddess: Three Emperors—Symbols of National Religion and National Greatness in Japan," *Asia*, Vol. 27 (March 1927), 177.
7. Ibid., 177–178.
8. Ibid., 178.
9. Circular Letter, Georgene Esther Brown, January 12, 1927, Tokyo, Japan, Harvard Divinity School Special Collections, Cambridge, MA, 1.
10. Circular Letter, Georgene Esther Brown, October 9, 1931, Tokyo, Japan, Harvard Divinity School Special Collections, 3.
11. Military Intelligence Summary No. 435, January 18, 1929, Far East, Office of Naval Intelligence, 12338.
12. Ibid., 12340.
13. Takashi Fujitani, *Splendid Monarchy: Power and Pageantry in Modern Japan*, 1–7.
14. K.K. Kawakami, "Japan's First Modern Emperor: Who Allows No Traditional Halo of Divinity to Obscure His Human Qualities," *Asia*, Vol. 28 (November 1928), 861.
15. Ibid.
16. Royama Masamichi, "The Meaning of the Manchoukuo Empire," *Contemporary Japan*, Vol. 3 (June 1934), 31.
17. Bix, *Hirohito*, 118–119. See Modris Eksteins, *Rites of Spring: The Great War and the Birth of the Modern Age* (New York: Anchor Books, 1989), 301–329,

for the Nazi invention of tradition, and Eric Hobsbawn, "Introduction: Invention of Tradition," *Invention of Tradition*, Eric Hobsbawn and Terrance Ranger, eds. (Cambridge: Cambridge University Press, 1983) for the invention of tradition on the British Isles.

18. Ian Nish, *Japanese Foreign Policy in the Interwar Period*, 55–60. "The Chino-Japanese Clash in Shantung," *Literary Digest*, Vol. 97, No. 7 (May 19, 1928), 5–6.

19. Bix, *Hirohito*, 215–220. Frederick R. Dickinson, *War and National Reinvention: Japan in the Great War, 1914–1919* (Cambridge, MA: Harvard University Press, 1999), 165–174. William Fitch Morton, *Tanaka Giichi and Japan's China Policy* (New York: St. Martin's Press, 1980), 122–134.

20. Ibid., 220.

21. "Why Japan Wants Manchuria," *Literary Digest* (September 1, 1928), 8.

22. Nish, *Japanese Foreign Policy*, 53–57. S. Komura, "Japan's Wish for China's Freedom," translated for *Literary Digest*, Vol. 95 (November 26, 1927), 15–16. For the rhetoric of progress toward Korea and Manchuria see Jon Thares Davidann, *A World of Crisis and Progress: The American YMCA in Japan, 1890–1930*, Chapter 5.

23. Letter, Ibuka Kajinosuke and Kakehi Mitsuaki to David Z. T. Yui, *Kaitakusha*, August 1928, 3, KFYMCA.

24. Foreign Comment, "Japan Talks Back to Uncle Sam," *Literary Digest*, Vol. 98 (July 21, 1928), 14–15.

25. "America's Mean Trick to Japan," *Literary Digest*, Vol. 98 (September 8, 1928), 17.

26. K.K. Kawakami, "Manchuria: The Crux of Chino-Japanese Relations," *Foreign Affairs*, Vol. 6 (April 1928), 389–394. K.K. Kawakami, "Japan Looks at the Russo-Chinese Dispute," *The Nineteenth Century*, Vol. 106 (September 1929), 328–334.

27. Shigeyoshi Obata, "China, Japan, and Manchuria," *The Nation*, Vol. 128, No. 3313 (January 2, 1929), 11–12.

28. Tomoko Akami, *Internationalizing the Pacific: The United States and Japan, and the Institute of Pacific Relations in War and Peace*, 147.

29. Ibid., 147. Yamaoka Michio, "The Role and Activities of the Japanese-American Relations Committee in the Formation of the Japan Pacific Council," *Rediscovering the IPR: Proceedings from the First International Research Conference on the Institute of Pacific Relations*, Paul Hooper, ed., 46.

30. Nobuo Katagiri, "A Reappraisal of the Japan IPR: With a Focus on the Period from the Establishment in 1925 to Withdrawal in 1936," *Rediscovering the IPR*, 55.

31. Akami, *Internationalizing the Pacific*, 148.

32. Davidann, *A World of Crisis and Progress*, Chapter 4.

33. Quoted from Akami, *Internationalizing the Pacific, 140–141.*

34. Ibid., 146.

35. "Explosion Hits Kyoto Parley As Chinese Explicitly Blame Japanese for Death of Chang," *The Japan Advertiser*, October 29, 1929, 1.

36. Matsuoka Yôsuke, "An Address on Manchuria, Its Past and Present," IPR Proceedings, 1929 Kyoto Conference, 3–16. Tomoko Akami, *Internationalizing the Pacific*, 151.

CHAPTER 8 "ORIENTAL" DUPLICITY OR PROGRESS AND ORDER: THE MANCHURIAN INCIDENT

1. Rodney Gilbert, "Japan Goes into Reverse Against Russia." *Asia*, Vol. 32, No. 5 (May 1932), 299–303.

2. Hartwell C. Davis, Naval Intelligence Report, Pearl Harbor, June 28, 1927, Office of Naval Intelligence, 1–2.

3. Letter, A. Ardlicaq to Henry Stimson, Henry L. Stimson Papers, Manuscript Division, Library of Congress, Reel 82, No. 327, 1–2. Letter, Col. V. M. Elmore to Senator William E. Borah, Henry Stimson Papers, Manuscript Division, Library of Congress, Reel 82, No. 604.

4. Isaac F. Marcosson, "The Japanese Smoke Screen," *The Saturday Evening Post*, Vol. 204, No. 45, May 7, 1932, 4.

5. Paul Hutchinson, "What Japan Really Wants," *The Forum*, Vol. 87 (April 1932), 194–196.

6. Upton Close, "Straws in the Wind: Significant Notes on World Affairs Today," *Scribner's Magazine*, Vol. 91 (April 1932), 227–228.

7. Ibid., 228.

8. Commander J.M. Kenworthy, "Japan—Conqueror of Asia?" *Outlook*, Vol. 160 (March 1932), 172.

9. Rene Lavigne and Edouard Ciprut, "Persons and Personages: The Japanese Colonel Lawrence," *The Living Age* (February 1936), 501–505.

10. Wilbur Burton, "Japan's Bid for Far Eastern Supremacy," *Current History*, Vol. 35 (February 1932).

11. Mauritz Hallgren, "Japan Defies the Imperialists," *The Nation*, Vol. 133, No. 3462 (November 11, 1931), 514–516.

12. Sherwood Eddy, T*he Challenge of the East* (New York: Farrar and Rinehart, 1931), 134.

13. Justus Doenecke, *When the Wicked Arise: American Opinion-Makers and the Manchurian Crisis of 1931–1933*, 28–29.

14. Richard Current, *Secretary Stimson: A Study in Statecraft* (New Brunswick, NJ: Rutgers University Press, 1954), 92–93. Godfrey Hodgson, *The Colonel: The Life and Wars of Henry Stimson, 1867–1950* (New York: Alfred A. Knopf, 1990), 156–157.

15. Dorothy Borg and Shumpei Okamoto, ed., *Pearl Harbor As History: Japanese-American Relations, 1932–1941* (New York: Columbia University Press, 1973), 423–429. Doenecke, *When the Wicked Arise*, 47–52.

16. Roy Mathew Frisen, "Japanophobia," *The Forum and Century*, Vol. 90, No. 4 (October 1933), 237–241.

17. Eleanor Tupper and George E. McReynolds, *Japan in American Public Opinion* (New York: MacMillan Company, 1937), 306–307.

18. Lincoln Colcord, "The Realism of Japanese Diplomacy," *Harpers Magazine*, Vol. 164 (April 1932), 513–524.

19. Doenecke, *When the Wicked Arise*, 38.

20. Arthur Schlesinger, "Japan's Destiny in the Orient," *American Mercury*, Vol. 32, No. 127 (July 1934), 293.

21. Circular Letter, Kathryn Fanning, January 2, 1932, Mission to Japan, Vol. 56, ABCFM Archives (1–91), Houghton Library, Harvard College Library, Harvard University, Cambridge, MA, 2. By Permission of Houghton Library, Harvard University. Also used with permission of Wider Church Ministries of the United Church of Christ.

22. William Axling, "Be Just to Japan!" *The Christian Century*, Vol. 49 (April 13, 1932), 474–476.

23. Editorial, "The Case for Japan," *The Christian Century*, Vol. 49 (April 27, 1932), 548.

24. Correspondence, "From 135 Missionaries in Japan," *The World Tomorrow* (May 1932), 156.

25. "The Truth about the Mukden Incident of September 18th," June 1932, Northeastern Affairs Research Institute, Peiping, China. "The Case for China: A Summary of Recent Events in Manchuria," April 1933, American Committee for Justice in China, New York. Letter, Howard Haag to Charles Herschleb, February 26, 1933, Harbin YMCA Papers, KFYMCA, 2.

26. "Telling Tokyo Where we Stand," *Literary Digest* (January 23, 1932), 5–6. "Roosevelt with Honor on Japan," *Literary Digest* (January 28, 1933), 7. Armin Rappport, *Henry L. Stimson and Japan, 1931–1933*, 26–27.

27. Letter, Secretary of State Henry Stimson to Frederic Coudert, Esq., Henry Stimson Papers, November 20, 1931, Reel 82, No. 150, 1. Letter, Secretary of State Henry Stimson to Honorable Elihu Root, Henry Stimson Papers, December 14, 1931, Reel 82, No. 210, 2–8. Rappport, *Henry L. Stimson and Japan*, 96.

28. Henry Stimson, *The Far Eastern Crisis: Recollections and Observations*, 10, 237.

29. Ibid., 3, 238–240.

30. Robert Dallek, *Franklin D. Roosevelt and American Foreign Policy, 1932–1945*, 27.

31. Cable, Sherwood Eddy, October 13, 1931, Sherwood Eddy Biographical File, KFYMCA.

32. Sherwood Eddy, "Japan Threatens the World," *Christian Century*, Vol. 49 (March 16, 1932), 346–347.

33. Charles Herschleb to Arthur Jorgensen, December 5, 1931, Arthur Jorgensen Biographical File, KFYMCA, 1.

34. Cable, Nitobe Inazô and Soichi Saito to C.A Herschleb, E.T. Colton, G.W. Birks, F.W. Ramsey, F.S. Harmon., October 21, 1931, Sherwood Eddy Biographical File, KFYMCA.

35. Eddy, "Japanese Threatens the World," 347.

36. Letter, Arthur Jorgensen to Charles Herschleb, October 24, 1931, Arthur Jorgensen Biographical File, KFYMCA, 1. Charles Herschleb to Arthur

Jorgensen, December 5, 1931, Arthur Jorgensen Biographical File, KFYMCA, 1.

37. Extracts from a Letter to a Friend in America, G.S. Phelps, May 29, 1933, Historical Files, Japanese YMCA Archives, Tokyo, Japan, 2.

38. G.S. Phelps, "We Visit Manchuria," unpublished article, May 15, 1933, G.S. Phelps Biographical File, KFYMCA, 1–2. Letter, G.S. Phelps to his children, April 12, 1993, G.S. Phelps Biographical File, KFYMCA, 1.

39. Howard W. Hackett, Diary of China Trip, Summer 1932, Mission to Japan, Vol. 56, ABCFM Archives, 3.

40. Sidmary Travelog—Geneva, April 15, 1932, G.S Phelps Biographical File, KFYMCA, 1.

41. Ibid., 2.

42. W.W. Gethman, "The Sino-Japanese Dispute and the Christian Conscience: Memorandum and Explanatory Note prepared by a representative group of Christians in Geneva," Document C, February 4, 1993, Soichi Saito File, Japanese YMCA Archives, 2.

43. Letter, Soichi Saito to Mr. W.W. Gethman, March 17, 1933, Soichi Saito File, Japanese YMCA Archives, 3.

44. *International Gleanings*, Vol. 8, No. 10 (October 15, 1932), 2.

45. Tomoko Akami, *Internationalizing the Pacific: The United States and Japan, and the Institute of Pacific Relations in War and Peace*, 164–166.

46. Ibid., 203–204, 229–230, 277–278.

47. Dr. Wilhelm H.H. Roth, "Japanese Public Opinion," *Los Angeles Times*, April 1932, Office of Naval Intelligence.

48. Letter to Editor, Hugh Byas, "What Shall We Call Japan?" *Contemporary Japan*, Vol. 3 (June 1934), 132.

49. Mark R. Peattie, *Ishiwara Kanji and Japan's Confrontation with the West*, 81–82. George M. Wilson, *Radical Nationalist in Japan: Kita Ikki, 1883–1937*, 65–80.

50. Intelligence Report, Excerpts from an Emergency Reader for Popular Use, Report No. 6638, February 9, 1932, Office of Naval Intelligence, 1–2.

51. "Japan's Appeal to World Opinion," *Literary Digest* (January 9, 1932), 14–15.

52. "Sees Japan in Grip of Internal Strife," *The New York Times*, April 26, 1932, 1.

53. *International Gleanings*, Vol. 8, No. 4 (April 15, 1932), 6.

54. *International Gleanings*, Vol. 8, No. 9 (September 15, 1932), 1–2. It was in this issue that the Japanese League of Nations (LNA) also suggested that there ought to be a regional branch of the League of Nations for Asia. Hugh Byas, "Japanese Warned of Hostility Here," *The New York Times*, February 25, 1932, 1.

55. K.K. Kawakami, "America Teaches, Japan Learns," *The Atlantic Monthly*, Vol. 140 (June 1932), 652.

56. Reference Material, Henry Stimson Papers, June 1, 1934, Reel 126, 923–924.

57. Nitobe Inazô, "Editorial Jottings," *The Works of Nitobe Inazô, Vol. II*, No. 347 and "Japan and the United States," *The Works of Nitobe Inazô, Vol. IV*, No. 259.

58. Tsurumi Yusuke, "Japanese Policy and Opinion," *The Yale Review*, Vol. 21, No. 4 (June 1932), 765–766.

59. "Japan's Appeal to World Opinion," *Literary Digest* (January 9, 1932), 14–15.

60. Jon Thares Davidann, *A World of Crisis and Progress: The American YMCA in Japan, 1890–1930*, 103–105.

61. Hugh Byas, "Japanese Compel Critic to Apologize," *The New York Times*, March 4, 1932, 1.

62. Thomas W. Burkman, "The Geneva Spirit," *Nitobe* Inazô: *Japan's Bridge Across the Pacific*, John R. Howes, ed., 204–205.

63. Kitasawa Sukeo, *The Life of Dr. Nitobe* (Tokyo: Hokuseido Press, 1953), 79.

64. Raymond Leslie Buell, "An Open Letter to Dr. Inazô Nitobe," *The New Republic*, May 25, 1932, 42.

65. Miwa Kimitada, "Colonial Theories and Practices in Japan," *Nitobe* Inazô: *Japan's Bridge*, 172.

66. Buell, "An Open Letter," 43.

67. Nitobe Inazô, *Lectures on Japan: An Outline of the Development of the Japanese People and their Culture* (Tokyo: Kenkyusha, 1936), 267.

68. Thomas W. Burkman, "The Geneva Spirit," *Nitobe* Inazô: *Japan's Bridge*, 204–205.

69. Ibid., 253–258.

70. Ogata Sadako, "The Role of Liberal Nongovernmental Organizations in Japan," *Pearl Harbor As History*, 485.

CHAPTER 9   "AMERICA IS VERY DIFFICULT TO GET ALONG WITH": ANTI-AMERICANISM, JAPANESE MILITARISM, AND SPYING, 1934–1937

1. Statement, Naval Intelligence Report, May 10, 1936, Office of Naval Intelligence, 1.

2. Matsuoka Yôsuke, "Dissolve the Political Parties," *Contemporary Japan*, Vol. 2, (March 1934), 664.

3. Anesaki Masaharu, "The Present Crisis of Culture in Japan," *Asia*, Vol. 36, No. 9 (September 1936), 579–582.

4. "Japan in the National Emergency," National Archives, Maryland Division, Catalogue Number 238–10, 1933.

5. Herbert Bix, *Hirohito and the Making of Modern Japan*, 273–277. See Leslie Pincus, *Authenticating Culture in Imperial Japan: Kuki Shûzô and the Rise of National Aesthetics* (Berkeley: University of California Press, 1995).

6. Statement, Naval Intelligence Reports, May 10, 1936, Office of Naval Intelligence, 2.

7. Mr. Honda Kumataro, 1936–1937 Does Not Present a Crisis for Japan, Lecture, Office of Naval Intelligence, 6.

8. Japan's Reaction to Japanese Training Squadron's Reception in the United States, 1936, Report No. 220, Office of Naval Intelligence, 1.

9. Takaki Yasaka, "International Reconciliation," *Contemporary Japan*, Vol. 4 (September 1935), 233, 238.

10. Forward by Konoe Fumimaro, *Kokusai Bunka Shinkokai Quarterly* Vol. 1, No. 1 (April–June 1935), 1, 4. Akira Iriye, *Cultural Internationalism and World Order*, 119, 122.

11. The Influence of the Senior Statesmen, September 6, 1935, Report No. 217, Office of Naval Intelligence, 2.

12. *The Autobiography of Ozaki Yukio: The Struggle for Constitutional Government in Japan*, trans. Fujiko Hara (Princeton: Princeton University Press, 2001), 390–391.

13. Ben-Ami Shillony, *Revolt in Japan: The Young Officers and the February 26, 1936 Incident* (Princeton: Princeton University Press, 1973), 123.

14. Ibid., 146–147.

15. Ibid., 135–140.

16. Tsurumi Yusuke, "Japan Today and Tomorrow," *International Affairs*, Vol. 15, No. 6 (November–December 1936), 816–819.

17. Ibid., 816, 821–822.

18. "Japan: Democratic Legislators Stun Military Fascists with Diet Uproar," *Newsweek*, January 30, 1937, 16.

19. Miner Searle Bates, Friendly Caution—and a Little Information, Spring 1937, Miner Searle Bates Papers, 3.

20. Robert Shildgen, "How Race Mattered: Kagawa Toyohiko in the United States," *Journal of American-East Asian Relations*, Vol. 5, No. 3–4 (Fall–Winter 1996), 229.

21. Wilbur L. Roe, Jr., "Kagawa Appraises Modern Japan," *The Christian Century*, Vol. 53 (February 5, 1936), 225, 231–234.

22. Ibid., 240–242.

23. Editorial, "Japan's Crisis," *The Christian Century*, Vol. 53 (March 11, 1936), 394. Hamish Ion, *The Cross in the Dark Valley: The Canadian Protestant Missionary Movement in the Japanese Empire, 1931–1945* (Waterloo, Canada: Wilfrid Laurier University Press, 1999), 215.

24. Editorial, "Japan Turns toward Peace," *The Christian Century*, Vol. 54 (May 19, 1937), 641.

25. Galen Fisher, "Revisiting Japan," *Amerasia*, Vol. 1, No. 5 (July 1937), 219–224.

26. Ibid., 221–222.

27. Quoted from Nakamura Masanori, *The Japanese Monarchy, 1931–1991: Ambassador Joseph Grew and the Making of the Symbol Emperor System*, trans. Herbert Bix, Derek Bowen, and Jonathan Baker-Bates (New York: M.E. Sharpe, 1992), 42–43, 46.

28. John Mott, "Reasons for Japanese-American Friendship," *Missionary Review of the World*, Vol. 58 (December 1935), 597. C. Howard Hopkins, *John R. Mott, 1865–1955: A Biography* (Grand Rapids, MI: William B. Eerdmans Publishing House, 1979), 699.

29. Edgar Snow, "The Japanese Juggernaut Rolls on," *The Saturday Evening Post*, No. 92, May 9, 1936, 8.

30. Harold S. Quigley, "Feudalism Reappears in Japan," *Christian Science Monitor Magazine*, March 3, 1936, 1.

31. Ibid., 2.
32. "Book Reviews," *Contemporary Japan*, Vol. 4 (December 1935), 419.
33. Winston Churchill, "The Mission of Japan," *Collier's*, February 20, 1937, 12.
34. "Book Reviews," *Contemporary Japan*, Vol. 4 (June 1935), 104–105.
35. "The Rising Sun of Japan," *Reader's Digest*, Condensed from *Fortune Magazine*, Vol. 29 (November 1936), 17.
36. Ibid., 21–22.
37. Shillony, *Revolt in Japan*, 212.
38. Bruce Wallace, "Charlie Chaplin's Japan Connection," *Honolulu Advertiser*, April 30, 2006, D1, D7.
39. J.G. McIlroy, Military Attaché, Naval Intelligence Report, October 27, 1932, Office of Naval Intelligence, 1–3.
40. Japanese Reaction to Congressional Anti-Japanese Speeches, February 19, 1936, Report No. 39, Office of Naval Intelligence, 1.
41. W.K. Kilpatrick, American-Born Japanese Boy Scouts Selected to be Educated in Japan, August 25, 1936, Pearl Harbor, T.H. (Territory Hawai'i), Serial No. 171–72, File No. 103–400, Office of Naval Intelligence, 1.
42. John K. Davis, Allegation of a Plot to Embroil the United States with Japan, March 14, 1934, File No. 711, Office of Naval Intelligence, 1.
43. American Consulate, Official Explanation for Arrest of Mr. A.L. Caron, June 27, 1938, Office of Naval Intelligence. S. Ohtaka, Massie Incident, July 4, 1938, Office of Naval Intelligence.
44. Zhang Kaiyuan, ed., *Eyewitnesses to Massacre: American Missionaries Bear Witness to Japanese Atrocities in Nanjing* (New York: M.E. Sharpe, 2001), 3.
45. Robert S. Morton, Review of "Japan and China: A War of Minds," Box 90, folder 718, Miner Searle Bates Papers.
46. Memorandum on Policy toward Japan, November 1935, Box 90, folder 718, Miner Searle Bates Papers, 1–5.
47. Ibid., 1–2.
48. Suggestions for Constructive Contacts, undated (c. 1937), Box 90, folder 718, Miner Searle Bates Papers, 1–2.
49. A.E.M., Notes on Dr. Bates' Report of his Trip to Japan, Ginling College, February 16, 1936, Miner Searle Bates Papers, 1.
50. Miner Searle Bates, Report on Present Day Japan: With Particular Reference to Policy toward China, March 1936 with changes in August 1936, Miner Searle Bates Papers, 4.
51. Miner Searle Bates, Cover Letter, 1936, Miner Searle Bates Papers, 1. The missionaries on the list were Miss A.E. Moffat of the Presbyterian Mission of Nanjing, Reverend R. Rees in Shanghai, Y.T. Wu and E.E. Barnet of the Chinese YMCA, C.S. Miao and E.H. Cressy of the Chinese Christian Educational Association in Shanghai.
52. Bates, Report on Present Day Japan.
53. Robert S. Morton (Miner Searle Bates), "Japan and China: A War of Minds," *Pacific Affairs*, Vol. 10, No. 3 (September 1937), 313.
54. Robert S. Morton (Miner Searle Bates), Japan's Great Adventure, unpublished paper, November 1937, Miner Searle Bates Papers, 7.

CHAPTER 10   "A CERTAIN PRESENTIMENT OF
FATAL DANGER": THE SINO-JAPANESE WAR AND
U.S.-JAPANESE RELATIONS, 1937–1939

1. John Hunter Boyle, *China and Japan at War: The Politics of Collaboration*, 52–54. "Press Demands Action," *The New York Times*, July 18, 1937, 1, 3.

2. Boyle, *China and Japan at War*, 49–54. Barbara J. Brooks, *Japan's Imperial Diplomacy: Consuls, Treaty Ports and War in China* (Honolulu: University of Hawai'i Press, 2000), 1, Chapter 5.

3. "China Will Pay $14.50 for Japanese Generals," *The New York Times*, October 3, 1937, 32.

4. George H. Gallup, *The Gallup Poll: Public Opinion, 1935–1948*, Vol. 1 (New York: Random House, 1972), 72.

5. "Japan Denounced at Rally of 10,000," *The New York Times*, October 2, 1937, 8. "Bootblacks Aid Chinese Army," *The New York Times*, August 29, 1937, 29.

6. Jonathan Utley, *Going to War with Japan*, 14.

7. Letter, Frank Slack to Arthur Jorgensen, November 14, 1938, Correspondence and Reports, Japanese YMCA Archives, 1. Letter, Galen Fisher to Saito Soichi, October 23, 1937, Correspondence and Reports, Japanese YMCA Archives, 1.

8. Frederick Field, Review, "The Far Eastern Crisis: Recollections and Observations," *The American Historical Review*, Vol. 43, No. 1 (October 1937), 145–146.

9. Letter, William S. Dodd, Jr. to Henry Stimson, October 30, 1937, Henry Stimson Papers, Reel 94, 21.

10. Henry Stimson, *The Far Eastern Crisis: Recollections and Observations*, 238–239.

11. Richard Current, *Secretary Stimson: A Study in Statecraft*, 135.

12. Robert Dallek, *Franklin D. Roosevelt and American Foreign Policy, 1932–1945*, 148–152.

13. Letter to Editor, Henry Stimson, *The New York Times*, October 7, 1937, 12.

14. Ibid., 12. Letter, Henry Stimson to Cordell Hull, August 30, 1937, Henry Stimson Papers, Reel 93, 644–650.

15. Cable, Halford Hoskins to Henry Stimson, October 7, 1937, Henry Stimson Papers, Reel 93, 814. Utley, *Going to War with Japan*, 21.

16. Letter, Henry Stimson to Hon. Franklin D. Roosevelt, November 15, 1937, Henry Stimson Papers, Reel 94, 372–376.

17. Walter LaFeber, *The Clash: U.S.-Japanese Relations throughout History*, 168.

18. Letter, Hu Shih to Henry Stimson, November 6, 1937, Henry Stimson Papers, Reel 94, 204–205.

19. Letter, Henry Stimson to Franklin D. Roosevelt, November 15, 1937, Henry Stimson Papers, Reel 94, 372–376.

20. D.A. Farnie, "Freda Utley, Crusader for Truth and Freedom," *Britain and Japan, Biographical Portraits*, Volume 4, Hugh Cortazzi, ed. (London: Japan Society, 2002), 361–374.

21. William Henry Chamberlin, "How Strong Is Japan?" *The Atlantic Monthly*, Vol. 160 (December 1937), 788–789.
22. Ibid., 788.
23. Pearl Buck, "Asia Book Shelf, Review of Japan over Asia," *Asia* Vol. 38, No. 2 (February 1938), 115.
24. Nathaniel Peffer, "Japan Counts the Cost," *Harper's Magazine*, Vol. 175 (September 1937), 354–355.
25. Ibid., 360.
26. Nathaniel Peffer, "Japan and China: Second Year," *Harpers Magazine*, Vol. 177 (September 1938), 339.
27. "Congress Leaders Decry Jingoism," *The New York Times*, December 14, 1937, 18. "Grew Gets Panay Fund," *The New York Times*, January 12, 1938, 13.
28. Letter, M.S. Bates to Officers of the Japanese Embassy, December 18, 1937, Miner Searle Bates Papers, 1.
29. Two of Bates' first letters bear the same date (December 16 and addressee), Japanese Embassy. The second letter was sent later in the day on the sixteenth and it is from this that the quote is taken. Both of them detail rapes. Letter, Miner Searle Bates to Japanese Embassy, December 16, 1937, Miner Searle Bates Papers, 1.
30. Letter, Charlotte DeForest to Sisters, November 17, 1938, Mission to Japan, Vol. 61, ABCFM Archives, 1.
31. Lawrence Rees, *Horror in the East: Japanese Atrocities in World War II*, (New York: Da Capo Press, 2002), 84. John Dower, *War Without Mercy: Race and Power in the Pacific War*, 9, 203–205.
32. Waldo Heinrichs Jr., *American Ambassador: Joseph Grew and the Development of the United States Diplomatic Tradition*, 244–245.
33. Ibid., 247, 253–254. James T.C. Liu, "German Mediation in the Sino-Japanese War, 1937–1938," *Far Eastern Quarterly*, Vol. 8, No. 2 (February 1949), 157–171.
34. Letter, Galen Fisher to Saito Soichi, Correspondence and Reports, October 23, 1937, Japanese YMCA Archives, 1.
35. Ibid., 2.
36. Letter, H.W. Hackett to Unnamed, October 9, 1937, Mission to Japan, Vol. 60, ABCFM Archives, 1.
37. A.L. Warnshuis, "Prospects of Peace in the Far East," Correspondence and Reports, Unpublished manuscript, Japanese YMCA Archives, 1, 3.
38. Letter, Arthur Jorgensen to A.L. Warnshuis, January 17, 1938, Jorgensen Biographical File, KFYMCA, 2–3. Letter A.L. Warnshuis, February 14, 1938, Jorgensen Biographical File, KFYMCA, 2.
39. Open Letter, A Message to Fellow Christians in the United States, Undated, Japanese YMCA Archives, Tokyo Japan, 1–2.
40. Japanese Christian Leaders, An Open Letter to Christian Brethren throughout the World, January 1938, Correspondence and Reports, Japanese YMCA Archives, 1. Open Letter, Japanese Christians to the Christians of the World, Undated, Correspondence and Reports, Japanese YMCA Archives, 1–2.

41. Open letter from Doshisha faculty, December 10, 1937, Arthur Jorgensen Biographical File, KFYMCA, 1–6. Memorandum, Dr. Fairfield to All Departments, ABCFM Former Missionaries and Japanese Workers, January 17, 1938, Mission to Japan, Vol. 61, ABCFM Archives, 1.

42. Jon Thares Davidann, *A World of Crisis and Progress: The American YMCA in Japan, 1890–1930*, Chapter 2.

43. Kan Kikuchi, "Japan and America," O*saka Young Men*, eds. Osaka YMCA, June 1938, 3.

44. Student Leader's Conference, Correspondence and Reports, Unpublished manuscript, Japanese YMCA Archives, Tokyo, Japan, 1.

45. Letter, Arthur Jorgensen to Frank Slack, August 26, 1937, Arthur Jorgensen Biographical File, KFYMCA, 1–2.

46. Letter, Charlotte B. DeForest to Mrs. Wilson, March 13, 1938, Mission to Japan, Vol. 60, ABCFM Archives, 1, 3–5.

47. Davidann, *A World of Crisis and Progress*, Chapter 4.

48. Tagawa D., undated report, The Sino-Japanese Incident, Correspondence and Reports, Japanese YMCA Archives, Tokyo Japan, 1. Letter, Eugene E. Barnett to Arthur Jorgensen, January 31, 1938, Arthur Jorgensen Biographical File, KFYMCA, 2. Anonymous Report, Japanese Christian Delegation to Beijing, May 12–17, 1938, Correspondence and Reports, Japanese YMCA Archives, 1–4.

49. Galen Fisher, A Ten Year History of the Institute of Pacific Relations, unpublished manuscript, 1935, IPR Collection, Rare Book and Manuscript Library, Columbia University, New York, 4–5.

50. Paul E. Hooper, *Rediscovering the IPR*, 37. Tomoko Akami, *Internationalizing the Pacific: The United States and Japan, and the Institute of Pacific Relations in War and Peace*, 204.

51. Letter, William Holland to E.C. Carter, November 24, 1937, IPR Collection, Rare Book and Manuscript Library, Columbia University, 5–6.

52. International Secretariat Inquiry: Its Origins and Progress, September 30, 1938, IPR Collection, University of Hawai'i at Manoa, Box A-4, folder 3, 1.

53. International Secretariat Inquiry, Statement of Project, June 28, 1938, IPR Collection, University of Hawai'i at Manoa, Box A-4, folder 3, 1. Statement of Project, IPR Collection, June 28, 1938, Rare Book and Manuscript Library, Columbia University, 1–2.

54. Ibid., 7, 10.

55. Ibid., 9.

56. Letter, Tadao Yamakawa, Concerning the Objections of the Japanese Council to the International, Secretariat Inquiry, 1938, July 19, 1938, IPR Collection, University of Hawai'i at Manoa, A-4 folder 3, Appendix K, 1–2.

57. Ibid., 1–2.

58. Unpublished Report, The Institute of Pacific Relations: Trends and Personnel of the American and Pacific Councils, IPR Collection, University of Hawai'i at Manoa, 1.

59. Ibid., 11–18.

60. Unpublished Report, The Institute of Pacific Relations: Trends and Personnel of the American and Pacific Councils, IPR Collection, University of Hawai'i at Manoa, 19–20.

61. Ibid., 2. Letter, EC Carter, Concerning Personnel departures from IPR, October 21, 1941, IPR Collection, University of Hawai'i at Manoa, A-4 folder 4.

62. Barak Kushner, *The Thought War: Japanese Imperial Propaganda*, 41–42.

63. Ibid., 42–42.

64. Unpublished Flyer, Yenji Takeda, Answers to Questions Asked by American Friends regarding the Current China Affair, 1937, Correspondence and Reports, Japanese YMCA Archives, Tokyo Japan, 1.

65. "Why Defend China?" 1938, Produced by International Cinema Association of Japan, Seized Enemy Records, 242 MID 3247, National Archives-Maryland Branch.

66. Barak Kushner, *The Thought War*, 6.

67. Letter, Arthur Jorgensen to Frank Slack, August 26, 1937, Jorgensen Biographical File, KFYMCA, 1.

68. M.S. Bates, Friendly Caution—and A Little Information, April 15, 1937, M.S. Bates Papers, Yale Divinity School Archives, 7.

69. Letter, Ernest T. Shaw to Rev. Wynn Fairfield, December 29, 1937, IPR Collection, Rare Book and Manuscript Library, Columbia University, 1.

70. Secret Japanese Press News in North China Issued by the Special Military Mission, September 1937, 1–2.

71. Ibid., 4.

72. Ibid., 3.

73. Memorandum, Eugene E. Barnett to S.M. Kearny, March 12, 1938, Japan Correspondence and Reports, KFYMCA, 1.

74. Russell Durgin, Memo regarding the Luther Tucker Case, November 4, 1939, Russell Durgin Biographical Files, KFYMCA, 1. Statement of Luther Tucker to the Press on Arrival in Shanghai, December 21, 1939, M.S. Bates Collection, 1–2. K. Yuasa, "The Lessons of the Tucker Case," *The Japan Weekly Chronicle*, December 28, 1939, 737–738.

75. "Japan's Periodicals—Extracts," *Contemporary Japan*, Vol. 6 (December 1937), taken from Toshio Shiratori, *The Kaizo*, 495–496.

76. Louise Young, *Japan's Total Empire: Manchuria and the Culture of Wartime Imperialism* (Berkeley: University of California Press, 1998), Chapter 6.

77. Mikasa Shobo, "Book Reviews," *Contemporary Japan*, Vol. 7 (September 1938), 333.

78. Commander Kawanami, "After a Battle in Kiangwan," *Asia*, Vol. 38, No. 4 (April 1938), 224.

79. Takeuchi Tatsuji, "The Background of the Sino-Japanese War," *Amerasia*, Vol. 2, No. 4 (June 1938), 183–191.

80. Frederick Field, "Reply to Dr. Takeuchi," *Amerasia*, Vol. 2, No. 4 (June 1937), 191–197.

81. Prince Tadashige Shimadzu, "The Japanese Motives," *Asia*, Vol. 38, No. 4 (April 1938), 220–224.

82. Ibid., 220.
83. Letter, Tetsutaro Hasegawa, November 14, 1937, Henry Stimson Papers, Reel 94, 201–202.

CHAPTER 11   THE MARCH TO WAR

1. John Hersey, "Joseph Grew, Ambassador to Japan: America's Top Career Diplomat Knows How to Appease the Japanese or be Stern with Them," *Life*, July 15, 1941, 77–78.
2. John W. Masland, "American Attitudes toward Japan," *Annals of the American Academy*, May 1941, 164–165.
3. Hersey, "Joseph Grew," 78.
4. Harold Fey, "Rise Again Amaterasu," *The Christian Century* (August 14, 1940), 998–1000.
5. William R. Hutchison, *Many Are Chosen: Divine Election and Western Nationalism* (Minneapolis, MN: Fortress Press, 1994). Ivan Hall, *Mori Arinori* (Cambridge, MA: Harvard University Press, 1973).
6. Robert Aura Smith, "The Japanese Don't Understand Us," *American Mercury*, (May 1941), 542.
7. Ibid., 543.
8. Ibid., 545–546.
9. Galen M. Fisher, "Understanding and Misunderstanding Japan," *Annals of the American Academy*, May 1941, 122–123.
10. Ibid., 122.
11. Ibid., 123.
12. Toshi Go, "Japanese Attitudes toward America," *Annals of American Academy*, May 1941, 166.
13. Ibid., 167. Smith, The Japanese Don't Understand Us," 546–547.
14. George H. Gallup, *The Gallup Poll: Public Opinion, 1935–1948* (New York: Random House, 1972), 159–160, 177.
15. "What Japan Thinks," Business Abroad Section, *Business Week*, August 3, 1940, 45.
16. Tyler Dennett, "Japan's 'Monroe Doctrine' Appraised," *Annals of the American Academy*, May 1941, 62. Harold S. Quigley, "The Drift in the Pacific," *Atlantic Monthly*, September 1940, 334–335.
17. Waldo Heinrichs Jr., *Threshold of War: Franklin D. Roosevelt and American Entry into World War II*, 133.
18. Kenneth Latourette, "A Church-Made War with Japan?" *The Christian Century* (January 31, 1940), 140. Masland, "American Attitudes toward Japan," 164.
19. Latourette, "A Church-Made War with Japan?" 141.
20. Kiyo Sue Inui, "American Public Opinion toward Japan," *Contemporary Japan*, Vol. 10 (February 1941), 150.
21. Masland, "American Attitudes toward Japan," 163.
22. Kiyo Sue Inui, "President Roosevelt's Fireside Chat," *Contemporary Japan*, Vol. 10 (July 1941), 863.

23. Heinrichs, *Threshold of War*, 132–135.
24. Walter Lafeber, *The Clash: U.S.-Japanese Relations throughout History*, 200.
25. Smith, "The Japanese Don't Understand Us," 549.
26. Nozaki Ryushichi, "American Freezing of Japanese Assets," *Contemporary Japan*, Vol. 10 (October 1941), 1341–1346.
27. LaFeber, *The Clash*, 197.
28. Nish, *Japanese Foreign Policy in the Interwar Period*, 157–163.
29. Heinrichs, *The Threshold of War*, 49–50.
30. Ibid., 51–52.
31. Robert Shildgen, "How Race Mattered," *Journal of American-East Asian Relations*, Vol. 5, No. 3–4 (Fall-Winter 1996), 243–244.
32. Haruo Iguchi, *Unfinished Business: Ayukawa Yoshisuke and U.S.-Japan Relations, 1937–1953*, 144–165.
33. Letter, Tsurumi Yusuke, Pax Japonica, April 28, 1939, no. 362–604, Tsurumi Yusuke Papers, National Diet Library, Tokyo, Japan, 1. Barak Kushner, *The Thought War: Japanese Imperial Propaganda*, 48–50.
34. James J. Halsema, unpublished diary of the 1940 Japan-American Student Conference, found at http://halsema.org/people/JamesJuliusHalsema/Japan Diary.html, accessed October 10, 2006.
35. Mark R. Mullins, "The Social and Legal Status of Religious Minorities in Japan," International Coalition for Religious Freedom Conference on "Religious Freedom and the New Millenium," Tokyo, Japan May 23–25, 1998, 2. Hamish Ion, *The Cross in the Dark Valley: The Canadian Protestant Missionary Movement in the Japanese Empire, 1931–1945* (Waterloo, Canada: Wilfird Laurer Press, 1999), 256–258.
36. Sheldon Garon, *Molding Japanese Minds: The State in Everyday Life*, 5–7, 206–207.
37. Jon Thares Davidann, *A World of Crisis and Progress: The American YMCA in Japan, 1890–1930*, 63–68.
38. Letter, Alice Cary to Wynn Fairfield, April 15, 1940, Mission to Japan, Vol. 69, ABCFM Archives, 2–3. Garon, *Molding Japanese Minds*, 206–207, 68–78.
39. Letter, William Axling to A.L Warnshuis, March 10, 1941, Mission to Japan, Vol. 69, ABCFM Archives, 1–2.
40. Suggestions regarding the Meeting of Japanese and American Christians, April 2, 1941, Mission to Japan, Vol. 68, ABCFM Archives, 2.
41. Some Negative Aspects of Christianity in America, [ca. 1941], Mission to Japan, Vol. 68, ABCFM Archives, 1–2. Recommendation—Itinerary of Japanese Visitors, (UN 105), [ca. 1941], Mission to Japan, Vol. 68, ABCFM Archives, 2.
42. Address given by Bishop Y. Abe of the Japan Methodist Church at the Luncheon Meeting at the Aldine Club, New York, May 21, 1941, Mission to Japan, Vol. 68, ABCFM Archives, 1.
43. "Conferring with Japanese Christians," *The Christian Century* (April 2, 1941), 446.

EPILOGUE   IMPACT ON THE POSTWAR WORLD

1. John Dower, *War Without Mercy: Race and Power in the Pacific War*, 124–128.
2. Ruth Benedict, *The Chrysanthemum and the Sword*, 10.
3. Dower, *War Without Mercy*, 119. Rudolf V.A. Janssens, *"What Future for Japan?" U.S. Wartime Planning for the Postwar Era, 1942–1945*, 206–213, Chapter 1.
4. Ibid., 14–15.

BIBLIOGRAPHY

MANUSCRIPT AND OTHER COLLECTIONS

American Board of Commissioners for Foreign Missions (ABCFM) Archives (1–91). Mission to Japan. Houghton Library, Harvard College Library, Harvard University, Cambridge, Massachusetts.

Beard, Charles Papers. Archives of Depauw University and Indiana United Methodism, Greencastle, Indiana.

Brown, Georgene Esther Papers. Harvard Divinity School Special Collections, Cambridge, Massachusetts.

Institute of Pacific Relations Collection. Hamilton Library Annex, University of Hawai'i at Manoa, Honolulu, Hawai'i.

Institute of Pacific Relations Collection. Rare Book and Manuscript Library, Columbia University, New York.

Japanese YMCA Archives. Tokyo, Japan.

Kautz Family YMCA Archives (KFYMCA). University of Minnesota, Minneapolis, Minnesota.

National Archives. Collections of videos about Japan. Record Groups 200, 226, 238, 242. Motion Picture, Sound, and Video Records LICON, Special Media Archives Services Division, National Archives, College Park, Maryland.

National Archives. Naval Intelligence Reports, Office of Naval Intelligence, Record Group 45, Washington, DC.

Special Collections, Yale Divinity School Library (YDSL), New Haven, Connecticut.

Stimson, Henry Papers. Manuscript Division, Library of Congress, Reels 93 and 94, Washington, DC.

Tsurumi Yusuke Papers. National Diet Library, Tokyo, Japan.

SELECT SOURCES

See endnotes for all books, articles, and primary source collections used. Articles from 70 different journals and magazines were used.

BOOKS

Akami, Tomoko. *Internationalizing the Pacific: The United States and Japan, and the Institute of Pacific Relations in War and Peace.* London: Routledge Press, 2002.

Barshay, Andrew E. *The Social Sciences in Modern Japan: The Marxist and Modernist Tradition.* Berkeley and Los Angeles: University of California Press, 2004.

Benedict, Ruth. *The Chrysanthemum and the Sword.* Boston: Houghton Mifflin Co., 1946.

Bix, Herbert. *Hirohito and the Making of Modern Japan.* New York: Harper Collins, 1999.

Borg, Dorothy and Shumpei Okamoto. eds. *Pearl Harbor As History: Japanese-American Relations, 1932–1941.* New York: Columbia University Press, 1973.

Boyle, John Hunter. *China and Japan at War: The Politics of Collaboration.* Stanford: Stanford University Press, 1972.

Brooks, Barbara J. *Japan's Imperial Diplomacy: Consuls, Treaty Ports and War in China.* Honolulu: University of Hawai'i Press, 2000.

Chang, Gordon ed. *Morning Glory, Evening Shadow: Yamato Ichihashi and His Internment Writings, 1942–1945.* Stanford: Stanford University Press, 1997.

Current, Richard. *Secretary Stimson: A Study in Statecraft.* New Brunswick, NJ: Rutgers University Press, 1954.

Dallek, Robert. *Franklin Roosevelt and American Foreign Policy, 1932–1945.* New York: Oxford University Press, 1979.

Davidann, Jon Thares. *A World of Crisis and Progress: The American YMCA in Japan, 1890–1930.* Bethlehem, PA: Lehigh University Press, 1998.

Dickinson, Frederick R. *War and National Reinvention: Japan in the Great War, 1914–1919.* Cambridge, MA: Harvard University Press, 1999.

Dingman, Roger. *Power in the Pacific.* Chicago: University of Chicago Press, 1976.

Doenecke, Justus. *When the Wicked Arise: American Opinion-Makers and the Manchurian crisis of 1931–1933.* Lewisburg: Bucknell University Press, 1984.

———. *Storm on the Horizon: The Challenge to American Intervention, 1939–1941.* Lanham, MD: Rowman Littlefield, 2003.

Dower, John. *War Without Mercy: Race and Power in the Pacific War.* New York: Pantheon Books, 1986.

———. *Embracing Defeat: Japan in the Wake of World War II.* New York: W.W. Norton, 1999.

Fujitani, Takashi. *Splendid Monarchy: Power and Pageantry in Modern Japan.* Berkeley: University of California Press, 1998.

Garon, Sheldon. *Molding Japanese Minds: The State in Everyday Life.* Princeton: Princeton University Press, 1997.

Goldstein, Erik and John Maurer. *The Washington Conference, 1921–22: Naval Rivalry, East Asian Stability and the Road to Pearl Harbor.* Essex, UK: Frank Cass, 1994.

Gordon, Andrew. *Labor and Imperial Democracy in Prewar Japan.* Berkeley: University of California Press, 1991.

Heinrichs Jr., Waldo. *American Ambassador: Joseph Grew and the Development of the United States Diplomatic Tradition.* Boston: Little, Brown and Company, 1966.

———. *Threshold of War: Franklin D. Roosevelt and American Entry into World War II.* New York: Oxford University Press, 1988.

Hennings, Joe. *Outposts of Civilization: Race, Religion, and the Formative Years of American-Japanese Relations.* New York: New York University Press, 2000.

Hirobe, Izumi. *Japanese Pride, American Prejudice: Modifying the Exclusion Clause of the 1924 Immigration Act.* Stanford: Stanford University Press, 2001.

Hobsbawn, Eric. "Introduction: Invention of Tradition." *Invention of Tradition.* Eric Hobsbawn and Terrance Ranger, ed. Cambridge: Cambridge University Press, 1983.

Hodgson, Godfrey. *The Colonel: The Life and War of Henry Stimson, 1867–1950.* New York: Alfred A. Knopf, 1990.

Hooper, Paul E. *Rediscovering the IPR: Proceedings of the First International Research Conference on the Institute of Pacific Relations.* Department of American Studies, Center for Arts and Humanities Occasional Papers, University of Hawai'i at Manoa, 1994.

Howes, John W. *Nitobe Inazô: Japan's Bridge across the Pacific.* Boulder, CO, Westview Press, 1995.

Iguchi, Haruo. *Unfinished Business: Ayukawa Yoshisuke and U.S.-Japan Relations, 1937–1953.* Cambridge, MA: Harvard University Press, 2003.

Iriye, Akira. *Cultural Internationalism and World Order.* Baltimore, MD: Johns Hopkins Press, 1997.

Iriye, Akira and Cohen Warren I. eds. *The United States and Japan in the Postwar World.* Lexington, KY: The University Press of Kentucky, 1989.

Janssens, Rudolf V.A. *"What Future for Japan?" U.S. Wartime Planning for the Postwar Era, 1942–1945.* Atlanta, GA: Rodopi, 1995.

Johnson, Sheila K. *The Japanese through American Eyes.* Palo Alto, CA: Stanford University Press, 1988.

Kahn, David. *The Reader of Gentlemen's Mail: Herbert O. Yardley and the Birth of American Codebreaking.* New Haven, CT: Yale University Press, 2004.

Kennedy, Thomas C. *Charles Beard and American Foreign Policy.* Gainesville: University Presses of Florida, 1975.

Kushner, Barak. *The Thought War: Japanese Imperial Propaganda.* Honolulu: University of Hawai'i Press, 2006.

Lafeber, Walter. *The Clash: U.S.-Japanese Relations throughout History.* New York: W.W. Norton, 1997.

MacMillan, Margaret. *Paris, 1919.* New York: Random House, 2002.

Martin, Jay. *The Education of John Dewey.* New York: Columbia University Press, 2002.

Masanori, Nakamura. *The Japanese Monarchy, 1931–1991: Ambassador Joseph Grew and the Making of the Symbol Emperor System.* Herbert Bix, Derek Bowen, Jonathan Baker-Bates, trans. New York: M.E. Sharpe, 1992.

Nish, Ian. *Japanese Foreign Policy in the Interwar Period* Westport, CT: Praeger, 2002.

Nobuya, Bamba. *Japanese Diplomacy in a Dilemma: New Light on Japan's China Policy, 1924–1929.* Kyoto, Japan: Minerva Press, 1972.

Ozaki, Yukio. *The Autobiography of Ozaki Yukio: The Struggle for Constitutional Government in Japan.* Fujiko Hara, trans. Princeton: Princeton University Press, 2001.

Peattie, Mark R. *Ishiwara Kanji and Japan's Confrontation with the West.* Princeton: Princeton University Press, 1975.

Rapport, Armin. *Henry L. Stimson and Japan, 1931–1933.* Chicago: The University of Chicago Press, 1963.

Reed, James. *The Missionary Mind and American East Asia Policy, 1911–1915.* Cambridge, MA: Harvard University Press, 1983.

Reischauer, Edwin O. *The United States and Japan.* Cambridge, MA: Harvard University Press, 1950.

Said, Edward. *Orientalism.* New York: Vintage, 1979.

Shillony, Ben-Ami. *Revolt in Japan: The Young Officers and the February 26, 1936 Incident.* Princeton: Princeton University Press, 1973.

Smethurst, Richard. *A Social Basis of Prewar Japanese Militarism: The Army and the Rural Community.* Berkeley: University of California Press, 1974.

Stimson, Henry. *The Far Eastern Crisis: Recollections and Observations.* Harpers & Brothers Publishers, 1936.

Tanaka, Stefan. *Japan's Orient: Rendering Pasts into History.* Berkeley: University of California Press, 1993.

Taylor, Sandra C. *Advocate of Understanding: Sidney Gulick and the Search for Peace with Japan.* Kent, OH: Kent State Press, 1984.

Thomson, James. *Sentimental Imperialists.* New York: Harper Collins, 1981.

Utley, Jonathan. *Going to War with Japan.* Knoxville: University of Tennessee Press, 1985.

Wilson, George M. *Radical Nationalist in Japan: Kita Ikki, 1883–1937.* Cambridge, MA: Harvard University Press, 1969.

Yoshihara, Mari. *Embracing the East: White Women and American Orientalism.* New York: Oxford University Press, 2000.

Young, Louise. *Japan's Total Empire: Manchuria and the Culture of Wartime Imperialism.* Berkeley: University of California Press, 1998.

INDEX